TEST PREPARATION
A STUDY GUIDE

Brenda Fonseca
Mesa Community College

PSYCHOLOGY

SAUNDRA K. CICCARELLI
Gulf Coast Community College

GLENN E. MEYER
Trinity University

PEARSON

Prentice
Hall

Upper Saddle River, New Jersey 07458

© 2006 by PEARSON EDUCATION, INC.
Upper Saddle River, New Jersey 07458

10 9 8 7 6 5 4 3 2

ISBN 0-13-195275-7

Printed in the United States of America

Table of Contents

CHAPTER 1 LEARNING OBJECTIVES

SUMMARY

Psychology is defined as the scientific study of behavior and mental processes. The goals of psychology are to describe, explain, predict, and control the behaviors and mental process of both humans and animals. The goals of psychology can be thought of in terms of what, why, when and how behaviors and mental processes occur.

The field of psychology is relatively new (around 125 years old), but has its origins in the much older fields of physiology and philosophy. Wilhelm Wundt formed the first psychology laboratory in Germany in 1879. Wundt used the method of **introspection** in an attempt to objectively study human thought processes. Because of his innovative efforts, Wundt is often referred to as the father of psychology. The reality, however, is that multiple people in multiple locations began studying psychology and promoting their particular perspective around the same time. Five historical perspectives are discussed in the text.

Edward Titchener, a student of Wundt's, expanded on Wundt's ideas and brought the method of introspection to the U.S. Titchener called his approach **structuralism** because his ultimate goal was to describe the precise structure of our mental processes. At the same time in the U.S., William James was focused on discovering how our mental processes help us to function in our daily lives and began to promote his viewpoint known as **functionalism**. The terms structuralism and functionalism are no longer used to describe specific viewpoints in the field of psychology. Meanwhile, back in Germany, the **Gestalt** psychologists were studying how sensation and perception create a whole pattern that is greater

1

than the sum of the individual components. Max Wertheimer was a major proponent of Gestalt psychology. In neighboring Austria, Sigmund Freud developed his theory of **psychoanalysis** based on the concept of the unconscious. Freud believed the unconscious played an important role in controlling our day to day behaviors and thoughts. Freud's theory is also referred to as the **psychodynamic** perspective. On the opposite end of the spectrum, and back in the United States, was John Watson. Watson expanded the findings of Russian physiologist Ivan Pavlov to promote the perspective of **behaviorism**. The behaviorists believed that psychology should focus on concepts that could be studied scientifically and they felt that the only area of psychology that could be approached scientifically was observable behavior.

Today there are seven major perspectives within the field of psychology. **Psychodynamics** focuses on the role of the unconscious. **Behaviorism** attempts to study psychology by focusing on observable actions and events. The **humanistic** perspective emphasizes human potential and free will. **Biopsychology** focuses on the biology underlying our behavior and thoughts, while **cognitive** psychologists focus on the thoughts or "cognitions" themselves. The **sociocultural** perspective explores the role of social and cultural factors on our behaviors and thoughts, while **evolutionary** psychologists attempt to explain behavior and thoughts in terms of their adaptive or "survival" qualities.

There are many professional opportunities within the field of psychology. **Psychiatrists** receive a medical degree (M.D.), treat serious psychological disorders, and can prescribe medication for their patients. A **psychologist** attends graduate school to obtain a doctorate degree (either a Ph.D., Ed.D. or Psy.D.) and can select one of many career options from research to counseling to consulting for a business. A **psychoanalyst** is a psychiatrist or psychologist who has received special training in Freud's method of psychoanalysis. A **psychiatric social worker** receives a master of social work degree (M.S.W.) and provides counseling to patients or possibly conducts research.

Psychologists use the **scientific method** to reduce bias and error in their observations. The steps of the scientific method include asking a question, turning your question into a hypothesis, testing your hypothesis, drawing a conclusion and reporting your findings. The method you use to test your hypothesis depends on which of the four goals of psychology you are attempting to achieve. If you would like to answer the question of "what" (goal = describe), you would use a descriptive method. **Naturalistic observation** provides a realistic picture of behavior but can become biased through the **observer effect** (subjects act differently when they know they are being watched) and **observer bias** (the researcher only sees what he or she wants to see). Laboratory observation is similar to naturalistic observation, but the participants are observed in a laboratory setting instead of "out in nature." A **case study** is a detailed investigation of one individual, or case, and can provide a great deal of information about that one person but is hard to generalize to a larger population. For a **survey**, researchers ask a group of subjects a series of questions. Surveys allow researchers to gather a lot of information quickly. However, with a survey there is no guarantee that the subjects will answer the questions truthfully. Also, researchers must be sure to take a representative sample of the population they are interested in. A researcher interested in discovering the relationship between two variables would use the **correlational method**. A correlation coefficient tells the researcher the direction and strength of the relationship. The coefficient will always be a number between -1.00 and +1.00. A correlation shows that a relationship between two variables exists, but can not explain the cause of the relationship. In order to answer the question of "why," a researcher must conduct an experiment. Remember the example with the churches and the bars. The new churches did not cause the construction of the new bars. In an **experiment**, the researcher manipulates a variable (the **independent variable**) and measure some response from the participants (the **dependent variable**). In order to measure the dependent variable, the researcher must come up with an **operational definition** for the variable. An operational definition is a set of instructions that explains exactly how to measure the variable. For example, aggressive behavior could be operationally defined as the number of times a subject swings a toy sword in a five minute observation period. The overall goal of the experiment is to keep everything the same except the independent variable. In order to accomplish this, the researcher usually observes two groups: an **experimental group** and a **control group**. The researcher will most likely use **random assignment** to determine which participants will go in which group. Often, the control group receives a fake treatment in order to control for the **placebo effect**, in which the participant's expectations actually influence the results of the experiment. Normally, the subjects are not told which group they are in (**single-blind study**). In order to control for any expectations the experimenter might have (**the experimenter effect**), the study is often designed so that neither the participants nor the experimenter know who is in what group (**double-blind study**). All psychological research must follow the ethical guidelines specified by the American Psychological Association.

Understanding the scientific method can help you in your daily life as you apply the four principles of **critical thinking** to problems you face day to day. The four criteria are that (1) most truths need to be tested, (2) all evidence is not equal, (3) authorities are not always right, and (4) an open mind is still important.

KEY POINTS

- Define psychology and describe the goals that psychologists hope to achieve.
- Describe the history of psychology.
- Discuss the current state of psychology, including the most common perspectives and major professions in the field.
- Describe the scientific method.
- Introduce the concept of critical thinking.

KEY CONCEPTS

psychology	The scientific study of behavior and mental processes.
introspection	The process of examining and measuring one's own thoughts and mental activities.
structuralism	Early perspective in psychology associated with Wilhelm Wundt and Edward Titchener, in which the focus of study is the structure or basic elements of the mind.
functionalism	Early perspective in psychology associated with William James, in which the focus of study is how the mind allows people to adapt, live, work, and play.
Gestalt psychology	Early perspective in psychology focusing on perception and sensation, particularly the perception of patterns and whole figures.
psychoanalysis	The theory and therapy based on the work of Sigmund Freud.
psychodynamic perspective	Modern version of psychoanalysis that is more focused on the development of a sense of self and the discovery of other motivations behind a person's behavior than sexual motivations.
behaviorism	The science of behavior that focuses on observable behavior only.

humanistic perspective	Perspective that emphasizes human potential and the idea that people have the freedom to choose their own destiny.
biopsychological perspective	Perspective that attributes human and animal behavior to biological events occurring in the body, such as genetic influences, hormones, and the activity of the nervous system.
cognitive perspective	Modern perspective that focuses on memory, intelligence, perception, problem-solving, and learning.
sociocultural perspective	Perspective that focuses on the relationship between social behavior and culture.
evolutionary perspective	Perspective that focuses on the biological bases of universal mental characteristics that all humans share.
psychiatrist	A medical doctor who has specialized in the diagnosis and treatment of psychological disorders.
psychologist	A professional with an academic degree and specialized training in one or more areas of psychology.
psychoanalyst	Either a psychiatrist or a psychologist who has special training in the theories of Sigmund Freud and his method of psychoanalysis.
psychiatric social worker	A social worker with some training in therapy methods who focuses on environmental conditions that can have an impact on mental disorders, such as poverty, overcrowding, stress, and drug abuse.
scientific method	System of gathering data so that bias and error in measurement are reduced.
naturalistic observation	Study in which the researcher observes people or animals in their normal environment.
observer effect	Tendency of people or animals to behave differently from normal when they know they are being observed.
observer bias	Tendency of observers to see what they expect to see.
case study	Study of one individual in great detail. Modern perspective that focuses on memory, intelligence, perception, problem-solving, and learning.
survey	Study conducted by asking a series of questions to a group of people.
correlation	A measure of the relationship between two variables.
experiment	A deliberate manipulation of a variable to see if corresponding

changes in behavior result, allowing the determination of cause and effect relationships.

independent variable	Variable in an experiment that is manipulated by the experimenter.
dependent variable	Variable in an experiment that represents the measurable response or behavior of the subjects in the experiment.
operational definition	Definition of a variable of interest that allows it to be directly measured.
experimental group	Subjects in an experiment that are subjected to the independent variable.
control group	Subjects in an experiment that are not subjected to the independent variable and who may receive a placebo treatment.
random assignment	Process of assigning subjects to the experimental or control groups randomly, so that each subject has an equal chance of being in either group.
placebo effect	The phenomenon in which the expectations of the participants in a study can influence their behavior.
single-blind study	Study in which the subjects do not know if they are in the experimental or the control group.
experimenter effect	Tendency of the experimenter's expectations for a study to unintentionally influence the results of the study.
double-blind study	Study in which neither the experimenter nor the subjects knows if the subjects are in the experimental or control group.
critical thinking	Making reasoned judgments about claims.

HINTS

1. This chapter presents a large number of theoretical perspectives. Five historical and seven current perspectives are presented. Keep in mind that a perspective is simply an outlook a psychologist has on what he or she feels is the right way to study behavior and mental processes. For example, a developmental psychologist could approach the study of child development from any of the seven current perspectives discussed. In reality, psychologists often adhere to a combination of one or more perspectives. To keep all the different viewpoints straight, try listing them out on a sheet of paper in two columns. The first column should consist of the historical perspectives and the second column should be the current perspectives. See if you can speculate on which historical perspectives contributed to psychology's modern day viewpoints.

2. Be careful not to confuse the independent variable (i.v.) with the dependent variable (d.v.). The

independent variable is the variable the researcher manipulates her or himself. If you think about it as if you were the researcher conducting the experiment, the independent variable is the one that **I** control. Another way to make sure you have correctly labeled the variables in an experiment is to insert the variable names into the following phrase and make sure it still makes sense. The test phrase is:

$$\text{How } \underline{\hspace{2cm}} \text{ affects } \underline{\hspace{2cm}} \text{ .}$$
$$\quad\quad\quad (i.v.) \quad\quad\quad\quad\quad (d.v.)$$

Here is an example for you to practice using the test phrase.

> *A researcher conducts a study looking at the color of different rooms and aggressiveness. She takes a group of 40 college students and randomly assigns 20 to the red room and 20 to the blue room. After the students have been in the rooms for 30 minutes, she measures each person's aggressiveness level on a scale of 1 to 10. In this experiment, which variable is the independent variable and which is the dependent? Try inserting the variable names into the phrase above.*

You can see that "How aggressiveness affects room color" does not make sense and is not what the researcher is interested in. However, "How room color affects aggressiveness" does correspond to the researchers' goals. So in this case, the room color is the independent variable and aggressiveness is the dependent variable.

Try one more example.

> *A researcher conducts an experiment to study memory skills and caffeine intake. The researcher has a total of 20 volunteer subjects. He gives 10 subjects a can of caffeinated soda and the other 10 subjects receive a can of decaffeinated soda. He then has all the subjects complete a memory task. What are his independent and dependent variables? Try inserting the variable names into the phrase above.*

Again, you can see that "How memory skills affect caffeine intake" does not make sense and is not what the researcher is interested in. However, "How caffeine intake affects memory skills" does correspond to the researchers' goals. So in this case, the caffeine intake is the independent variable and memory skill is the dependent variable.

3. The phrase "correlation does not prove causation" is an important concept to understand. One way to think about it is in terms of the four goals of psychology. If your goal is to describe or predict, then a correlation is an excellent choice. A correlation can tell you students who sit in the front row of class are also the students who get A's, or that a high SAT score is a fairly good predictor of college success. However, if your goal is to explain something (in other words, to answer the question of "why"), then a correlation will not help you. A correlation cannot tell you why the front row students get A's. It could be that good students are drawn to the front, or sitting in the front forces you to pay more attention, or perhaps there is some third variable that we have not considered, such as students who sit in the front are more likely to find a study partner and studying together is what leads to the good grade.

4. The concept of operational definitions is introduced in this chapter. An operational definition can be thought of as a recipe telling a researcher precisely how to make her observations. In other words, they define the operations or procedures the researcher should go through in order

to record her data. Operational definitions are based on behaviors and actions that can be observed, and they are much different than the definitions given in a standard dictionary. For example, the dictionary might define fear as feeling anxious or apprehensive about a possible situation. However, that definition does not tell the researcher how to measure one individual's level of fear. On the other hand, the researcher might operationally define fear as the percent increase in heart rate from a baseline level during a two-minute observation period.

Try this example yourself.

Dictionary Definition of anger: _____

Operational Definition of anger: _____

The dictionary might define anger as a strong feeling of displeasure. However, an operational definition of anger might be something like the number of times an adult slams his or her fists on the table.

Now, try to figure out what variable is being operationally defined below.

The number of times a person laughs within a five minute period.

Operational Definition of _____:

The score an individual receives on an IQ test.

Operational Definition of _____:

The first example is operationally defining the variable of happiness and the second example gives an operational definition for intelligence.

SAMPLE EXAM

For the following multiple choice questions, select the answer you feel best answers the question and explain the rationale or reason for your selection in the space provided.

Objective 1.1

1. How is psychology different from philosophy?
   a) Psychology uses the scientific method to answer questions.
   b) Psychology is interested in questions related to human behavior.
   c) There is no difference between philosophy and psychology.
   d) The field of psychology is much older than the field of philosophy.

   Rationale:
   Psychology bases its answers on observations, while philosophy answers its questions using logic and reasoning. Both fields are interested in human behavior. The field of psychology is only 125 years old, while philosophy is much older.

2. A researcher is attempting to design a program to help people stop smoking. The goal she is attempting to achieve is to
   a) describe
   b) predict
   c) explain
   d) control

   Rationale:
   She is trying to change people's behaviors. This corresponds to the question of "how" (in other words, "how" do I help people to stop smoking?).

3. A researcher is interested in finding out the percentage of adolescents in the U.S. who have depression. The goal he is attempting to achieve is to
   a) describe
   b) predict
   c) explain
   d) control

   Rationale:

   _____

   _____

4. Which of the following research questions would NOT fall within the field of psychology?
    a) How can you increase the amount of time a female bird stays with its mate after the birdlings hatch?
    b) What changes occur in the brain of a rat that has been deprived of sleep?
    c) Why do students perform better on exams when the exam is given in the same room in which the learned the material?
    d) All of the questions above could be studied by a psychologist.

Rationale:

_____

_____

5. The first psychology laboratory was opened in _____ in order to study _____.
    a) 1065, psychological disorders
    b) 1946, learning
    c) 1879, introspection
    d) 1809, biopsychology

Rationale:

_____

_____

6. Which of these is the most accurate definition of the discipline of psychology?
    a) the science of behavior
    b) the science of mental processes
    c) the science of behavior and mental processes
    d) the science of human behavior and mental processes

Rationale:

_____

_____

Objective 1.2

7. The psychological perspective of structuralism focused on
    a) how the whole structure is bigger than the individual parts.
    b) understanding each individual structure of human thought.
    c) how mental thought helps us structure our daily activities.
    d) the structure of society at large.

Rationale:

_____

_____

8. The school of psychology called *structuralism* used a technique called _____, which involved reporting the contents of consciousness to study a person's experiences.
   a) intervention
   b) introspection
   c) insight inventory
   d) induction

   Rationale:

   _____

   _____

9. William James believed that mental processes could not be studied as an isolated, static event but instead needed to be viewed in terms of how they helped people perform in their daily lives. James was a strong proponent for
   a) structuralism.
   b) functionalism.
   c) behaviorism.
   d) the humanistic perspective.

   Rationale:

   _____

   _____

Objective 1.3

10. Freud said phobias were _____, whereas Watson said phobias were _____.
    a) learned; inherited
    b) repressed conflicts; learned
    c) sexual; unconscious
    d) conditioned; unconditioned

    Rationale:

    _____

    _____

11. Which of the following statements would Sigmund Freud have most likely been overheard saying:
    a) "Human behavior is largely determined by our own free will."
    b) "The only way to understand behavior is to study behavior."
    c) "We will never understand why people do the things they do."
    d) "The key to understanding behavior is in the unconscious."

    Rationale:

    _____

    _____

12. What was John Watson's biggest complaint about the field of psychology?
    a) Psychologists were attempting to study non-observable events using the scientific method.
    b) Psychology was not focused enough on the free will of humans.
    c) Psychologists were ignoring the role of the unconscious in determining behavior.
    d) Psychologists were spending too much time doing research.

    Rationale:

    _____

    _____

Objective 1.4

13. A researcher who studies the chemical changes in the brains of patients with depression would be approaching psychology from which perspective?
    a) behaviorist
    b) psychodynamic
    c) cognitive
    d) biopsychological

    Rationale:

    _____

    _____

14. One of the reasons psychodynamic theories have persisted over the years is that they are _____.
    a) supported by significant scientific research
    b) based on facts
    c) difficult to scientifically test and, thus, difficult to disprove
    d) used by the majority of psychologists

    Rationale:

    _____

    _____

15. A humanistic psychologist would be interested in which of the following research questions?
    a) Describing a group of people who claim to have reached their full potential.
    b) Understanding the role of the unconscious in a child's decision to disobey her parents.
    c) Investigating the role of hormones in the mating behavior of birds.
    d) Figuring out visual illusions are possible.

    Rationale:

    _____

    _____

16. Cognitive psychologists are interested in
    a) social interactions.
    b) the adaptive value of particular behaviors.
    c) mental processes.
    d) the unconscious.

    Rationale:

    _____

    _____

Objective 1.5

17. Self-actualization was part of which of the following perspectives?
    a) behaviorism
    b) cognitive perspective
    c) functionalism
    d) humanism

    Rationale:

    _____

    _____

Objective 1.6

18. Taylor received her degree from a medical school and now meets with patients on a daily basis. Most of her patients have a serious psychological disorder, and often Taylor will prescribe medication to treat the disorder. Taylor is a
    a) psychologist.
    b) psychiatrist.
    c) psychiatric social worker.
    d) school nurse.

    Rationale:

    _____

    _____

19. Vido has an M.S.W. and is interested in working on the causes of poverty. What type of professional is Vido most likely to become?
    a) educational psychologist
    b) psychiatrist
    c) school psychologist
    d) psychiatric social worker

    Rationale:

    _____

    _____

20. Why do psychologists use the scientific method?
     a) It is easier to use than other methods.
     b) All academic fields must use the scientific method.
     c) It is the only method available to answer questions.
     d) It reduces bias and error in measurement.

     Rationale:

     _____

     _____

21. The tendency to look for information that supports one's own belief is called _____ .
     a) the principle of falsifiability
     b) confirmation bias
     c) criterion validity
     d) volunteer bias

     Rationale:

     _____

     _____

Objective 1.8

22. Deb spent the entire day at the park observing children with their parents to see whether fathers or mothers spent more time playing with their kids. Deb used the method of
     a) naturalistic observation.
     b) laboratory observation.
     c) survey.
     d) case study.

     Rationale:

     _____

     _____

Objective 1.9

23. Which of the following topics would be best studied using the case study method?
     a) The reaction times of adults in a stressful situation.
     b) The sleep pattern of adolescents.
     c) The impact of club sports involvement on female adolescent self-esteem.
     d) The personality characteristics of a man accused of killing five people.

     Rationale:

     _____

     _____

24. What is an advantage of the survey method?
    a) non-representative samples
    b) courtesy bias
    c) large amounts of information
    d) observer bias

    Rationale:

    _____

    _____

25. A researcher stops people at the mall and asks them questions about their attitudes toward gun control. Which research technique is being used?
    a) survey
    b) experiment
    c) case study
    d) naturalistic observation

    Rationale:

    _____

    _____

26. A group of randomly selected subjects that matches the population on important characteristics such as age and sex is called _____.
    a) volunteer bias
    b) a representative sample
    c) the experimental group
    d) the control group

    Rationale:

    _____

    _____

Objective 1.10

27. The word *correlation* is often used as a synonym for _____.
    a) validity
    b) reliability
    c) variable
    d) relationship

    Rationale:

    _____

    _____

28. Which of the following correlation coefficients represents the strongest relationship between two variables?
    a) +0.62
    b) -0.98
    c) +0.01
    d) +1.24

    Rationale:

    _____

    _____

29. A researcher finds that as the number of classes missed increases, the students' grades decrease. This is an example of a
    a) positive correlation.
    b) negative correlation.
    c) zero correlation.
    d) case study.

    Rationale:

    _____

    _____

Objective 1.11

30. Marcy is trying to define *anxiety* in a way that can be empirically tested. She is attempting to find an appropriate _____.
    a) hypothesis
    b) operational definition
    c) double-blind study
    d) theory

    Rationale:

    _____

    _____

31. A researcher is investigating the effects of exercise on weight. What are the independent and dependent variables in this experiment?
    a) The dependent variable is weight; the independent variable is exercise.
    b) The independent variable is calories consumed; the dependent variable is diet.
    c) The independent variable is weight; the dependent variable is calories consumed.
    d) The dependent variable is amount of exercise; the independent variable is calories consumed.

    Rationale:

    _____

    _____

32. In a laboratory, smokers are asked to "drive" using a computerized driving simulator equipped with a stick shift and a gas pedal. The object is to maximize the distance covered by driving as fast as possible on a winding road while avoiding rear-end collisions. Some of the participants smoke a real cigarette immediately before climbing into the driver's seat. Others smoke a fake cigarette without nicotine. You are interested in comparing how many collisions the two groups have. In this study, the *cigarette without nicotine* is _____.
    a) the control group
    b) the driving simulator
    c) the experimental group
    d) the no-control group

    Rationale:

    _____

    _____

33. A psychology professor feels that her students will do better on her exams if there is music playing while they take their exams. To test her hypothesis, she divides her class in half. One half takes the exam in a room with music playing and the other half takes the exam in a similar room, but without the music playing. In this case, the independent variable is
    a) the room the exam is taken in.
    b) the absence or presence of music playing.
    c) the exam.
    d) the students' scores on the exam.

    Rationale:

    _____

    _____

34. For the experiment described in Question 33, the dependent variable is
    a) the room the exam is taken in.
    b) the absence or presence of music playing.
    c) the exam.
    d) the students' scores on the exam.

    Rationale:

    _____

    _____

35. Twenty volunteers are brought into a sleep laboratory in the evening. Ten are allowed eight hours of sleep while the other ten are only allowed two hours of sleep. In the morning, all 20 subjects are tested for their reaction time in a driving simulation program. For this experiment, the reaction time in the simulation program is the
    a) independent variable.
    b) dependent variable.
    c) confounding variable.
    d) random variable.

Rationale:

_____

_____

36. For the experiment described in Question 35, the amount of sleep allowed is the
    a) independent variable.
    b) dependent variable.
    c) confounding variable.
    d) random variable.

Rationale:

_____

_____

Objective 1.12

37. Which of the following situations best illustrates the placebo effect?
    a) You sleep because you are tired.
    b) You throw up after eating bad meat.
    c) You have surgery to repair a defective heart valve.
    d) You drink a nonalcoholic drink and become "intoxicated" because you think it contains alcohol.

Rationale:

_____

_____

38. _____ is an experiment in which neither the participants nor the individuals running the experiment know if participants are in the experimental or the control group until after the results are tallied.
    a) The double-blind study
    b) Field research
    c) The single-blind study
    d) Correlational research

Rationale:

_____

_____

Objective 1.13

39. Dr. Teresa Amabile conducted an actual experiment in which she had two groups of girls aged 7 to 10 years create artwork in the classroom. One group was told that the girl with the best artwork would receive a prize at the end of the session and the other group was told that prizes would be raffled off when the session was over. Amabile then measured the level of creativity for the artwork in both groups and found that the second group had higher levels of creativity. In this experiment, the dependent variable is the
    a) prize.
    b) level of creativity.
    c) way the prize was distributed.
    d) group of girls.

Rationale:

_____

_____

Objective 1.14

40. Each of the following is a common ethical guideline suggested by the American Psychological Association EXCEPT _____.
    a) participants must be informed of the nature of the research in clearly understandable language
    b) participants cannot be deceived or have information concealed from them at any time during an experiment
    c) risks, possible adverse effects, and limitations on confidentiality must be spelled out in advance
    d) informed consent must be documented

Rationale:

_____

_____

Objective 1.15

41.　Which of the following is NOT one of the four principles of critical thinking?
　　a)　all truths need to be tested
　　b)　an open mind is always important
　　c)　authorities can almost always be trusted
　　d)　all evidence is not equal

Rationale:

_____

_____

Objective 1.16

42.　Which of the following questions applies the concept of critical thinking to the real world pseudo-psychology of astrology?
　　a)　What is my astrological sign?
　　b)　What does my astrological sign predict will happen to me today?
　　c)　How up-to-date are the charts used by astrologists today?
　　d)　Should I marry someone that is the same sign as me?

Rationale:

_____

_____

SAMPLE EXAM ANSWERS & RATIONALES

1.   a   Psychology bases its answers on observations, while philosophy answers its questions using logic and reasoning. Both fields are interested in human behavior. The field of psychology is only 125 years old, while philosophy is much older.

2.   d   She is trying to change people's behaviors. This corresponds to the question of "how" (in other words, "how" do I help people to stop smoking).

3.   a   He would like to describe this particular group with regards to depression rates. He is trying to answer the question of "what." What is the current depression rate among U.S. teenagers?

4.   d   All of the questions fall under the category of describing, predicting, explaining, or controlling behavior and/or mental processes of humans and animals.

5.   c   Wilhelm Wundt opened his laboratory in Germany in 1879 and used the method of introspection to study the basic elements of mental processes.

6.   c   Psychology deals with both behavior and mental processes and includes other animals besides humans.

7.   b   Structuralists felt that mental processes had to be broken down into their most basic or elemental form in order to be understood.

8.   b   Introspection was used in an attempt to self-examine the structure of the mind. Although the word "intervention" looks similar, it has a completely different meaning.

9.   b   James believed we need to understand the <u>function</u> of mental processes.

10.   b   Freud studied repressed (unconscious) conflict and Watson studied observable behavior. Watson did not believe that the unconscious could be studied scientifically.

11.   d   Sigmund Freud was a major proponent of the perspective of psychoanalysis which emphasizes the role of the unconscious on human behavior.

12.   a   John Watson started the idea of behaviorism, which states that the only subject matter that can be scientifically studied is observable behavior.

13.   d   The biopsychological perspective focuses on studying the biological changes that underlie behavior and mental processes.

14.   c   Since it is very hard to scientifically test the psychodynamic theories, there is little scientific data to support the theories.

15.   a   The humanistic perspective focuses on the uniqueness and potential of human beings and tries to suggest ways for humans to maximize their potential.

16.   d   Cognitive psychologists focus on "cognitions" or mental processes, including topics such as memory, decision-making, problem-solving, perception, language comprehension, creativity and reasoning.

17.   d   Humanists talk about self-actualization.

18.   b   Psychiatrists have M.D.s, counsel patients with serious disorders, and can prescribe medications.

19.   d   Psychiatric Social Workers typically have their Masters of Social Work (M.S.W.) and counsel patients with less severe disorders or focus on social issues such as poverty.

20.   d   The scientific method is based on observations so that the influence of the researcher's bias is minimized.

21.   b   The principle of falsifiability is not an actual principle in psychology.

22.   a   Naturalistic observation consists of recording behaviors as they occur in their normal settings.

23.   d   A case study focuses on one individual (or "case") and provides a detailed description of that individual.

24.   c   A survey allows the researcher to collect a large amount of information quickly. The other three options are all potential disadvantages of the survey method.

25.   a   A survey asks the same questions to many people, while naturalistic observation never involves asking questions.

26.   b   A representative sample is a randomly selected group that matches the population on important characteristics. An experimental group is not necessarily representative of the population.

27.   d   Correlation means relationship between two variables.

28.   b   The correlation coefficient must be between +1.00 and -1.00, so option D is automatically excluded. The sign of the coefficient indicates the direction of the relationship and the absolute value of the coefficient indicates the strength. Therefore, 0.98 is the largest absolute value listed between 0 and 1.

29.   b   For a negative correlation, the variables move in the opposite direction. As one variable increases, the other one decreases. In this case, as the number of absences increase the grade in class decreases.

30.   b   An operational definition defines responses in terms that allow them to be measured, while a hypothesis is an educated guess, not a definition.

31.   a   The exercise is controlled by the experimenter and is, therefore, *independent* of anything the participants do, while the participants' weight is expected to *depend* on the amount of exercise.

32.   a   A control group gets either no treatment or treatment that has no effect (in this case, experimenters are controlling for the possibility that the cigarette itself, and not the nicotine, might cause people to get into collisions).

33.   b   The independent variable is the variable the researcher manipulates. In this case, the instructor manipulated whether there was music playing or not.

34.   d   Recall the test phrase, "How _____(*i.v.*) affects _____ (*d.v.*). The professor is testing "How music affects student test scores." The dependent variable is the subjects' responses. The room the test is taken in and the test itself should be the same for both groups.

35.   b   The reaction time is the response observed in the subject. It is not manipulated by the experimenter.

36.   a   Recall the test phrase, "How hours slept affects driving reaction time."

37.   d   The placebo effect is brought on by expectations, and in this case you felt drunk only because you believed you were drinking alcohol.

38.   a   The double-blind study is an experiment in which neither the participants nor the individuals running the experiment know if the participants are in the experimental or control group. In a single-blind study, only the participants are "blind."

39.   b   Dr. Amabile was looking at "how <u>method of reward</u> affects <u>creativity</u>," and creativity serves as the dependent variable.

40.   b   Participants may be deceived or have information concealed from them at any time during an experiment.

41.   c   Simply because someone is an authority does not mean they should automatically be trusted.

42.   c   Critical thinking involves making reasoned judgments and questioning the basis that others are using to make judgments, such as in response c.

APPLY IT

This section will help you use the concepts you are learning in this class to improve your study skills.

Recall that the four goals of psychology are to describe, predict, explain, and control behavior and mental processes. Why not start with your own behavior? In order to do well in any of your college courses, you should plan on spending around 3-4 hours OUTSIDE of the class for every hour spent IN the class. This means that for a 3 credit hour psychology course, you should plan on spending between 9 to 12 hours per week studying and preparing for class. Sound impossible? Now's your chance to start to think like a psychologist. You have a behavior that you would like to control – your own! How can you get yourself to spend that amount of time each week on this course? We will use two simple methods to try to control your behavior. One is a schedule and the second will be a reward.

The first step in controlling your behavior will be in figuring out exactly what your daily schedule looks like and figuring out when you can fit in your studying. On the following page is a sample schedule called "Proposed Weekly Schedule." Feel free to tear this schedule out and make copies of it so you can use it throughout the course of the semester. If you already have a schedule you prefer, go ahead and use that. The important thing is that you sit down and fill in all your activities and responsibilities. Be sure to include the following:

> The meeting times for all of your classes
> Work hours
> Family responsibilities
> Free time or personal time
> Travel time to get to and from your appointments

The second step in figuring out how to control your behavior has to do with rewards. In chapter 7 we will learn even more about the powerful effect of rewards. For now, select a reward that you will give yourself if you adhere to the proposed schedule for one week. The reward can be simple or big. Some rewards students have used in the past have been going for a cup of coffee with a friend, giving yourself an hour to browse around in a book store, purchasing a new CD., going out one night with your friends, sleeping in on Saturday morning, buying a new piece of clothing for yourself, spending an hour on the phone with an old friend, or going out to your favorite restaurant. You get the point. The only requirement for the reward is that it be something that will truly be rewarding for you. Select the reward and write it down at the top of your Proposed Weekly Schedule.

Now the third step is for you to post your Proposed Weekly Schedule someplace where you will see it often. This can be on the refrigerator, your bathroom mirror, or the dashboard of your car. Next to your Proposed Weekly Schedule, you should place a copy of the Actual Weekly Schedule. You can find a template for this on the page right after the Proposed Weekly Schedule. On the Actual Weekly Schedule, you will write down what actually happens during the week. Be sure to record how much time your events actually take. Try to record this at least once a day to keep your records as accurate as possible.

Finally, the fourth step comes at the end of the week. Now you can compare your proposed and actual schedule. How close were you to achieving your goals? If you came pretty close, go ahead and give yourself the reward you selected. Be sure not to skip this step, as it is extremely important in shaping your behavior in the way you would like to. Spend some time seeing where the actual schedule differed from the proposed. If there are extreme differences, you might want to create another, more realistic, proposed schedule for the following week. Once again, don't forget the reward! Keep going with this process throughout the course of the semester and by the end of the semester you will be very pleased with how you have managed to control your own behavior. Good luck!

Proposed Weekly Schedule   Week # ___   Reward:_____

	Mon.	Tue.	Wed.	Thur.	Fri.	Sat.	Sun.
6:00 am							
7:00 am							
8:00 am							
9:00 am							
10:00 am							
11:00 am							
12:00 pm							
1:00 pm							
2:00 pm							
3:00 pm							
4:00 pm							
5:00 pm							
6:00 pm							
7:00 pm							
8:00 pm							
9:00 pm							
10:00 pm							
11:00 pm							
12:00 am							

Actual Weekly Schedule   Week # ___   Reward:_____

	Mon.	Tue.	Wed.	Thur.	Fri.	Sat.	Sun.
6:00 am							
7:00 am							
8:00 am							
9:00 am							
10:00 am							
11:00 am							
12:00 pm							
1:00 pm							
2:00 pm							
3:00 pm							
4:00 pm							
5:00 pm							
6:00 pm							
7:00 pm							
8:00 pm							
9:00 pm							
10:00 pm							
11:00 pm							
12:00 am							

CHAPTER 2 LEARNING OBJECTIVES

2.1 *How do all the parts of the nervous system relate to one another?*

2.2 *What are neurons and nerves, and how do they work?*

2.3 *How do neurons communicate with each other and with the body?*

2.4 *What are the different neurotransmitters?*

2.5 *How do the brain and spinal cord interact?*

2.6 *How does the somatic nervous system allow people and animals to interact with their surroundings?*

2.7 *How does the autonomic system control the body's automatic functions and its reaction to stress?*

2.8 *How do psychologists study the brain and how it works?*

2.9 *What are the different structures of the bottom part of the brain, and what do they do?*

2.10 *What are the structures of the brain that control emotion, learning, memory, and motivation?*

2.11 *What parts of the cortex control the different senses and the movement of the body?*

2.12 *What parts of the cortex are responsible for higher forms of thought, such as language?*

2.13 *How does the left side of the brain differ from the right side?*

2.14 *How do the hormones released by glands interact with the nervous system and affect behavior?*

SUMMARY

The **nervous system** is made up of a complex network of cells throughout your body. Since psychology is the study of behavior and mental processes, understanding how the nervous system works provides fundamental information about what is going on inside your body when you engage in a specific behavior, feel a particular emotion or have an abstract thought. The role of the nervous system is to carry information. Without your nervous system, you would not be able to think, feel, or act. The cells in the nervous system that carry information are called **neurons**. Information enters a neuron at the **dendrites**, flows through the cell body (or **soma**) and down the **axon** in order to pass the information on to the next cell. Although neurons are the cells that carry the information, most of the nervous system consists of **glial cells**. Glial cells provide food, support, and insulation to the neuron cells. The insulation around the neuron is called **myelin** and works in a way very similar to the plastic coating of an electrical wire.

Neurons use an electrical signal to send information from one end of its cell to the other. At rest, a neuron has a negative charge inside and a positive charge outside. When a signal arrives, gates in the cell wall next to the signal open and the positive charge moves inside. The positive charge inside the cell causes the next set of gates to open and those positive charges move inside. In this way, the electrical signal makes its way down the length of the cell. The movement of the electrical signal is called an **action potential**. After the action potential is over, the positive charges get pumped back out of the cell and the neuron returns to its negatively-charged state. This condition is called the **resting potential**. A neuron acts in an **all-or-none** manner. This means the neuron either has an action potential or it does not. The neuron indicates the strength of the signal and how many action potentials are produced or "fired" within a certain amount of time.

Neurons pass information on to target cells using a chemical signal. When the electrical signal travels down the axon and reaches the other end of the neuron, it enters the **axon terminal** and causes the **neurotransmitters** in the **synaptic vesicles** to be released into the fluid-filled space between the two cells. This fluid-filled space is called the **synaptic gap**. The neurotransmitters are the chemical signals the neuron uses to communicate with its target cell. The neurotransmitters fit into the receptor sites of the target cell and create a new electrical signal that then can be transmitted down the length of the target cell. The neurotransmitters are cleared out of the synaptic gap through the process or **reuptake**, diffusion, or by being broken apart by an enzyme.

Neurotransmitters can have two different effects on the target cell. If the neurotransmitter increases the likelihood of an action potential in the target cell, it is called an **excitatory neurotransmitter**. If the neurotransmitter decreases the likelihood of an action potential, it is call an **inhibitory neurotransmitter**. **Agonists** and **antagonists** are chemicals that are not naturally found in our body but can fit into the receptor sites of target cells if they get into our nervous system. Agonists lead to a similar response in the target cell as the neurotransmitter itself, while antagonists block or reduce the action of the neurotransmitter on the target cell. There are at least 50-100 different types of neurotransmitters in the human body. **Acetylcholine** was the first to be discovered; it is an excitatory neurotransmitter that causes your muscles to contract. Gamma amino butyric acid (**GABA**) is an inhibitory neurotransmitter that decreases the activity level of neurons in your brain. **Serotonin** is both an excitatory and inhibitory neurotransmitter and has been linked with sleep, mood and appetite. Low levels of the neurotransmitter **dopamine** have been found to cause Parkinson's disease, and increased levels of dopamine have been linked to the psychological disorder known as schizophrenia. **Endorphin** is a special neurotransmitter called a neural regulator that controls the release of other neurotransmitters. When endorphin is released in the body, the neurons transmitting information about pain are not able to fire action potentials.

The **central nervous system (CNS)** is made up of the brain and the **spinal cord**. The spinal cord is a long bundle of neurons that transmits messages between the brain and the body. The cell bodies or somas of the neurons are located along the inside of the spinal cord and the cell axons run along the outside of the spinal cord. **Sensory neurons** send information from our senses to the spinal cord. For example, sensory neurons would relay information about a sharp pain in your finger. **Motor neurons** send commands from the spinal cord to our muscles, such as a command to pull your finger back. **Interneurons** connect sensory and motor neurons and help to coordinate the signals. All three of these neurons act together in the spinal cord to form a reflex arc.

The **peripheral nervous system (PNS)** is made up of all the nerves and neurons that are NOT in the brain or spinal cord. This includes all the nerves that connect to your eyes, ears, skin, mouth and muscles. The PNS is divided into two parts, the **somatic nervous system** and the **autonomic nervous system**. The somatic nervous system consists of all the nerves coming from our sensory systems and all the nerves going to the skeletal muscles that control our voluntary movements. The autonomic nervous system is made up of the nerves going to and from our organs, glands and involuntary muscles and is divided into two parts: the **sympathetic division** and the **parasympathetic division**. The sympathetic division turns on the body's fight-or-flight reactions, which include responses such as increased heart rate, increased breathing, and dilation of your pupils. The parasympathetic division controls your body when you are in a state of rest to keep the heart beating regularly, breathing normally, and to coordinate digestion. The parasympathetic division is active most of the time.

Researchers have developed several methods to observe the structure and activity of a living brain. If a researcher wants a picture of the structure of the brain, he might choose a **CT scan** or an **MRI**. Computed tomography (CT) scans use x-rays to create images of the structures within the brain. Magnetic resonance images (MRIs) use a magnetic field to "take a picture" of the brain. MRIs provide much greater detail than CT scans. On the other hand, if a researcher wants to record the activity of the brain, she might select an **EEG**, **fMRI**, or **PET scan**. An electroencephalogram (EEG) provides a record of the electrical activity of groups of neurons just below the surface of the skull. A functional magnetic resonance image (fMRI) uses magnetic fields in the same way as an MRI, but goes a step further and pieces the pictures together to show changes over a short period of time. A positron emission tomography (PET) scan involves injecting a person with a low dose of a radioactive substance and then recording the activity of that substance in the person's brain.

The brain can be roughly divided into three sections: the brainstem, the cortex, and the structures under the cortex. The **brainstem** is the lowest part of the brain that connects to the spinal cord. The outer wrinkled covering of the brain is the **cortex**, and the structures under the cortex are essentially everything between the brainstem and the cortex. The brainstem contains four important structures. The **medulla** controls life-sustaining functions such as heart beat, breathing and swallowing. The **pons** influences sleep, dreaming and coordination of movements. The **reticular formation** plays a crucial role in attention and arousal, and the **cerebellum** controls all of the movements we make without really "thinking" about it.

One main group of structures under the cortex is the **limbic system**. The limbic system includes the **thalamus**, **hypothalamus**, **hippocampus**, and **amygdala**. The thalamus receives input from the sensory systems, processes it and then passes it on to the appropriate area of the cortex. The hypothalamus interacts with the endocrine system to regulate body temperature, thirst, hunger, sleeping, sexual activity and mood. It appears that the hippocampus is critical for the formation of long-term memories and for memories of the locations of objects. The amygdala is a small almond-shaped structure that is involved in our response to fear.

The outer part of the brain, or cortex, is divided into a right and a left section called **cerebral hemispheres**. The two hemispheres communicate with each other through a thick band of neurons called the **corpus callosum**. Each cerebral hemisphere can be roughly divided into four sections. These sections are called lobes. The **occipital lobes** are at the back of the brain and process visual information. The **parietal lobes** are located at the top and back half of the brain and deal with information regarding touch, temperature, body position and possibly taste. The **temporal lobes** are just behind your temples and process auditory information. The **frontal lobes** are located at the front of your head and are responsible for higher mental functions, such as planning, personality and decision making, as well as language and motor movements. **Association areas** are the areas within each of the lobes that are responsible for "making sense" of all the incoming information. Two association areas involved with language are **Broca's area,** which controls the production of speech, and **Wernicke's area,** which controls the comprehension of speech. The two cerebral hemispheres are not identical. The left hemisphere is typically more active when a person is using language, math, and other analytical skills, while the right hemisphere shows more activity during tasks of perception, recognition, and expression of emotions.

The **endocrine glands** represent a second communication system in the body. The endocrine glands secrete chemicals called **hormones** directly into the bloodstream. The **pituitary gland** is located in the brain and secretes the hormones that regulate milk production, salt levels, and the activity of other glands. The **pineal gland** is also located in the brain and regulates the sleep cycle through the secretion of melatonin. The **thyroid gland** is located in the neck and releases a hormone that regulates metabolism. The **pancreas** controls the level of blood sugar in the body while the gonads regulate sexual behavior and reproduction. The **adrenal glands** play a critical role in regulating the body's response to stress.

KEY POINTS

- Explain what neurons are and how they work to transfer and process information.
- Introduce the peripheral nervous system and describe its role in the body.
- Describe the methods used to observe the structure and activity of the brain.
- Introduce the basic structures of the brain.
- Discuss the role of the endocrine system.

KEY CONCEPTS

nervous system	An extensive network of specialized cells that carry information to and from all parts of the body.
neurons	The basic cell that makes up the nervous system, which receives and sends messages within that system.

27

dendrites	Branch-like structures that receive messages from other neurons.
soma	The cell body of the neuron, responsible for maintaining the life of the cell.
axon	Long tube-like structure that carries the neural message to other cells.
glial cells	Grey fatty cells that provide support for the neurons to grow on and around, deliver nutrients to neurons, produce myelin to coat axons, and clean up waste products and dead neurons.
myelin	Fatty substances produced by certain glial cells that coat the axons of neurons to insulate, protect, and speed up the neural impulse.
action potential	The release of the neural impulse consisting of a reversal of the electrical charge within the axon.
resting potential	The state of the neuron when not firing a neural impulse.
all-or-none	Referring to the fact that a neuron either fires completely or does not fire at all.
axon terminals	Branches at the end of the axon.
neurotransmitter	Chemical found in the synaptic vesicles which, when released, has an effect on the next cell.
synaptic vesicles	Sack-like structures found inside the synaptic knob containing chemicals.
synaptic gap	Microscopic fluid-filled space between the rounded areas on the end of the axon terminals of one cell and the dendrites or surface of the next cell.
reuptake	Process by which neurotransmitters are taken back into the synaptic vesicles.
excitatory neurotransmitter	Neurotransmitter that causes the receiving cell to fire.
inhibitory neurotransmitter	Neurotransmitter that causes the receiving cell to stop firing.
agonists	Chemical substances that mimic or enhance the effects of a neurotransmitter on the receptor sites of the next cell, increasing or decreasing the activity of that cell.
antagonists	Chemical substances that block or reduce a cell's response to the action of other chemicals or neurotransmitters.
Acetylcholine	The first neurotransmitter to be discovered. Found to regulate

memories in the CNS and the action of skeletal and smooth muscles in the PNS.

GABA	Abbreviation for gamma-aminobutyric acid, the major inhibitory neurotransmitter in the brain.
serotonin	Neurotransmitter involved in pain disorders and emotional perceptions. Is also known as 5-hydroxytryptamine (5-HT).
dopamine	Neurotransmitter that regulates movement, balance and walking and is involved in the disorders of schizophrenia and Parkinson's disease.
endorphin	Neurotransmitter that is found naturally in the body and works to block pain and elevate mood. It is chemically similar to morphine and its name is short for "endogenous morphine."
central nervous system (CNS)	Part of the nervous system consisting of the brain and spinal cord.
spinal cord	A long bundle of neurons that carries messages to and from the body to the brain and that is responsible for very fast, life-saving reflexes.
sensory neuron	A neuron that carries information from the senses to the central nervous system. Also called afferent neuron.
motor neuron	A neuron that carries messages from the central nervous system to the muscles of the body. Also called efferent neuron.
interneuron	A neuron found in the center of the spinal cord that receives information from the sensory neurons and sends commands to the muscles through the motor neurons. Interneurons also make up the bulk of the neurons in the brain.
peripheral nervous system (PNS)	All nerves and neurons that are not contained in the brain and spinal cord but run through the body itself.
somatic nervous system	Division of the PNS consisting of nerves that carry information from the senses to the CNS and from the CNS to the voluntary muscles of the body.
autonomic nervous system	Division of the PNS consisting of nerves that control all of the involuntary muscles, organs, and glands.
sympathetic division	Part of the autonomic nervous system that is responsible for reacting to stressful events and bodily arousal. Also known as the fight-or-flight system.
parasympathetic division	Part of the autonomic system that restores the body to normal functioning after arousal and is responsible for the day-today functioning of the organs and glands. Sometimes referred to as

the rest-and-digest system.

electroencephalograph (EEG)	Machine designed to record the brain wave patterns produced by electrical activity of the surface of the brain.
functional magnetic resonance imaging (fMRI)	A method used to observe activity in the brain. It shows which structures are active during particular mental operations using the same basic procedure as MRI.
positron emission tomography (PET)	Brain imaging method in which a radioactive sugar is injected into the subject and a computer compiles a color-coded image of the activity of the brain, with lighter colors indicating more activity.
computed tomography (CT)	Brain imaging method using computer-controlled x-rays of the brain.
magnetic resonance imaging (MRI)	Brain imaging method using radio waves and magnetic fields of the body to produce detailed images of the brain.
brainstem	Section of the brain that connects directly to the spinal cord and regulates vital functions such as breathing, the heart, reflexes and level of alertness.
cortex	Outermost covering of the brain consisting of densely packed neurons, responsible for higher thought processes and interpretation of sensory input.
medulla	The first large swelling at the top of the spinal cord, forming the lowest part of the brain, which is responsible for life-sustaining functions such as breathing, swallowing, and heart rate.
pons	The larger swelling above the medulla, which connects the top of the brain to the bottom, and plays a part in sleep, dreaming, left-right body coordination, and arousal.
reticular formation	An area of neurons running through the middle of the medulla and the pons and slightly beyond, responsible for selective attention.
cerebellum	Part of the lower brain located behind the pons that controls and coordinates involuntary, rapid, fine motor movement.
limbic system	A group of several brain structures located under the cortex and involved in learning, emotion, memory, and motivation.
thalamus	Part of the limbic system located in the center of the brain, this structure relays sensory information from the lower part of the brain to the proper areas of the cortex, and processes some sensory information before sending it to its proper area.
hypothalamus	Small structure in the brain located below the thalamus and directly above the pituitary gland, responsible for motivational

behavior such as sleep, hunger, thirst, and sex.

hippocampus	Curved structure located within each temporal lobe, responsible for the formation of long term memories and the storage of memory for location of objects.
amygdala	Brain structure located near the hippocampus, responsible for fear responses and memory of fear.
cerebral hemispheres	The two sections of the cortex on the left and right sides of the brain.
corpus callosum	Thick band of neurons that connects the right and left cerebral hemispheres.
occipital lobes	Sections of the brain located at the rear and bottom of each cerebral hemisphere, containing the visual centers of the brain.
parietal lobes	Sections of the brain located at the top and back of each cerebral hemisphere, containing the centers for touch, taste, and temperature sensations.
temporal lobes	Areas of the cortex located just behind the temples, containing the neurons responsible for the sense of hearing and meaningful speech.
frontal lobes	Areas of the cortex located in the front and top of the brain, responsible for higher mental processes and decision making, as well as the production of fluent speech.
association areas	Areas within each lobe of the cortex responsible for the coordination and interpretation of information, as well as higher mental processing.
Broca's area	Association area of the brain located in the frontal lobe that is responsible for language production and language processing.
Wernicke's area	Association area of the brain in the temporal lobe that has been found to be involved in the comprehension of spoken language.
endocrine glands	Glands that secrete chemicals called hormones directly into the bloodstream.
hormones	Chemicals released into the bloodstream by endocrine glands.
pituitary gland	Gland located in the brain that secretes human growth hormone and influences all other hormone-secreting glands (also know as the master gland).
pineal gland	Endocrine gland located near the base of the cerebrum that secretes melatonin.

thyroid gland	Endocrine gland found in the neck that regulates metabolism.
pancreas	Endocrine gland that controls the levels of sugar in the blood.
adrenal glands	Endocrine glands located on top of each kidney that secrete over thirty different hormones to deal with stress, regulate salt intake, and provide a secondary source of sex hormones affecting the sexual changes that occur during adolescence.

HINTS

1. As you can see in the "New Terms and Concepts" section, this chapter introduces a large number of new vocabulary terms. You should plan on spending additional time working on these new terms and committing them to memory. Some students find flash cards and study partners helpful for learning this material. For additional assistance, work through the "Study Challenge" at the end of this section. Many students have found it extremely helpful.

2. Some students have a hard time keeping the various research methods straight. It might be helpful to divide the methods into two categories: (1) methods that provide a picture of the structures of the brain and (2) methods that measure the activity of the brain. CT scans were developed before MRIs and do not provide as many details as the MRI does. If you've ever had a CT scan or an MRI performed, you will know that getting an MRI is a much more expensive procedure than a CT scan, although neither procedure is cheap. EEGs only provide information about activity in the outermost part of your brain. PET scans can provide information about activity anywhere in your brain but typically don't provide details about the exact location of the activity. fMRIs show the activity and the detailed location where the activity is taking place.

Structure of the brain	Activity of the brain
CT scan	EEG
MRI	PET scan
	fMRI

    Think of some instances when a researcher would want to use the methods in the left column and write them in the space here:

    _____

    _____

    _____

    You might have listed examples such as attempting to locate a tumor in the brain, comparing the size of a brain structure between males and females, looking for abnormalities in brain structures for patients with a particular psychological disorder.

Now think of some instances when a researcher would want to use the methods in the right column and write them in the space here:

_____

_____

_____

You might have listed examples such as recording the activity of the brain in a patient with epilepsy, locating the area of the brain that is active when a person is solving complex word problems, observing the activity of the brain during a normal night of sleep, determining if women and men use the same part of the brain when solving math problems.

3. Students sometimes have trouble remembering the functions of the peripheral nervous system (PNS). Recall that the PNS is divided into two main sections: the somatic nervous system and the autonomic nervous system. The somatic nervous system deals with the senses and the skeletal muscles (all "S's") and is fairly straight-forward to understand. The autonomic nervous system is slightly more complicated. First, understand that the *autonomic* nervous system deals with all the *automatic* functions of your body. What are some functions that are controlled automatically in your body? List them here:

    _____ , _____ , _____ , _____ ,

    You probably mentioned functions such as digestion, heart rate, pupil dilation, breathing, salivation, or perspiration, to name a few. These are the functions controlled by the autonomic system.

    There are two components of the autonomic system, and they serve to balance each other out. The two divisions are the sympathetic and parasympathetic divisions. Most of the time, the parasympathetic division is in control. Some people have called the parasympathetic division the rest-and-digest system because it controls the digestive processes, maintains a resting heart and breathing rate and in general keeps your body in its normal relaxed state. The sympathetic division goes into action when your body needs to react to some type of threat. It might be helpful to associate **s**ympathetic with **s**urprise, since the sympathetic division is the part of your nervous system that responds when you are surprised. This system is often referred to as the fight-or flight system. What happens to your body when you are surprised? List some of the responses here:

    _____ , _____ , _____ , _____ ,

    You probably mentioned responses such as your heart rate increases, you breathe faster, your pupils dilate, you begin to sweat, to name a few. All of these responses are "turned on" by the sympathetic division of your autonomic nervous system and aid in your survival by allowing you to respond quickly to a threat.

4. Two of the brain structures most commonly confused with each other are the hippocampus and the hypothalamus. Both of the structures are located in the limbic system in the area of your brain above your brainstem and below the outer surface, however the two structures are involved are in charge of very different functions in your body. The hippocampus has been found to be important in helping us form memories that last more than just a few seconds. Patients with damage to the hippocampus often cannot remember information for longer than a few seconds. Also, the hippocampus is very important in storing memories of where things are located, called a spatial map. On the other hand, the hypothalamus is important in controlling many of our basic bodily functions, such as sleeping, drinking, eating, and sexual activities. The structures are often confused because the two words sound so similar to each other. Can you think of any memory device or "trick" to help you keep these two brain structures separate? List your idea in the space below:

hippocampus: _____

hypothalamus: _____

One suggestion might be as follows: If you look at the word hippocampus you can think of the last part of the word – campus. In order to get around on your college campus, you need to keep in mind where certain buildings and areas are located. This is exactly what your hippocampus is involved in. Without your hippo-<u>campus</u>, you would have a very hard time finding your way around your college <u>campus.</u>

To remember the hypothalamus, first it might help to understand how the name came about. "Hypo" means under or below. For example, if someone has "hypothermia" their body temperature is under the normal amount and the person is probably feeling very cold. If someone has "hypoglycemia," they have under or lower than the normal amount of blood sugar (glycemia refers to the sugar found in your blood). What do you think "hypothalamus" means?

_____

If you wrote under the thalamus, then you are correct. The hypothalamus is located directly underneath the thalamus. You might also look at the name to try to remember some of the activities the hypothalamus regulates. Recall that we said the hypothalamus plays a role in hunger, sleep, thirst and sex. If you look at the "hypo" of hypothalamus you might memorize "h" – hunger, "y" – yawning, "p" – parched (or very, very thirsty) and "o" – overly excited.

SAMPLE EXAM

For the following multiple choice questions, select the answer you feel best answers the question and explain the rationale or reason for your selection in the space provided.

Objective 2.1

1.   The function of the _____ is to carry information to and from all parts of the body.
        a) soma
        b) synapse
        c) nervous system
        d) endorphins

    Rationale:
    The nervous system is the correct answer because sending information to and from all parts of the body is the primary function of the nervous system. The soma and the synapse are both parts of an individual neuron and endorphins are one type of neurotransmitter found in the body.

2.   The central nervous system is made of which two components?
        a) the somatic and autonomic systems.
        b) the brain and the spinal cord.
        c) the sympathetic and parasympathetic divisions.
        d) neurotransmitters and hormones.

    Rationale:
    The central nervous system is composed of the nerves and neurons in the center of your body. Choices A and C are both components of the peripheral nervous system. Hormones are the chemical messengers for the endocrine system..

Objective 2.2

3. A specialized cell that makes up the nervous system that receives and sends messages within that system is called a _____.
        a) glial cell
        b) neuron
        c) cell body
        d) myelin sheath

    Rationale:
    B is the correct answer because neurons are a specialized cell that makes up the nervous system that receives and sends messages within that system. A is incorrect because glial cells serve as a structure for neurons.

4. What type of signal is used to relay a message from one end of a neuron to the other end?
    a) chemical
    b) hormonal
    c) biochemical
    d) electrical

Rationale:

_____

_____

Objective 2.3

5.
    A chemical found in the synaptic vesicles which, when released, has an effect on the next cell is called a_____.
    a) glial cell
    b) neurotransmitter
    c) precursor cell
    d) synapse

Rationale:

_____

_____

6. What event causes the release of chemicals into the synaptic gap?
    a) an agonist binding to the dendrites
    b) an action potential reaching the axon terminal
    c) the reuptake of neurotransmitters
    d) excitation of the glial cells

Rationale:

_____

_____

Objective 2.4

7. Sara has been experiencing a serious memory problem. An interdisciplinary team has ruled out a range of causes and believes that a neurotransmitter is involved. Which neurotransmitter is most likely involved in this problem?
    a) GABA
    b) dopamine
    c) serotonin
    d) acetylcholine

Rationale:

_____

_____

8. A neuron releases neurotransmitters into the synaptic gap that reduce the frequency of action potentials in the neighboring cell. The neuron most likely released is:
       a) an inhibitory neurotransmitter
       b) an excitatory neurotransmitter
       c) acetylcholine
       d) an agonist

Rationale:

_____

_____

Objective 2.5

9. Which part of the nervous system takes the information received from the senses, makes sense out of it, makes decisions, and sends commands out to the muscles and the rest of the body?
       a) spinal cord
       b) brain
       c) reflexes
       d) interneurons
Rationale:

_____

_____

Objective 2.6

10. Every deliberate action you make, such as pedaling a bike, walking, scratching, or smelling a flower involves neurons in the _____ nervous system.
       a) sympathetic
       b) somatic
       c) parasympathetic
       d) autonomic
Rationale:

_____

_____

Objective 2.7

11. Involuntary muscles are controlled by the _____ nervous system.
       a) somatic
       b) autonomic
       c) sympathetic
       d) parasympathetic
Rationale:

_____

_____

12. Which of the following responses would occur if your sympathetic nervous system has been activated?
   a) increased heart rate
   b) pupil constriction
   c) slowed breathing
   d) increased digestion

Rationale:

_____

_____

Objective 2.8

13. Small metal disks are pasted onto Miranda's scalp and they are connected by wire to a machine that translates the electrical energy from her brain into wavy lines on a moving piece of paper. From this description, it is evident that Miranda's brain is being studied through the use of_____.
   a) CT scans
   b) functional magnetic resonance imaging (fMRI)
   c) a microelectrode
   d) an electroencephalograph

Rationale:

_____

_____

14. Which method would a researcher select if she wanted to determine if her patient's right hemisphere was the same size as his left hemisphere?
   a) EEG
   b) deep lesioning
   c) CT scan
   d) PET scan

Rationale:

_____

_____

15. Which of the following is responsible for the ability to selectively attend to certain kinds of information in one's surroundings and become alert to changes in information?
    a) reticular formation
    b) pons
    c) medulla
    d) cerebellum

    Rationale:

    _____

    _____

16. When a professional baseball player swings a bat and hits a home run, he is relying on his _____ to coordinate the practiced movements of his body.
    a) pons
    b) medulla
    c) cerebellum
    d) reticular formation

    Rationale:

    _____

    _____

Objective 2.10

17. Eating, drinking, sexual behavior, sleeping, and temperature control are most strongly influenced by the
    a) hippocampus
    b) thalamus
    c) hypothalamus
    d) amygdala

    Rationale:

    _____

    _____

18. After a brain operation, a laboratory rat no longer displays any fear when placed into a cage with a snake. Which part of the rat's brain was most likely damaged during the operation?
    a) amygdala
    b) hypothalamus
    c) cerebellum
    d) hippocampus

    Rationale:

    _____

    _____

19. Darla was in an automobile accident that resulted in an injury to her brain. Her sense of touch has been affected. Which part of the brain is the most likely site of the damage?
    a) frontal lobes
    b) temporal lobes
    c) occipital lobes
    d) parietal lobes

    Rationale:

    _____

    _____

20. If a person damages their occipital lobes, which would be the most likely problem they would report to their doctor?
    a) trouble hearing
    b) problems with their vision
    c) decreased sense of taste
    d) numbness on the right side of their body

    Rationale:

    _____

    _____

Objective 2.12

21. Damage to what area of the brain would result in an inability to comprehend language?
    a) occipital lobes
    b) Broca's area
    c) Wernicke's area
    d) parietal lobe
    Rationale:

    _____

    _____

Objective 2.13

22. If Darren's brain is like that of most people, then language will be handled by his
    a) corpus callosum
    b) occipital lobe
    c) right hemisphere
    d) left hemisphere

    Rationale:

    _____

    _____

23. The two hemispheres of the brain are identical copies of each other.
    a) true
    b) false

    Rationale:

    _____

    _____

Objective 2.14

24. The hormone released by the pineal gland that reduces body temperature and prepares you for sleep is
    a) melatonin
    b) DHEA
    c) parathormone
    d) thyroxin

    Rationale:

    _____

    _____

25. Which endocrine gland regulates your body's response to stress?
    a) pancreas
    b) thyroid gland
    c) pineal gland
    d) adrenal gland

    Rationale:

    _____

    _____

SAMPLE EXAM ANSWERS & RATIONALES

1.   c   The nervous system is the correct answer because sending information to and from all parts of the body is the primary function of the nervous system. The soma and the synapse are both parts of an individual neuron and endorphins are one type of neurotransmitter found in the body.

2.   b   The central nervous system is composed of the nerves and neurons in the center of your body. Choices A and C are both components of the peripheral nervous system. Hormones are the chemical messengers for the endocrine system.

3.   b   B is the correct answer because neurons are a specialized cell that makes up the nervous system that receives and sends messages within that system. A is incorrect because glial cells serve as a structure for neurons.

4.   d   Neurons use electrical signals to communicate within their own cell. The electrical signal is called an action potential.

5.   b   Neurotransmitters are stored in the synaptic vesicles. D is incorrect because the synapse is the space between the synaptic knob of one cell and the dendrites.

6.   d   When the electrical signal (called an action potential) reaches the axon terminal, the synaptic vesicles release their contents into the synaptic gap.

7.   d   Acetylcholine is found in a part of the brain responsible for forming new memories.

8.   a   Inhibitory neurotransmitters inhibit the electrical activity of the receptor cell.

9.   b   The spinal cord carries messages to and from the body to the brain, but it is the job of the brain to make sense of all the information.

10.   b   The somatic nervous system controls voluntary muscle movement, whereas the autonomic nervous system consists of nerves that control all of the involuntary muscles, organs, and glands.

11.   b   The autonomic nervous system controls involuntary muscles like the heart, stomach, and intestines.

12.   a   The sympathetic division is responsible for controlling your body's fight-or-flight response, which prepares your body to deal with a potential threat. The responses include increased heart rate and breathing, pupil dilation, and decreased digestion, among others.

13.   d   An electroencephalograph or EEG records brain wave patterns. CT scans take computer-controlled x-rays of the brain.

14.   c   C is the only selection that would allow the researcher to take a picture of the structure of the brain. All other options listed would provide information about the activity of the brain.

15.   b   The reticular formation plays a role in selective attention.

16.   c   The cerebellum is responsible for controlling the movements that we have practiced repeatedly, the movements that we don't have to really "think about."

17.   c   The hypothalamus is regulates sleep, hunger, thirst, and sex.

18.   a   The amygdala has been found to regulate the emotion of fear. The amygdala is found within the limbic system, a part of our brain responsible for regulating emotions and memories.

19.   d   The parietal lobes contain the centers for touch, taste, and temperature.

20.   b   The occipital lobes are responsible for processing visual information.

21.   c   Wernicke's area is located in the temporal lobe and is important in the comprehension of language. Broca's area is located in the frontal lobe and plays a role in the production of language.

22.   d   For most people, the left hemisphere specializes in language.

23.   b   The left hemisphere is more active during language and math problems, while the right hemisphere appears to play a larger role in non-verbal and perception based tasks.

24.   a   The pineal gland secretes melatonin.

25.   d   The adrenal glands secrete several hormones in response to stress.

APPLY IT

This section will help you use the concepts you are learning in this class to improve your study skills.

Think about what you have learned about the brain in this chapter. How can this knowledge help you enhance your study skills? As mentioned in the Study Hints section, there is a lot of new information presented in this chapter. How will you be able to keep all of this information straight? One thing you learned in this chapter is that most of our higher mental processing goes on in the cortex of your brain. You also learned that the cortex contains association areas that are important for piecing all the information together and making sense of it. Often the association areas coordinate input from multiple sensory systems. Typically, when you learn information from the textbook, you are receiving information as written words. In order to incorporate additional areas of your cortex, try using the following lecture aids during class. Take notes on the lecture aids in addition to writing down words. You might be surprised how much the additional visual input will enhance your memory of the information.

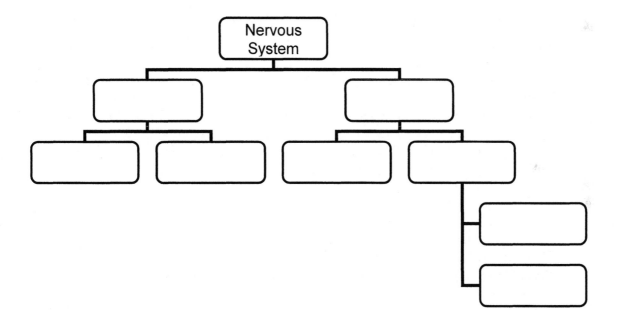

THE NEURON

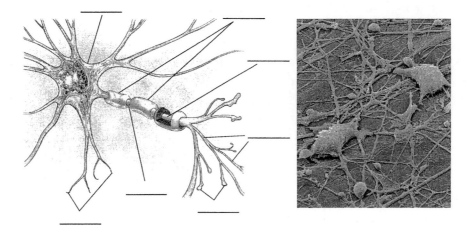

THE SYNAPSE

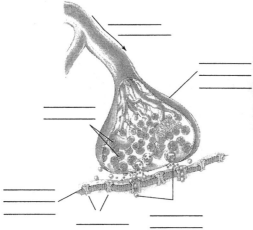

A micrograph of synaptic knobs (small mushroom-like fibers) clustering around another neuron's cell body.

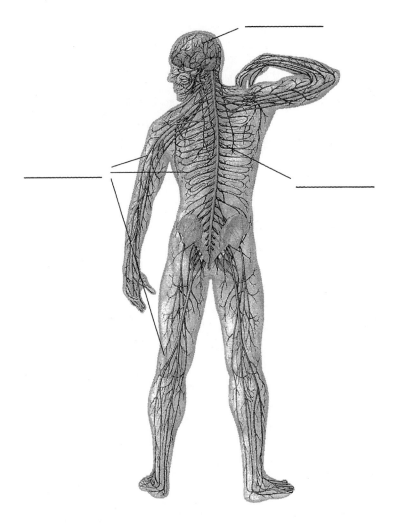

CHAPTER 3 LEARNING OBJECTIVES

3.1	What is sensation and how does it enter the central nervous system?	3.10	How do the senses of taste and smell work?
3.2	How can some sensations be ignored?	3.11	How does the sense of touch work and what happens when people experience pain?
3.3	What is light?		
3.4	How do the parts of the eye work together?		
3.5	How do the eyes see, and how do the eyes see different colors?	3.12	What sense allows the body to know how it is moving and when it is balanced?
3.6	What is sound?	3.13	What are perception and perceptual constancies?
3.7	How do the parts of the ear work together to hear sounds?	3.14	What are the Gestalt principles of perception?
3.8	What is a hearing impairment?	3.15	How do people perceive the world in three dimensions?
3.9	What can be done to help people with a hearing impairment?	3.16	How do visual illusions work?
		3.17	What factors can influence perception?

SUMMARY

Sensation allows us to receive information from the world around us. Outside stimuli (such as the sound of your mother's voice) activate **sensory receptors** that convert the outside stimulus into a message that our nervous system can understand – electrical and chemical signals. The sensory receptors are specialized forms of neurons and make up part of our somatic nervous system. **Ernst Weber** and **Gustav Fechner** were two pioneers in the study of sensory thresholds. Weber studied the smallest difference between two stimuli that a person could detect fifty percent of the time. He called this difference a **just noticeable difference (jnd),** and he discovered that the jnd is always a constant. For instance, if a person needs to add 5% more weight to notice the difference in the heaviness of a package, then this person's jnd is 5%. If the initial weight of the package is 10 lbs, then 0.5 lbs would need to be added to detect a difference (5% of 10 lb = 0.5lb). If the initial weight is 100 lbs, then 5 lbs would need to be added in order for the person to detect a difference in weight (5% of 100 lb = 5 lb). The fact that the jnd is always a constant is known as **Weber's Law**. Fechner investigated the lowest level of a stimulus that a person could detect fifty percent of the time. He called this level the **absolute threshold**. **Habituation** and **sensory adaptation** are two methods our body uses to ignore unchanging information. Habituation takes place when the lower centers of the brain prevent conscious attention to a constant stimulus, such as the humming of a desktop computer. Sensory adaptation occurs in the sensory receptors themselves when the receptors stop responding to a constant stimulus, such as the feeling of your shirt on your skin.

The visual sensory system is activated by light waves. There are three psychological aspects to our experience of light. **Brightness** is determined by the height, or amplitude, of the wave. **Color**, or hue, is determined by the length of the light wave and **saturation**, or purity, is determined by the mixture of wavelengths of varying heights and lengths. Light enters your eye through the cornea, which protects your eye and helps to focus the light, and then travels through a hole in your iris, called your pupil. The iris is a group of muscles that control the size of the pupil. The light then passes through the lens, which focuses the light and travels through the vitreous humor in the middle of your eyeball to reach the **retina** at the very back of your eye. The retina is the size of a postage stamp and contains the sensory receptor neurons that convert the incoming light waves into an electrical-chemical signal that the nervous system can understand. Your eye contains two types of sensory receptors, **rods** and **cones**. About seventy percent of the sensory receptors in your eyes are rods. Rods detect the brightness of light and send information about the levels of black, white, and shades of gray. The rods are located over the entire retina except at the very center. Rods are extremely sensitive to light but produce images with low acuity, or sharpness. Cones make up the remaining 30% of the sensory receptors in your eyes and are located mainly in the center of the retina. Cones transmit information about color and produce images with very high acuity.

The exact method the cones use to transmit information about color is still unknown. Two theories are currently proposed. The **trichromatic theory** was originally proposed by Thomas Young and later modified by Hermann Helmholtz. The theory suggests that there are three types of cones, red, green and blue, that combine to produce sensation of color much like three spotlights would combine to produce the full spectrum of colors. The trichromatic theory most likely is an accurate description of the cones but cannot explain certain visual phenomena such as the **afterimage**. The afterimage is the image you see after staring at something and then looking away. For example, stare at something red, then look away and you see a green afterimage. A different theory of color perception known as the **opponent-process theory** was developed to explain phenomena such as the afterimage. The theory states that cones are arranged in pairs with a red-green pair and a blue-yellow pair. If one member of the pair is firing, then the other member cannot. When you stare at something red, the red member sends information and the green member is inhibited. When you look away, the green member is no longer inhibited and sends information even though you are not looking at anything green. Both the trichromatic theory and the opponent-process theory are probably correct. The trichromatic theory most likely explains the actions of cones in the retina, while the opponent-process theory explains the actions higher up in the visual system in the thalamus of the brain.

After light is converted to an electrical-chemical signal by the rods and cones, the message travels out of the eye through the **optic nerve**, crosses over at the optic chiasm, enters the medulla, and then the thalamus. From the thalamus the signal is sent to the occipital lobes, which, if you recall from the previous chapter, are responsible for processing visual information. **Color blindness** is caused by defective cones in the retina and can be one of three types.

Our sense of hearing, the **auditory system**, is activated by the vibrations of molecules in the air that surrounds us. These vibrations are called sound waves, and like light waves, we respond to three features of sound waves. **Pitch** corresponds to the frequency of the wave, **volume** is determined by the amplitude of the wave and **timbre** relates to the purity of the wavelengths. Humans can only respond to wavelengths of a certain frequency. The average range for humans is between 20 and 20,000 **Hertz** (Hz) or waves per second. Sound waves enter our auditory system through the **pinna**, vibrate the eardrum, which causes the hammer, anvil and stirrup to vibrate. The vibrations of the stirrup cause the oval window to move back and forth, which causes the fluid in the **cochlea** to vibrate. The fluid causes the **basilar membrane** to vibrate which causes the **organ of Corti** to move up, and this causes the **hair cells** to bend. The hair cells are the sensory receptors of the auditory system and the movement of the hair cells triggers an action potential in the axon. A louder noise causes the hair cell to fire more action potentials.

There are three theories that explain how the brain receives information about pitch. **Place theory** states that pitch is determined by the place on the organ of Corti that is stimulated. The **frequency theory** suggests that the speed of vibrations of the basilar membrane determine the pitch heard by the person. The **volley principle** suggests that hair cells take turns firing in a process called volleying. All three theories are correct. Frequency theory holds true for wavelengths of 100 Hz or less, volley theory covers the wavelengths from 100 to 1000 Hz, and place theory seems to account for the wavelengths faster than 1000 Hz. Hearing impairment is the term used to describe difficulties in hearing. **Conduction hearing impairment** occurs from damage to the eardrum or the bones of the middle ear. **Nerve hearing impairment** is caused by problems in the inner ear or in the auditory pathways and cortical areas of the brain. Ordinary hearing aids are designed to assist with conduction hearing impairment, whereas **cochlear implants** can be used to restore some hearing for people with nerve hearing impairment.

The sense of taste, or **gustation**, is activated by chemicals that dissolve in the mouth. The sensory receptors are receptor cells found within the **taste buds** that are located on the little bumps on the tongue, cheek and roof of your mouth. The little bumps that you can actually see with your eye are called

48

papillae. Five basic tastes have been proposed; they are sweet, sour, salty, bitter and **umami**. Umami is the newest taste and corresponds to a "brothy" taste like the taste from chicken soup.

The sense of smell, or olfaction, is also a chemical sense. Humans have about 10 million olfactory receptor cells located in a 1 square inch area at the top of the nasal passage. Olfactory receptor cells send their axons directly to the olfactory bulbs, which are located right under the frontal lobes.

The sense of touch is actually composed of several sensations and is more accurately referred to as **somesthetic senses**. The three somesthetic senses are **skin**, **kinesthetic**, and **vestibular**. The skin contains at least six different types of sensory receptors and transmits information about touch, pressure, temperature and pain. The currently accepted theory about pain is called **gate-control theory** and suggests that pain information is regulated by a number of factors in the brain and spinal cord. Two chemicals involved with pain messages are **substance P** and endorphins. Substance P transmits information about pain to the brain and spinal cord while endorphins inhibit the transmission of signals of pain. The kinesthetic sense relays information about your body's sense of position in space. The information comes from sensory receptors called **proprioceptive receptors** located in your skin, joints, muscles and tendons. Our sense of balance, or **vestibular sense**, is regulated by receptor cells in the **otolith organs** and the **semicircular canals**. Both structures are located near the cochlea of the inner ear. The otolith organs contain small crystals suspended in fluid. Movement causes the crystals to move and activates the sensory receptors. The semicircular canals are three fluid-filled cavities located in three different planes.

Perception is the interpretation of sensation and seems to follow some basic principles, although individual and cultural differences in perception have been recorded. One principle is that of **perceptual constancy**. We tend to view objects as the same **size**, **shape** and **brightness** even if the sensations we are receiving from our sensory systems are not constant in size, shape or brightness. An example of perceptual constancy is our perception of the size and shape of a door as it is opened and closed. Gestalt psychologists believe that when people are presented with visual information, they interpret the information according to certain expected patterns or rules. The patterns are called the Gestalt principles of perception, and they include the following seven rules: **figure-ground relationships**, **closure**, **similarity**, **continuity**, **contiguity**, **proximity**, and common region.

Visual perception of depth appears to be present at a very early age. Visual cues for depth that require the use of one eye are referred to as **monocular cues** and include **linear perspective**, **relative size**, **overlap** or interposition, **aerial perspective**, **texture gradient**, **motion parallax**, and **accommodation**. Visual cues that use two eyes are called **binocular cues** and include **convergence** and **binocular disparity**. An **illusion** is a perception that does not correspond to reality. Some famous visual illusions include the **Müller-Lyer illusion**, the moon illusion and illusions of motion. In addition to cultural and individual differences, perceptions can be influenced by **perceptual sets** or expectancies. One example of perceptual expectancy is **top-down processing** and occurs when a person uses pre-existing knowledge to fit individual features into an organized whole. If there is no expectancy to help organize information, a person might use **bottom-up processing** to build a complete perception by making sense of the smaller features piece by piece.

KEY POINTS

- Define sensation and introduce some of the key concepts developed by researchers in the study of sensation.
- Explain in detail how our sense of sight and our sense of hearing work and discuss some causes for impairments in these senses.
- Discuss the chemical senses of taste and smell and the lesser known somesthetic senses of touch, body position and balance.
- Describe our experience of perception, especially in relation to visual stimuli.

KEY CONCEPTS

sensation — The activation of receptors in the various sense organs.

sensory receptors — Specialized neurons designed to convey information regarding external stimuli to the nervous system.

Ernst Weber — 1795-1978. Pioneer in the study of sensory thresholds. Discovered the just noticeable difference and Weber's law.

Gustav Fechner — 1801-1887. Pioneer in the field of sensation and perception.

just noticeable difference (jnd) — The smallest difference between two stimuli that is detectable 50 percent of the time.

Weber's Law — States that the size of the just noticeable difference is a constant proportion.

absolute threshold — The smallest amount of energy needed for a person to consciously detect a stimulus 50 percent of the time it is present.

habituation — Tendency of the brain to stop attending to constant, unchanging information.

sensory adaptation — Tendency of sensory receptor cells to become less responsive to a stimulus that is unchanging.

brightness — Corresponds to the amplitude (or height) of a light wave.

color or hue — Determined by the frequency (or length) of a light wave.

saturation — Relates to the degree of mixture of light waves of varying frequency.

retina — Nerve tissue lining the inside of the back of the eye that contains sensory receptors that convert focused light into nerve impulses and transmits the information to the brain through the optic nerves.

rods — Visual sensory receptor found at the back of the retina, responsible for non-color sensitivity to low levels of light.

cones — Visual sensory receptor found at the back of the retina, responsible for color vision and sharpness of vision.

trichromatic theory — Theory of color vision that proposes three types of cones: red, blue, and green.

afterimage — Images that occur when a visual sensation persists for a brief time even after the original stimulus is removed.

opponent-process theory	Theory of color vision that proposes four primary colors with cones arranged in pairs: red and green, blue and yellow.
optic nerve	Bundle of axons carrying visual information from the retina to the brain.
color blindness	Reduced ability to distinguish colors due to damage to the cones of the retina.
audition (auditory system)	The sensation of hearing.
volume	Sensation of the loudness of sound determined by the amplitude (or height) of a sound wave.
pitch	Psychological experience of sound that corresponds to the frequency (or length) of the sound waves; higher frequencies are perceived as higher pitches.
timbre	(pronounced TAM-br) The quality of a sound that distinguishes it from other sounds with the same pitch and volume. Also referred to as sound quality. For example: thin, thick, light, dark, sharp, dull, smooth, rough, warm, or cold. It is this quality which allows you to distinguish between a flute and an oboe playing the same pitch at the same volume. Corresponds to the degree of mixture of varying wavelengths.
Hertz (Hz)	Cycles or waves per second, a measurement of frequency.
pinna	The outer ear that focuses sound waves for the middle and inner ears.
cochlea	Snail-like structure of the inner ear, filled with fluid.
basilar membrane	The cellular membrane in which the hair cells are embedded. It is a part of the organ of Corti.
organ of Corti	The structure in the inner ear that contains the hair cell sensory receptors.
hair cells	Sensory receptors of the auditory system. Specifically, specialized neurons that convert sound into an electrical-chemical signal.
place theory	Theory of pitch that states that different pitches are experienced by the stimulation of hair cells in different locations on the organ of Corti.
frequency theory	States that the perceived pitch is caused by the frequency of the incoming sound wave and subsequently the frequency of firing in the auditory nerve.

volley principle	Theory of pitch that states that frequencies are above 100 Hz cause the hair cells (auditory neurons) to fire in a volley pattern, or taking turns in firing.
conduction hearing impairment	Deficit in hearing cause by damage to the eardrum or the bones of the middle ear. Typically corrected by ordinary hearing aid.
nerve hearing impairment	Deficit in hearing caused by damage to the inner ear, auditory nerve, or cortical areas of the brain. Can sometimes be partially reversed with cochlear implants.
cochlear implants	Medical device surgically implanted to bypass damage in the inner ear and directly stimulate auditory nerve endings.
gustation (gustatory system)	The sensation of taste.
taste buds	Small structures located under the papillae in the mouth that contain the sensory receptors for the gustatory system.
papillae	Small projections on the tongue.
umami	Name for the taste sensation produced by foods such as parmesan, soy sauce, fish sauce, and the additive monosodium glutamate or MSG.
olfaction (olfactory system)	The sensation of smell.
somesthetic senses	The body senses consisting of the skin senses, the kinesthetic sense, and the vestibular senses.
skin senses	The sensations of touch, pressure, temperature, and pain.
kinesthetic senses	Sense of the location of body parts in relation to the ground and each other.
vestibular senses	The sensations of movement, balance, and body position.
gate-control theory	Theory of pain that states the psychological experience of pain is controlled by a series of "gates" in the central and peripheral nervous system that can allow or block the flow of the pain information depending on a number of factors.
Substance P	A newly discovered neurotransmitter that plays a role in transmitting information about pain.
proprioceptive receptors (proprioceptors)	Sensory receptors that detect pain and pressure in the organs.
otolith organs	Structures in the inner ear that send information to the brain about acceleration and tilt.

semicircular canals	Three circular tubes filled with fluid and lined with hair-like receptors that fire when the body moves in any circular pattern.
perception	The method by which the sensations experienced at any given moment are interpreted and organized in some meaningful fashion.
size constancy	The tendency to interpret an object as always being the same actual size, regardless of its actual distance.
shape constancy	The tendency to interpret the shape of an object as being constant, even when its shape changes on the retina.
brightness constancy	The tendency to perceive the apparent brightness of an object as the same even when the light conditions change.
figure-ground relationships	The tendency to perceive objects, or figures, as existing on a background.
closure	The tendency to complete figures that are incomplete.
similarity	The tendency to perceive things that look similar to each other as being part of the same group.
contiguity	The tendency to perceive two things that happen close together in time as being related.
continuity	The tendency to perceive things as simply as possible, with a continuous pattern rather than with a complex, broken-up pattern.
proximity	The tendency to perceive objects that are close to each other as part of the same grouping.
depth perception	The ability to perceive the world in three dimensions.
monocular cues	Cues for perceiving depth based on one eye only.
linear perspective	The tendency for parallel lines to appear to converge on each other.
relative size	Perception that occurs when objects that a person expects to be of a certain size appear to be small and are therefore assumed to be much, much father away.
interposition (overlap)	The assumption that an object that appears to be blocking part of another object is in front of the second object and closer to the viewer.
aerial perspective	The haziness that surrounds objects that are farther away from the viewer, causing the distance to be perceived as greater.

texture gradient	The tendency for textured surfaces to appear to become smaller and finer as distance from the viewer increases.
motion parallax	The perception of motion of objects in which close objects appear to move more quickly than objects that are farther away.
accommodation	As a monocular clue, the brain's use of information about the changing thickness of the lens of the eye in response to looking at objects that are close or far away.
binocular cues	Cues for perceiving depth based on both eyes.
Convergence	The rotation of the two eyes in their sockets to focus on a single object, resulting in greater convergence for closer objects and less convergence if objects are distant.
binocular disparity	The difference in images between the two eyes, which is greater for objects that are close and smaller for distant objects.
illusion	A perception that does not correspond to reality.
Müller-Lyer illusion	Illusion of line length that is distorted by inward-turning or outward-turning corners on the ends of the lines, causing lines of equal length to appear to be different.
perceptual sets	The tendency to perceive things a certain way because previous experiences or expectations influence those perceptions.
top-down processing	The use of pre-existing knowledge to organize individual features into a unified whole.
bottom-up processing	The analysis of the smaller features to build up to a complete perception.

HINTS

1. Chapter 3 presented information about seven different sensory systems. What information do you think will be important to know about each of the systems? Brainstorm a little in the space below:

_____

_____

_____

Some important concepts include the name of the system, the type of stimulus the system responds to, the sensory organ and sensory receptor, or proposed theories on how the system works. A chart can be extremely helpful in organizing these various components. See how much of the information you can fill in below and go to the textbook to find the remaining answers. The first row is filled in for you. A complete table can be found at the end of the Study Hints section.

Sensory System	External Stimulus	Sensory Organ	Sensory Receptor	Proposed Theories
Visual System	*Light waves*	*eyes*	*rods and cones*	*trichromatic theory opponent-process theory*

2.   Both the visual and auditory system respond to stimuli traveling as a wave. Each wave can be broken down into three components. The height or amplitude of the wave is the distance from the top of the peak to the bottom of the peak. The length or frequency of the wave is measured as the distance from peak to peak. The purity of the wave describes how many different waves are combined together. The wave drawn below is a single wave with no other waves combined.

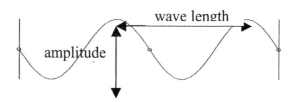

Fill in the chart with the correct psychological dimensions that correspond to each of the three physical dimensions of a wave.

	Light Waves	Sound Waves
amplitude		
frequency / length		
purity		

Now use this information, to compare Wave A and Wave B.

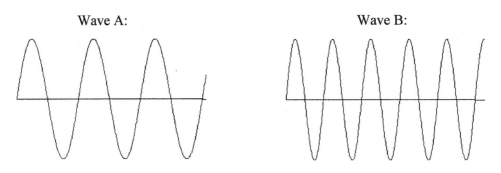

Wave A: Wave B:

If these were sound waves, how would Wave A sound different than Wave B?

_____

If these were light waves, how would Wave A look different than Wave B?

_____

If these waves are light waves, they would both have the same brightness (amplitude) but they would be seen as different colors (wave length). If these weaves were sound waves, they would both be the same loudness (amplitude) but Wave B would sound higher pitched (wave length) than Wave A.

3.   Many of the new terms and concepts of this chapter are easier to understand if you simply think about the words themselves. How do these terms "describe themselves"?

trichromatic theory: _____

opponent-process theory: _____

place theory: _____

frequency theory: _____

- *Trichromatic theory proposes 3 colors for the cones, tri = 3 and chromatic = colors.*
- *Opponent-process theory suggests the cones work against each other, they are opponents.*

- *Place* theory states that it is the *place* on the basilar membrane that is stimulated and that then determines the pitch that we perceive.
- *Frequency* theory states that it is the sensory receptor fires at the same *frequency* as sound wave and that is how we perceive the pitch of a sound.

4. Many students confuse the Gestalt principles of perception with the monocular cues for depth perception. The two are listed below. The principles of perception deal with the rules we use to decide which objects should be grouped together, while the monocular depth cues are used to determine how far away objects are.

Gestalt principles of perception	Monocular Depth Cues
closure	linear perspective
similarity	texture gradient
contiguity	aerial position
continuity	interposition
figure-ground relationship	motion parallax
proximity	relative size

In order to help clarify the difference, use these cues to draw two separate pictures.

Use one or more of the Gestalt principles to create a picture with at least two separate groups of objects.	Use one or more of the monocular depth cues to draw a picture of a tree, house and a person. Make sure the tree is the farthest object and the person is the closest object.

Sensory System	External Stimulus	Sensory Organ	Sensory Receptor	Proposed Theories
Visual System	Light waves	eyes	rods and cones	trichromatic theory opponent-process theory
auditory system	sound waves	ears	hair cells in the organ of Corti	place theory frequency theory volley theory
Gustatory system (taste)	soluble chemicals	tongue, cheeks, mouth	taste cells in the taste buds	
Olfactory system (smell)	airborne chemicals	nose	olfactory receptors	
skin senses	pressure, temperature, pain	skin	Six different types including free nerve endings and paucian corpculse	Gate-control theory of pain
Kinesthetic	body position	skin, joints, muscles, and tendons	propriocetive receptors	
Vestibular	acceleration and tilt	semicircular canals and otolith organs	hair cells	

SAMPLE EXAM

For the following multiple choice questions, select the answer you feel best answers the question and explain the rationale or reason for your selection in the space provided.

Objective 3.1

1.   The most important role of sensory receptors is to _____.
        a) coordinate communications within the body.
        b) regulate the body's response to pain.
        c) control skeletal muscle contractions.
        d) convert an external stimulus into an electrical-chemical message the nervous system can use.

Rationale:
D is the correct answer. Sensory receptors are the body's "antennae" to the outside world. Each sensory receptor type is specially designed to receive a specific external signal and convert it to an electrical-chemical signal.

2.   The point at which a person can detect a stimulus 50 percent of the time it is presented is called the

_____.
        a) absolute threshold
        b) range threshold
        c) differential threshold
        d) noticeable threshold

Rationale:
A is the correct answer. Gustav Fechner investigated the sensitivity of the human sensory systems and called the lowest level of a stimulus that a person could detect half of the time the absolute threshold.

3.   An automobile manufacturer has decided to add a little bit of horsepower to its cars. They have a device that alters horsepower one unit at a time. Suppose drivers first notice the increase on a 200 horsepower car when it reaches 220 horsepower. How much horsepower must be added to a 150 horsepower car for drivers to notice the difference?
        a) 5
        b) 10
        c) 15
        d) 25
Rationale:

_____

_____

Objective 3.2

4.   If you stared at a picture for a long period of time, you might think the image of the picture would fade due to sensory adaptation. This would be the case except for the tiny vibrations of your eye called:

        a) glissades
        b) saccades
        c) habituation movements
        d) light wave responses

Rationale:

_____

_____

Objective 3.3

5.   Light is said to have a dual nature, meaning it can be thought of in two different ways. These two ways are:

        a) particles and photons
        b) waves and frequencies
        c) photons and waves
        d) dark light and daylight

Rationale:

_____

_____

Objective 3.4

6.   When light waves enter the eye, they first pass through the

        a) iris.
        b) lens.
        c) pupil.
        d) cornea.

Rationale:

_____

_____

Objective 3.5

7.   Which of the following is true about cones?

        a) They are more sensitive to light than rods.
        b) They are found mainly in the center of the eye.
        c) They operate mainly at night.
        d) They respond only to black and white.

Rationale:

_____

_____

8. The existence of afterimages in complementary colors best supports the _____ theory of color vision.
    a) opponent-process
    b) place
    c) vibrational
    d) Hering trichromatic

    Rationale:

    _____

    _____

Objective 3.6

9. Which of the following properties of sound would be the most similar to the color or hue of light?
    a) pitch
    b) loudness
    c) purity
    d) timbre

    Rationale:

    _____

    _____

10. Vibrating molecules in the air are called
    a) light waves
    b) sound waves
    c) odor molecules
    d) taste sensations

    Rationale:

    _____

    _____

Objective 3.7

11. The membrane stretched over the opening to the middle ear is the
    a) pinna
    b) oval window
    c) tympanic membrane
    d) cochlea

    Rationale:

    _____

    _____

12.   Which is the correct order of the three bones of the middle ear, from the outside in?
a) anvil, hammer, stirrup
b) hammer, anvil, stirrup
c) stirrup, anvil, hammer
d) stirrup, hammer, anvil

Rationale:

_____

_____

13.   Which theory proposes that above 100 Hz but below 1000Hz, auditory neurons do not fire all at once but in rotation?
a) place theory
b) volley theory
c) frequency theory
d) rotational theory

Rationale:

_____

_____

14.   The _____ theory explains how we hear sounds above 1,000 Hz.
a) place
b) frequency
c) volley
d) adaptive

Rationale:

_____

_____

Objective 3.8

15.   Ringing or buzzing sensations in the ears may be a sign of:
a) noise produced hearing damage
b) habituation of the hair cells
c) rigidity of the ossicles
d) volley theory morbidity

Rationale:

_____

_____

16. _____is the term used to refer to difficulties in hearing.
        a) Hearing impairment
        b) Timbre blindness
        c) Acoustic stiffness
        d) Volley involution

Rationale:

_____

_____

17. If a severe ear infection damages the bones of the middle ear, you may develop _____ hearing impairedness.
        a) nerve
        b) stimulation
        c) brain pathway
        d) conduction

Rationale:

_____

_____

Objective 3.9

18. Cochlear implants bypass the:
        a) outer ear
        b) outer and middle ear
        c) outer, middle and inner ear
        d) none of the above

Rationale:

_____

_____

Objective 3.10

19. The "bumps" on the tongue that are visible to the eye are the _____
        a) olfactory receptors
        b) taste buds
        c) papillae
        d) taste receptors

Rationale:

_____

_____

20. An olfactory stimulus travels from receptor to _____.
   a) olfactory bulb
   b) thalamus
   c) amygdala
   d) pons

   Rationale:

   _____

   _____

Objective 3.11

21. In gate control theory, Substance P
   a) opens the spinal gates for pain.
   b) closes the spinal gates for pain.
   c) is unrelated to pain.
   d) is similar in function to endorphins.

   Rationale:

   _____

   _____

Objective 3.12

22. Which is the best description of the vestibular senses?
   a) having to do with touch, pressure, temperature, and pain
   b) having to do with the location of body parts in relation to the ground and to each other
   c) having to do with movement and body position
   d) having to do with your location as compared to the position of the sun

   Rationale:

   _____

   _____

23. We know when we are moving up and down in an elevator because of the movement of tiny crystals in the
   a) outer ear
   b) inner ear
   c) otolith organs
   d) middle ear

   Rationale:

   _____

   _____

24.   Which might be the best explanation of motion sickness, according to your textbook?
a) The conflict between vision and the vestibular organs
b) Fluid circulating in the semicircular canals
c) Human evolutionary history in that poisons make us dizzy, so when motion makes us dizzy we try to expel the poison
d) none of these

Rationale:

_____

_____

Objective 3.13

25.   The tendency to interpret an object as always being the same size, regardless of its distance from the viewer is known as _____
a) size constancy
b) shape constancy
c) brightness constancy
d) color constancy

Rationale:

_____

_____

Objective 3.14

26.   Closure is _____
a) the tendency to perceive objects, or figures, on some background.
b) the tendency to complete figures that are incomplete.
c) the tendency to perceive objects that are close to each other as part of the same grouping.
d) the tendency to perceive things a with a continuous pattern rather than with a complex, broken-up pattern.

Rationale:

_____

_____

27.   Which Gestalt principle is at work in the old phrase, "birds of a feather flock together?"
a) closure
b) similarity
c) expectancy
d) continuity

Rationale:

_____

_____

Objective 3.15

28.   Visual distance and depth cues that require the use of both eyes are called _____ .
        a) monocular cues
        b) diocular cues
        c) binocular cues
        d) dichromatic cues

Rationale:

_____

_____

Objective 3.16

29.   The Müller-Lyer illusion exists in cultures in which there are
        a) more men than women
        b) more women than men
        c) few buildings
        d) buildings with lots of corners

Rationale:

_____

_____

Objective 3.17

30.   People's tendency to perceive things a certain way because their previous experiences or expectations influence them is called
        a) a perceptual set
        b) binocular disparity
        c) motion parallax
        d) accommodation

Rationale:

_____

_____

31.   A recent review of studies on ESP using the Ganzfeld procedure concluded that _____ .
        a) no convincing evidence for psychic ability had emerged from any of the studies
        b) no convincing evidence for psychic ability had emerged from the majority of studies
        c) convincing evidence for psychic ability had been found in the majority of studies
        d) convincing evidence for psychic ability had been found in virtually all studies

Rationale:

_____

_____

SAMPLE EXAM ANSWERS & RATIONALES

1.   d   D is the correct answer. Sensory receptors are the body's "antennae" to the outside world. Each sensory receptor type is specially designed to receive a specific external signal and convert it to an electrical-chemical signal.

2.   a   Gustav Fechner investigated the sensitivity of the human sensory systems and called the lowest level of a stimulus that a person could detect half of the time the absolute threshold.

3.   c   According to Weber's law, the just noticeable difference (jnd) is a constant proportion. A change from 200 to 220 represents an increase of 20 units and a jnd of 20/200 or 0.10, which is 10%. If the company starts with 150 horsepower, they will need to increase it by 10% in order for the driver to notice a difference. Ten percent of 150 is 15.

4.   b   Saccades are the small quick movements your eye makes in order to keep the visual stimuli changing. When our sensory receptors receive unchanging, constant stimuli, they eventually stop responding to the stimulus. This process is known as sensory adaptation.

5.   c   Light can be thought of as a wave and as particles. Photons are the specific type of particles that light is composed of.

6.   d   The cornea is the outermost coating of the eye. It is transparent and serves to protect the eye and to help focus the light coming into the eye.

7.   b   Cones are the sensory receptors that respond to color and send visual information of high acuity or visual sharpness. The cones are located primarily in the center of the retina. Choices a and d more accurately describe the rods.

8.   a   The opponent process theory of color vision was introduced, in part, to explain the phenomenon of the afterimage.

9.   a   Pitch is determined by the length of the wave just as color is determined by the length of the wave. Both brightness and loudness are determined by the height of the wave.

10.   b   The outer and middle ear are designed to funnel the vibrating air molecules to the inner ear, where they are translated into an electrical signal and sent to the brain.

11.   c   The tympanic membrane is also known as the eardrum. Sound waves cause the tympanic membrane to vibrate, which then causes the bones of the middle ear to move back and forth.

12.   b   The order of the bones is hammer, anvil, stirrup which spells "has."

13.   b   Volley theory describes the perception of pitch for the middle frequencies (100 – 1000 Hz). Frequency theory describes the low frequencies (100 Hz and less) and place theory describes the fastest frequencies (1000 Hz and higher).

14.   a   The idea is that at very high sound frequencies, the action potential frequency can't keep up, so pitch has to be coded by the place on the basilar membrane that is activated.

15.   a   Damage to the hair cells can cause the receptors to fire action potentials even when no stimulus is present. This can cause a sensation of ringing in the ears.

16.   a   Hearing impairments are usually divided into impairments of conduction and nerve.

17.   d   Conduction hearing impairment is caused by damage to the outer or middle ear.

18.   b   Cochlear implants use an electronic device instead of the movements of the bones in the middle ear to convert the sound wave into a signal that is then sent to the auditory nerve in the inner ear.

19.   c   The bumps you can see with your eye are the papillae. The taste buds are located along the sides of the papillae. Each taste bud contains 10-20 taste receptors.

20. a   The olfactory system is the only system in which the receptors send their signal directly to the higher brain and bypass the filtering process of the lower brain.
21. d   The gate-theory of pain suggests that there are a number of factors in the central and peripheral nervous system that can inhibit or allow pain signals to be transmitted to the brain.
22. c   The vestibular sense provides you with a sense of balance and sends your brain information about acceleration and tilt.
23. c   Although the otolith organs are located in the inner ear, choice c is a more precise answer.
24. c   Although choice a is partially correct, the conflict between the visual and vestibular system only explains the sense of dizziness, not the sense of nausea. Probably the best explanation for that is human evolutionary theory.
25. a   Size constancy refers to the fact that our perception of the size of an object tends to remain constant.
26. b   Closure is one of the Gestalt principles of perception and refers to our tendency to "close" objects to form a complete picture.
27. b   The saying is emphasizing that objects with similar characteristics ("birds of a feather") tend to be grouped together ("flock together"). This is the principle of similarity.
28. c   The phrase "ocular" means having to do with the eyes. "Mono" refers to one and "bi" refers to two. Therefore the term binocular means seeing depth with two eyes.
29. d   The carpentered-world theory states that the Müller-Lyer illusion does not exist in certain "primitive" cultures because they are not surrounded by straight lines and corners.
30. a   An individual's expectations or perceptual set often influence perception of objects.
31. b   The majority of quality studies have found no evidence for ESP. The studies that reported positive results have been flawed.

APPLY IT

This section will help you use the concepts you are learning in this class to improve your study skills.

In the last chapter's Study Challenge, you were given several visual aids in order to help you organize the material in a format other than simply words. For this chapter, think about the topics you will be covering and the types of visual aids that would help you learn and remember the material. List some visual aids that you feel will be helpful in the space below.

_____

_____

_____

You might have listed some of the following aids: diagram of the eye, diagram of the visual system, a picture of the ear, a graphic of the tongue, or an illustration of the brain with the main sensory pathways highlighted, to name a few.

Your task for this challenge is to find these visual aids yourself and bring them with you to class. You may want to photocopy an image from your textbook or a friend's textbook, you can try searching online and printing out any images you find, or you can use the resources available at your library. A quick search under google images (www.images.google.com) with the search term "eye" brings up several graphics that would be excellent aids for the lecture on the visual system. See what you can find for yourself!

4.1   *What does it mean to be conscious, and are there different levels of consciousness?*

4.2   *Why do people sleep, and how does sleep work?*

4.3   *What is the purpose of sleep?*

4.4   *What are the different stages of sleep?*

4.5   *What is dreaming, and what happens if people don't dream?*

4.6   *Can sleepwalking be a defense for committing a crime?*

4.7   *What kinds of problems can happen during sleep?*

4.8   *Why do people dream, and what do they dream about?*

4.9   *What is hypnosis and how does it work?*

4.10   *What is the difference between a physical dependence and a psychological dependence on a drug?*

4.11   *What are some examples of stimulants and the dangers associated with taking them?*

4.12   *What are some different types of depressants and how can they be harmful?*

4.13   *What kind of drug is alcohol and what are the dangers of drinking too much?*

4.14   *How do narcotics work, and why are they so addictive?*

4.15   *How do hallucinogens work?*

4.16   *What is marijuana and what are the risks of using it?*

4.17   *How serious is the problem of sleep deprivation?*

SUMMARY

Consciousness is defined as a person's awareness of the world around them. **Waking consciousness** is defined as the state of awareness where our thoughts and feelings are clear and organized. **Altered states of consciousness** describe a shift in the quality or pattern of a person's awareness. Examples of altered states of consciousness include using drugs, daydreaming, being hypnotized, or simply sleeping.

The sleep-wake cycle is a **circadian rhythm,** meaning one cycle takes about a day to complete. The cycle is regulated by the **suprachiasmatic nucleus (SCN)** located in the hypothalamus. The SCN responds to changes in daylight and regulates the release of **melatonin** from the pineal gland and body temperature accordingly. By the end of the day, higher melatonin levels and lower body temperature cause people to feel sleepy. In addition, high levels of serotonin are believed to produce feelings of sleepiness. The sleep-wake cycle tends to shift to a 25-hour cycle when subjects do not have access to the sun or clocks. Sleep deprivation, or loss of sleep, results in an increase in **microsleeps**, concentration problems, and an inability to perform simple tasks. Participants in a number of sleep deprivation studies reported that they were unaware of their impaired functioning. Two theories are currently proposed for why we sleep. The **adaptive theory** suggests that we sleep to avoid predators while the **restorative theory** states that sleep is needed to replenish chemicals and repair cellular damage. Both theories are probably partially correct.

Based on brain wave activity recorded with the use of an EEG, sleep has been divided into two different types, **rapid eye movement (REM) sleep** and **non-REM sleep**. Non-REM sleep is a deep, restful sleep and consists of four stages. Stage 1 sleep is also called light sleep and occurs when brain activity begins to shift from **alpha** to **theta wave** activity. Many people experience a **hypnic jerk** in this stage when their body jerks suddenly and wakes them up. As body temperature continues to drop and heart rate slows, **sleep spindles** begin to appear on the EEG recording, signaling Stage 2 of non-REM sleep. Stage 3 occurs when the slow, large **delta waves** first appear, and when delta waves account for more than 50% of the total brain activity, the person is said to be in Stage 4, the deepest stage of sleep. **Sleepwalking**, or somnambulism, occurs in Stage 4 as well as the rare disorder of **night terrors**. Most people state that they are not aware of the actions they committed during a sleepwalking episode. The explanation of "sleepwalking" has been used as a successful defense in several trials for murder, but in these cases, the term sleepwalking is more likely referring to the condition known as REM behavior disorder.

After a person cycles through Stage 1-4 and back, instead of entering Stage 1, people experience REM sleep. During this type of sleep, the brain is active and displays **beta wave** activity, the eye exhibits rapid movements, and the skeletal muscles of the body are temporarily paralyzed. When a person is wakened from this type of sleep, they often report being in a dream state. Most likely, around 90% of dreams take place in REM sleep, although dreams also do occur in non-REM sleep. Contrary to popular belief, people do not go crazy when deprived of REM sleep; however, they do spend longer amounts of time in REM sleep when allowed to sleep normally again. This phenomenon is known as **REM rebound**. **Nightmares** are bad dreams and typically occur in REM sleep. **REM behavior disorder** is a rare disorder in which a person's muscles are not paralyzed during REM sleep, allowing them to thrash about and even get up and act out their dreams.

There are a large number of disorders associated with sleep. **Insomnia** is the inability to get to sleep, stay asleep, or get a good night of quality sleep. **Sleep apnea** is a disorder in which a person actually stops breathing for brief periods throughout the night. **Narcolepsy** is a genetic disorder in which a person suddenly enters REM sleep during the day. The attack can occur many times throughout the day and without warning. The attacks often occur with cataplexy, or a sudden loss of muscle tone.

Several theories have been proposed to explain why dreams occur. Sigmund Freud believed that dreams represented our unconscious thoughts and desires. He called the actual content of our dream the **manifest content** and the real meaning of the dream the **latent content**. The **activation-synthesis hypothesis** was originally proposed by Hobson and McCarley; it suggests that dreams are caused by lower brain areas activated by the cortex and the cortex fitting together (or synthesizing) the random input from the lower brain. The **activation-information mode model (AIM)** expands on the activation-synthesis model in an attempt to explain the meaningful, realistic and consistent nature of many dreams. AIM proposes that the cortex uses information from the previous day as it pieces together the input coming from the lower brain. A considerable amount of information is known about the content of dreams. Most dreams tend to reflect events in everyday life as well as the "personality" of the dreamer's culture. Men tend to dream about males, weapons, tools, cars, and roads, and their dream occur in outdoor or unfamiliar settings containing more physical aggression than women's dreams. Men also report more sexual dreams. Women tend to dream about men and women equally, and they also are more likely to report dreams about people they know, family, home, concern about their appearances, and more often report dreams in which they are the victims of aggressive acts. Dreams of being naked in public appear to be common in many cultures.

Hypnosis is a state of consciousness in which a person is especially susceptive to suggestion. Hypnosis can reduce the sensation of pain, create temporary states of amnesia and affect sensory perception, but it cannot increase physical strength, enhance memory or regress a person back to their childhood. One theory of hypnosis proposed by Ernst Hilgard suggests that the hypnotized person is in a state of **dissociation,** with one part of the brain unaware of the activities happening under hypnosis and another part aware and simply watching what is happening. Hilgard called the part of the conscious that was aware of the activities the hidden observer. The **social-cognitive explanation** of hypnosis states that people who are hypnotized are not in an altered state but are simply playing the role they feel is expected of them in the situation.

A **psychoactive drug** is any drug that alters a person's thinking, perception or memory. **Physical dependence** on a drug occurs when the user's body does not function normally without the drug. Two signs of physical dependence are drug tolerance and symptoms of withdrawal when deprived of the drug. **Psychological dependence** occurs when a drug is needed to maintain a feeling of emotional or psychological well-being. Psychoactive drugs can be classified into major categories including stimulants, depressants, narcotics, and psychogenic drugs.

Stimulants are a class of drugs that increase the activity of the nervous system and the organs connected to it. Specifically, stimulants activate the fight-or-flight response of the sympathetic nervous system. **Amphetamines** are man-made stimulants and include drugs such as benzedrine, methedrine and dexedrine. Large doses of amphetamines can lead to a severe mental disturbance and paranoia called amphetamine psychosis. **Cocaine** is a naturally occurring stimulant found in coca plant leaves. Cocaine produces feelings of happiness, energy, power and pleasure, and also reduces pain and suppresses appetite. Cocaine is highly addictive an can cause convulsions and death even in first-time users. Signs of cocaine abuse include compulsive use, loss of control, and disregard for the consequences of use. **Nicotine** is a mild yet toxic naturally-occurring stimulant that raises blood pressure, accelerates the heart rate and provides a rush of sugar into the bloodstream. Nicotine has been found to be more addictive than heroin or alcohol and is linked to nearly 430,000 deaths in the United States each year. **Caffeine** is a naturally occurring stimulant that increases alertness and can enhance the effectiveness of certain pain relievers.

Depressants are drugs that slow down the central nervous system and include **barbiturates**, **benzodiazepines** and **alcohol**. Barbituates have a strong sedative, or sleep-inducing, effect and are known as the major tranquilizers. The minor tranzuilizers, or benzodiazepines, have a relatively minor depressant effect and are used to lower anxiety and reduce stress. Some common benzodiazepines include Valium, Xanax, Halcion, Ativan, Librium and Rohypnol (also known as the date rape drug). The most commonly used and abused depressant is alcohol.

Narcotics reduce the sensation of pain by binding to and activating the receptor sites for endorphins. All narcotics are derived from the plant-based substance opium. **Opium** itself is made from the opium poppy and reduces pain as well as increases feelings of well-being. **Morphine** is made from opium and is used for the short-term relief of severe pain. Due to its highly addictive nature, the use of morphine is carefully controlled. **Heroin** is also made from opium but is not used as a medicine due to the fact that it is more addictive than morphine or opium. Narcotics are thought to be so addictive because they mimic the action of endorphins and subsequently cause the body to stop producing its own endorphins so that without the drug, there is no protection from pain. **Methadone** is made from opium but does not produce the feelings of euphoria produced by morphine and heroine. Methadone can be used to attempt to control heroin dependency. In addition to methadone treatment, heroin addiction is treated with behavioral therapies such as contingency management therapies and cognitive approaches such as cognitive-behavior interventions.

Hallucinogens are psychogenic drugs that create false sensory perceptions, also known as hallucinations. **Lysergic acid diethylamide (LSD)** is synthesized from a grain fungus and is one of the most potent hallucinogens. Phenyl cyclohexyl piperdine or **PCP** is a synthesized drug that can act as a hallucinogen, stimulant, depressant or analgesic, depending on the dosage. PCP has also been shown to lead to acts of violence against others or suicide. **MDMA** or Ecstasy is an amphetamine that also produces hallucinations. Because of their stimulant and hallucinogenic properties, PCP and MDMA are now classified as stimulatory hallucinogenics. Naturally occurring hallucinogenics include **mescaline**, **psilocybin** and **marijuana**. The effects of marijuana are milder than other hallucinogens, yet marijuana use can lead to a powerful psychological dependency.

Sleep deprivation is a serious and pervasive problem in the United States and has been linked to a large percentage of fatal road accidents in addition to higher levels of stress, anxiety and depression. Causes of sleep deprivation include sleep apnea, narcolepsy, sleep walking, night terrors, and personal choice.

KEY POINTS

- Define consciousness and discuss the different levels of consciousness.
- Explain the factors that control sleep, theories on the purpose of sleep, the stages of sleep and several disorders of sleep.
- Discuss dreams and three theories that attempt to explain the purpose of dreams.
- Introduce the phenomenon of hypnosis and two theories suggesting the underlying mechanism.
- Describe properties and potential dangers of psychoactive drugs including stimulants, depressants, narcotics and hallucinogens.

KEY CONCEPTS

consciousness	A person's awareness of everything that is going on around him or her at any given moment.
waking consciousness	State in which thoughts, feelings, and sensations are clear, organized, and the person feels alert.
altered states of consciousness	State in which there is a shift in the quality or pattern of mental activity as compared to waking consciousness.
circadian rhythm	A cycle of bodily rhythm that occurs over a 24 hour period.
suprachiasmatic nucleus (SCN)	Area in the hypothalamus that is sensitive to daylight and controls the body's sleep-wake cycle.
melatonin	Hormone released from the pineal gland that is associated with the sleep-wake cycle.
microsleeps	Brief episodes of sleep lasting only a few seconds.
adaptive theory	Theory of sleep proposing that animals and humans evolved sleep patterns to avoid predators, sleeping when predators are most active.
restorative theory	Theory of sleep proposing that sleep is necessary to the physical health of the body and serves to replenish chemicals and repair cellular damage.
rapid eye movement (REM) sleep	Stage of sleep in which the eyes move rapidly under the eyelids and the person is typically experiencing a dream.
non-REM sleep	Any of the stages of sleep that do not include REM.
beta waves	Brain waves that indicate a state of being awake and alert.
alpha waves	Brain waves that indicate a state of relaxation or light sleep.
theta waves	Brain waves indicating the early stages of sleep.
delta waves	Long, slow waves that indicate the deepest stage of sleep.
hypnic jerk	An involuntary muscle twitch that often occurs during the transition from wakefulness to sleep.
sleep spindles	Bursts of brain wave activity seen on the EEG during Stage 2 sleep.
sleepwalking (somnambulism)	Occurring during the deep sleep of Stage 4 non-REM sleep, an episode of moving around or walking around in one's sleep.

night terrors	Relatively rare disorder in which the person experiences extreme fear and screams or runs around during deep sleep, without waking fully.
REM rebound	Increased amounts of REM sleep after being deprived of REM sleep on earlier nights.
nightmares	Bad dreams occurring during REM sleep.
REM behavior disorder	A rare disorder in which the mechanism that blocks the movement of the voluntary muscles fails to function, allowing the person to thrash around and even get up and act out nightmares.
insomnia	The inability to get to sleep, stay asleep, or get a good quality of sleep.
sleep apnea	Disorder in which the person stops breathing for nearly half a minute or more during sleep.
narcolepsy	Sleep disorder in which a person falls immediately into REM sleep during the day, without warning.
manifest content	Term coined by Sigmund Freud to identify the actual or "apparent" content of a dream.
latent content	Term coined by Sigmund Freud to identify the real or "hidden" meaning of a dream.
activation-synthesis hypothesis	Explanation of dreaming that states that dreams are created by the higher centers of the cortex to explain the activation by the brainstem of cortical cells during REM sleep periods.
activation-information mode model (AIM)	Revised version of the activation-synthesis explanation of dreams in which information that is accessed during waking hours can have an influence on the synthesis of dreams.
hypnosis	State of consciousness in which the person is especially susceptible to suggestion.
dissociation	Theory of hypnosis that states part of our brain is aware of what we are doing under hypnosis while another part is unaware.
social-cognitive explanation	Theory that assumes that people who are hypnotized are not in an altered state but are merely playing the role expected of them in the situation.
psychoactive drug	Drugs that alter thinking, perception, and memory.
physical dependence	A physical state in which rapid discontinuation of consumption of a particular drug leads to a condition of withdrawal.

withdrawal	Physical symptoms that can include nausea, pain, tremors, crankiness, and high blood pressure, resulting from a lack of an addictive drug in the body systems.
psychological dependence	The feeling that a drug is needed to continue a feeling of emotional or psychological well-being.
stimulants	Drugs that increase the functioning of the nervous system.
amphetamines	Stimulants that are synthesized (made) in laboratories rather than being found in nature.
cocaine	A natural stimulant derived from the leaves of the coca plant.
nicotine	A natural stimulant and the active ingredient in tobacco.
caffeine	A mild stimulant found in coffee, tea, and several other plant-based substances.
depressants	Drugs that decrease the functioning of the nervous system.
barbiturates	Depressant drugs that have a sedative effect.
benzodiazepines	Depressant drugs that lower anxiety and reduce stress.
alcohol	Depressant drug resulting from fermentation or distillation of various kinds of vegetable matter.
narcotics	A class of opium-related drugs that suppress the sensation of pain by binding to and stimulating the nervous system's natural receptor sites for endorphins.
opium	Substance derived from the opium poppy from which all narcotic drugs are derived.
morphine	Narcotic drug derived from opium, used to treat severe pain.
heroin	Narcotic drug derived from opium that is extremely addictive.
methadone	Narcotic drug derived from opium used to treat heroin addiction.
hallucinogens	Drugs that cause false sensory messages, altering the perception of reality.
Lysergic acid diethylamide (LSD)	Powerful synthetic hallucinogen.
Phenyl cyclohexyl piperdine (PCP)	Synthesized drug now used as an animal tranquilizer and that can cause stimulant, depressant, narcotic, or hallucinogenic effects.
MDMA	Designer drug that can have both stimulant and hallucinatory

effects.

mescaline	Natural hallucinogen derived from peyote cactus buttons.
psilocybin	Natural hallucinogen found in certain mushrooms.
marijuana	Mild hallucinogen derived from the leaves and flowers of a particular type of hemp plant.
sleep deprivation	Any significant loss of sleep, resulting in problems in concentration and irritability.

HINTS

1. The purpose of Chapter 4 is to introduce and describe various states of consciousness that humans experience. Normally, we think of consciousness simply as waking consciousness. To expand your concept of the term, list as many different states of consciousness as you can and provide a brief description of each. The first example has already been completed.

State of consciousness	Brief Description
waking	*state in which you are aware of your thoughts and feelings and you feel alert.*

Be sure that your chart includes the states of consciousness such as sleep, hypnosis, daydreaming, meditation, and drugged. See the textbook for descriptions of each state.

2. Use the space below to create a visual summary of the brain wave and physiological changes that occur as your body moves from an awake state through the stages of sleep typical for one night of sleep. Use arrows to indicate the progression through the stages throughout the course of a night.

Stage	Brain wave activity	Other descriptions
Awake		
non-REM Stage 1		
non-REM Stage 2		
non-REM Stage 3		
non-REM Stage 4		
REM		

3. The textbook introduces six different sleep disorders. Pretend that you have each of the sleep disorders and write a brief description of a particular episode you experienced due to the disorder.

sleepwalking   *I don't remember anything that happened, but in the morning my mother told me that about 50 minutes after I had fallen asleep (right when I would be in the deepest stage of sleep, stage 4) I walked past her in the kitchen and I was carrying a bath towel. I put the towel in the refrigerator, looked right at her and then went back to bed in my bedroom. Supposedly I do this type of thing quite often.*

night terrors   _____

_____

_____

REM behavior
disorder   _____

_____

_____

insomnia _____

_____

_____

apnea _____

_____

_____

narcolepsy _____

_____

_____

4. The other piece of information that students often find confusing in this chapter is the drug types and actions on the nervous system. Use the chart below to organize the information for yourself.

Drug Category	Examples	Action on nervous system
Stimulants	*caffeine, cocaine, nicotine, amphetamines (such as Benzedrine, Methedrine, and Dexedrine)*	*increases activity, speeds up heart rate, speeds up breathing, raises blood pressure and suppresses appetite. Can produce feelings of power, happiness, energy, and increased alertness.*
Depressants		
Narcotics		
Hallucinogens		

Suggested solutions for Questions 2 and 4

Drug Category	Examples	Action on nervous system
Stimulants	caffeine, cocaine, nicotine and amphetamines (such as Benzedrine, Methedrine, and Dexedrine)	increases activity, speeds up heart rate, speeds up breathing, raises blood pressure and suppresses appetite. Can produce feelings of power, happiness, energy, and increased alertness.
Depressants	barbiturates, alcohol and benzodiazepines (such as Valium, Xanax, Ativan and Rohypnol)	decrease activity, induce sleep, lower anxiety, reduce stress
Narcotics	Opium, morphine, heroin, and methadone	reduce pain, activate endorphin receptor sites, cause feelings of well-being, and are highly addictive
Hallucinogens	LSD, PCP, MDMA, mescaline, psilocybin and marijuana	create false sensory perceptions (also known as hallucinations)

Stage	Brain wave activity	Other descriptions
Awake ⇩	beta	
non-REM Stage 1 ⇩	alpha	hypnic jerk occurs here
non-REM Stage 2 ⇩ ⇧	theta	sleep spindles are seen in this stage
non-REM Stage 3 ⇩ ⇧	delta waves	initial appearance of delta waves, they make up minority of brain wave activity
non-REM Stage 4 ⇩ ⇧	more than 50% delta waves	deepest stage of sleep, hardest to wake the person up, sleep walking and night terrors occur in this stage
REM	beta	skeletal muscles are paralyzed (except for people with REM behavior disorder), eyes dart back and forth rapidly below the eyelids

SAMPLE EXAM

For the following multiple choice questions, select the answer you feel best answers the question and explain the rationale or reason for your selection in the space provided.

Objective 4.1

1. What term do psychologists use to designate our personal awareness of feelings, sensations, and thoughts?
    a) thinking
    b) cognition
    c) conscience
    d) consciousness

    Rationale:
    D is the correct answer. Consciousness is defined as personal awareness of feelings, sensation and thoughts. Your <u>conscience</u> is your sense of morality or right and wrong.

Objective 4.2

2. A biological cycle, or rhythm, that is approximately 24 hours long is a(n) _____ cycle.
    a) infradian
    b) circadian
    c) diurnal
    d) ultradian

    Rationale:

    _____

    _____

3. The hormone melatonin reaches peak levels in the body during the _____.
    a) morning
    b) early evening
    c) afternoon
    d) night

    Rationale:

    _____

    _____

4.   Sid is taking part in research on the effects of sleep deprivation; he has been without sleep for 75 hours. Right now researchers have asked him to sit in front of a computer screen and hit a button each time he sees the letter "S" on the screen. A few days ago, Sid was a whiz at this task; however, he is doing very poorly today. How are sleep researchers likely to explain Sid's poor performance?
   a) Due to the sleep deprivation, Sid does not understand the task.
   b) Microsleeps are occurring due to the sleep deprivation and he is asleep for brief periods of time.
   c) He is determined to ruin the research because of the suffering he is enduring at the hands of the researchers.
   d) He is probably dreaming that he is somewhere else and has no interest in responding to the "here and now."

Rationale:

_____

_____

Objective 4.3

5.   According to this theory, sleep is a product of evolution.
   a) restorative theory
   b) adaptive theory
   c) psychoanalytic theory
   d) dream theory

Rationale:

_____

_____

Objective 4.4

6.   If the EEG record reveals evidence of very small and very fast waves, you are likely to conclude that the sleeping person is:
   a) really not sleeping and is awake.
   b) in stage 2.
   c) in stage 3.
   d) in stage 4.

Rationale:

_____

_____

7.   Each of the following is true of sleepwalking EXCEPT _____.
    a)   more boys than girls sleepwalk
    b)   sleepwalking is more common among children than adults
    c)   waking a sleepwalker is difficult
    d)   waking a sleepwalker is dangerous

Rationale:

_____

_____

Objective 4.5

8.   For several months, Ted has been taking increasingly larger doses of barbiturate sleeping pills to treat insomnia. He just decided to quit taking any barbiturate sleeping pills. What is likely to happen to Ted when he stops taking the barbiturate sleeping pills?
    a)   He will become depressed.
    b)   He will experience the REM rebound.
    c)   He will increase his intake of caffeine.
    d)   He will suffer the symptoms of narcolepsy.

Rationale:

_____

_____

9.   REM paralysis:
    a)   is a myth.
    b)   only occurs in the elderly.
    c)   prevents the acting out of dreams.
    d)   may become permanent.

Rationale:

_____

_____

10.   REM behavior disorder results from:
    a)   too much sleep.
    b)   not enough sleep.
    c)   failure of the pons to block brain signals to the muscles.
    d)   deterioration of the medial hypothalamus.

Rationale:

_____

_____

Objective 4.6

11.   What is the rationale for the use of "sleepwalking" as a defense for committing a crime?
   a) It was too dangerous to awaken the sleepwalking criminal.
   b) The suspect actually suffers from REM behavior disorder and was unknowingly acting out a dream.
   c) High levels of anxiety and stress were created by the sleep deprivation caused by the sleepwalking episodes.
   d) The suspect was highly susceptible to suggestion at the time of the crime.

Rationale:

_____

_____

Objective 4.7

12.   Mary is having insomnia. Which piece of advice would you give to help her deal with it?
   a) Take sleeping pills.
   b) Go to bed every night at the same time.
   c) Study in bed and then go immediately to sleep.
   d) Don't do anything but sleep in your bed.

Rationale:

_____

_____

13.   Sleep apnea is a disorder characterized by _____.
   a) difficulty falling or remaining asleep
   b) nodding off without warning in the middle of the day
   c) difficulty breathing while asleep
   d) experiencing temporary paralysis immediately after waking up from sleep

Rationale:

_____

_____

Objective 4.8

14.   What two categories of dream content did Sigmund Freud describe?
   a) poetic and realistic
   b) literal and symbolic
   c) latent and manifest
   d) delusional and hallucinatory

Rationale:

_____

_____

15. The activation-information-mode model suggests:
    a) events that occur during waking hours may influence dreams.
    b) nothing influences dreams.
    c) activation-synthesis is all wrong.
    d) dreams have more latent content then once thought.

Rationale: _____

_____

_____

16. According to the text, girls and women tend to dream about:
    a) animals
    b) cars
    c) people they know
    d) strangers

Rationale: _____

_____

_____

Objective 4.9

17. A social interaction in which one person responds to suggestions offered by another person for experiences involving alterations in perception, memory, and voluntary action defines
    a) hypnosis
    b) meditation
    c) truth induction
    d) extrasensory perception

Rationale: _____

_____

_____

18. Tests of 'hypnotic susceptibility' have been found to _____.
    a) be similar for almost everyone
    b) make use of a series of suggestions
    c) be almost completely inherited
    d) use deception

Rationale: _____

_____

_____

19. Hypnosis can:
    a) give people superhuman strength.
    b) reliably enhance accuracy of memory.
    c) regress people back to childhood.
    d) induce amnesia.

    Rationale:

    _____

    _____

20. The idea of "hidden observer" was suggested by:
    a) Freud
    b) Watson
    c) Hilgard
    d) Kirsch

    Rationale:

    _____

    _____

Objective 4.10

21. Psychoactive drugs are:
    a) drugs that speed up activity in the central nervous system.
    b) drugs capable of influencing perception, mood, cognition or behavior.
    c) drugs that slow down activity in the central nervous system.
    d) drugs derived from the opium poppy, which relieve pain and produce euphoria.

    Rationale:

    _____

    _____

22. Psychological dependence is best described as
    a) a desire to take a drug
    b) drug tolerance and signs of withdrawal when deprived of the drug
    c) needing a drug to maintain a feeling of emotional or psychological well-being
    d) feelings of euphoria following the ingestion of a drug

    Rationale:

    _____

    _____

23.   Drugs that speed up the functioning of the nervous system are called:
        a)   stimulants
        b)   depressants
        c)   narcotics
        d)   psychogenics

Rationale:

_____

_____

24.   The most addictive and dangerous (as defined by the number of deaths caused by the drug) stimulant in use today is _____.
        a)   alcohol
        b)   amphetamine
        c)   nicotine
        d)   cocaine

Rationale:

_____

_____

Objective 4.12

25.   Cathy has just taken a drug that has caused her heart rate and breathing to slow down considerably. Most likely, Cathy has taken a(n)
        a)   amphetamine
        b)   barbiturate
        c)   narcotic
        d)   hallucinogen

Rationale:

_____

_____

26.   Your doctor has decided to give you a prescription for a drug to reduce your anxiety levels. Most likely your doctor will prescribe a
        a)   narcotic
        b)   hallucinogen
        c)   depressant
        d)   stimulant

Rationale:

_____

_____

Objective 4.13

27. Which of the following is classified as a depressant?
    a) cocaine
    b) alcohol
    c) heroin
    d) marijuana

    Rationale:

    _____

    _____

28. Jane has a loss of equilibrium, decreased sensory and motor capabilities, and double vision. According to the table in the text, how many drinks has Jane had?
    a) 1-2
    b) 3-5
    c) 6-7
    d) 8-10

    Rationale:

    _____

    _____

Objective 4.14

29. Morphine, heroin, and methadone:
    a) are stimulants
    b) are derived from opium
    c) are often used with ADHD
    d) increase the action of the central nervous system

    Rationale:

    _____

    _____

Objective 4.15

30. LSD is similar to which of the following drugs?
    a) Cocaine
    b) methadone
    c) PCP
    d) CHT

    Rationale:

    _____

    _____

31. Bill is taken to the emergency room of the hospital after he reports hearing dogs screaming and seeing fire shooting across his shirt and pants. Assuming his condition is due to a drug overdose, which type of drug did Bill most likely consume?
   a) a depressant
   b) a stimulant
   c) a narcotic
   d) a hallucinogen

Rationale:

_____

_____

Objective 4.16

32. One of the greatest risks of using marijuana is
   a) physical dependency
   b) psychological dependency
   c) weight gain
   d) heart attack

Rationale:

_____

_____

Objective 4.17

33. A significant loss of sleep, resulting in problems in concentration and irritability, is known as
   a) sleep apnea
   b) narcolepsy
   c) sleep deprivation
   d) night terrors

Rationale:

_____

_____

SAMPLE EXAM ANSWERS & RATIONALES

1.   d   Consciousness is defined as personal awareness of feelings, sensation and thoughts. Your <u>conscience</u> is your sense of morality or right and wrong.

2.   b   If you break down the word, "circa" means about or around (such as circa 1960) and "dia" means day. So circa-dia means about one day long.

3.   d   High melatonin levels is one of the signals for our body that it is time to sleep. The release of melatonin is controlled by signals coming from the suprachiasmatic nucleus, which is light sensitive. In this way, the release of melatonin follows the light-dark patterns of the day.

4.   b   Microsleeps are brief episodes of sleep that we enter and exit rapidly. Sleep deprivation often leads to decreased performance in simple tasks.

5.   b   Adaptive theory states that a species sleeps during the time when its predators are most likely to be out hunting, thus increasing the likelihood of survival for that species.

6.   a   The faster the brain wave activity, the more alert and awake the person is. Another option would have been that the person was in REM sleep where fast small brain wave activity is also seen.

7.   d   Waking the sleepwalker is not dangerous, it just might be hard to do since they are in stage 4 deep sleep.

8.   b   Barbiturate sleeping pills interfere with REM sleep, so since Ted has been deprived of REM he is likely to spend a longer than usual amount of time in REM for the next few nights. This phenomenon is known as REM rebound.

9.   c   During REM sleep the pons sends messages to the spinal cord that inhibits the movements of skeletal muscles.

10.   c   REM behavior disorder occurs when REM paralysis does not work and a person acts out their dreams. The paralysis is mediated by the pons in the brainstem.

11.   b   The sleepwalking defense is actually referring to a suspect thought to have REM behavior disorder.

12.   d   The idea is that the only association you should have with your bed is sleeping and this will make it easier for you to fall asleep when you get in bed.

13.   c   Sleep apnea is a sleeping disorder in which a person actually stops breathing for brief periods throughout the night.

14.   c   Freud thought dreams had two levels – the actual content that he called the manifest content and then the real meaning, which he called the latent content.

15.   a   The activation-synthesis model proposes that dreams are caused by the activation of the cortex by lower areas of the brain.

16.   c   Women tend to dream about both men and women as well as people they know, while men tend to dream about men.

17.   a   This is simply another way of describing a state of consciousness in which the person is especially susceptible to suggestion.

18.   b   The tests used to determine how likely it is for a person to be hypnotized generally include a list of suggestions.

19.   d   Hypnosis has only been found to induce temporary amnesia, reduce pain and alter sensory perceptions.

20.   c   Ernst Hilgard suggested that hypnosis was possible because the subject dissociates himself into a part that is aware of what is going on (the hidden observer) and a part that is unaware.

21.   b   The rest of the choices describe a specific category of psychoactive drug.

22.   c   Choice c is the definition for psychological dependence.

23.	a	Stimulants speed up heart rate, blood pressure, and breathing, among other activities.
24.	c	Nicotine has been linked to nearly 430,000 deaths per year in the U.S. alone.
25.	b	Barbiturate is the only drug listed that is a depressant.
26.	c	The depressants known as the mild tranquilizers, or benzodiazepines, are often prescribed to lower anxiety levels.
27.	b	Alcohol slows down the activity of the central nervous system.
28.	d	See the table in the textbook.
29.	b	All narcotics are derived from the opium poppy. All three of the drugs listed are classified as narcotics.
30.	c	LSD and PCP are both hallucinogens.
31.	d	Hallucinogens produce false sensory perceptions.
32.	b	The effect of psychological dependence can be very powerful.
33.	c	Sleep deprivation affects a large number of people in the U.S. today.

APPLY IT

This section will help you use the concepts you are learning in this class to improve your study skills.

This chapter dealt with the different levels of consciousness we experience in our daily lives. One way to improve your effectiveness as a student is to increase your state of waking consciousness with regard to your upcoming lecture. Try the following technique for all the lectures of this chapter and see if your time spent in lecture is more worthwhile.

        <u>Goal: Think about the material right before class begins</u>
- ❑ Arrive five minutes early to class (make sure you bring your textbook with you).
- ❑ Look through your textbook and write down the main topics that you will most likely be covering in class that day.
- ❑ For each topic, write down something that you already know about it. This will help you form associations with the material and will greatly enhance your memory of the information.
- ❑ Also for each topic, write down one question that comes to mind. This will keep you engaged in the material as your instructor is lecturing on it. You might even want to ask the question in class.

Feel free to use the space below to list the main topics. An example has already been completed.

Consciousness

> ➤ I know that you can get knocked out and lose consciousness and then you are no longer aware of what is going on.
> ➤ I wonder what part of our brain controls whether we are conscious or not.

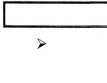

> ➤

> ➤

> ➤

> ➤

> ➤

> ➤

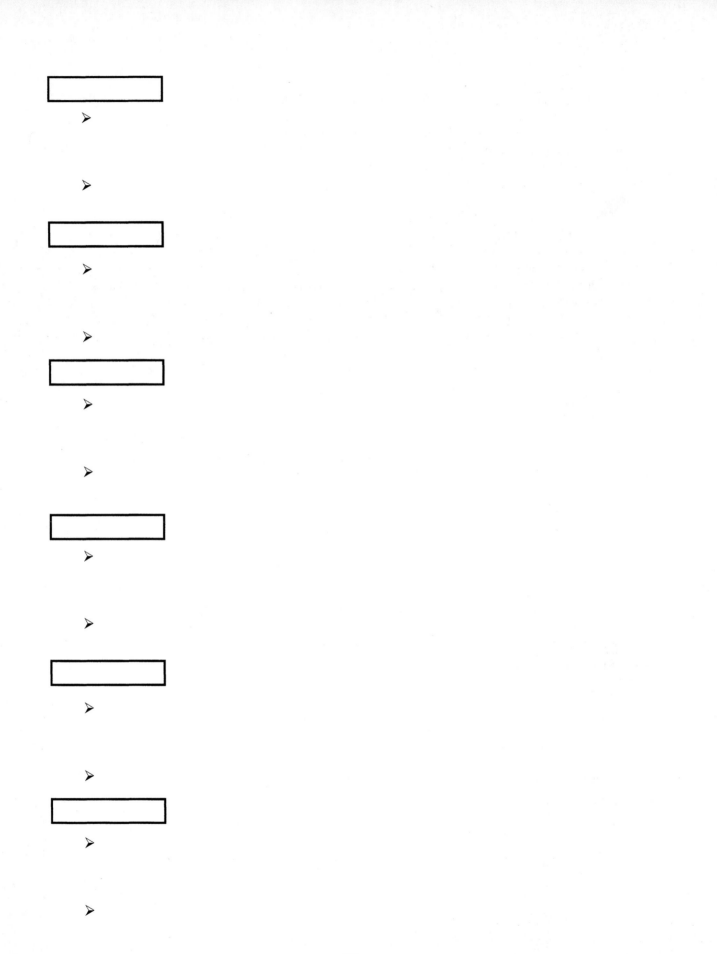

CHAPTER 5 LEARNING OBJECTIVES

SUMMARY

Learning is the process that allows us to adapt to the changing conditions of the environment around us and is defined as any relatively permanent change in behavior brought about by experience or practice (as opposed to changes brought about by maturation). **Ivan Pavlov**, a Russian physiologist, discovered one of the simplest forms of learning called **classical conditioning**. In classical conditioning, an organism learn to make a reflex response to a stimulus other than the original stimulus that produced the response in the first place. The original stimulus is called the **unconditioned (or "unlearned") stimulus (UCS)** and the reflex response is the **unconditioned response (UCR)**. If a **neutral stimulus (NS)** is repeatedly paired with the UCS, it will eventually produce the same kind of reflexive response. At this point, the NS is called a **conditioned stimulus (CS)** and the response is called a **conditioned, or learned, response (CR)**. The repeated pairing of the NS and UCS is known as **acquisition**. In order for classical conditioning to occur, the CS must occur before the UCS, the CS and UCS must occur close together in time, the CS and UCS must be paired together repeatedly and the CS should be distinctive. Two other principles of classical conditioning are **stimulus generalization**, the ability of a stimulus that resembles the CS to produce a CR and **stimulus discrimination**, learning to respond to different stimuli in different ways. In classical conditioning, **extinction** occurs after the CS is repeatedly presented without the UCS and no longer produces a CR. **Spontaneous recovery** occurs when the CS is presented after being absent for a period of time and produces a mild CR. When a powerful conditioned stimulus is paired with a neutral stimulus, the conditioned stimulus itself can function as an UCS and turn the neutral stimulus into a second conditioned stimulus. This process is called **higher order conditioning**.

John Watson demonstrated a particular type of classical conditioning called **conditional emotional response** with Little Albert and his learned phobia of white rats. **Vicarious conditioning** occurs when a person becomes classically conditioned simply by watching someone else respond to a stimulus. **Conditioned taste aversions** are a unique form of classical conditioning that can occur with only one neutral stimulus – unconditioned stimulus pairing. Conditioning is believed to occur so rapidly due to the **biological preparedness** of most mammals. Pavlov suggested that classical conditioning works through the process of **stimulus substitution**, in that the close pairing in time of the CS with the UCS eventually leads to the CS serving as a substitute stimulus for the UCS and activating the same brain area as the

UCS. Cognitive psychologists such as Robert Rescorla suggested that the CS must provide some information about the upcoming CUS and that it is this **expectancy** that causes the association to occur.

    Operant conditioning is a type of learning more strongly associated with voluntary behavior and is based on **Edward Thorndike's** work with cats and the puzzle box. Based on his research, Thorndike formulated the **Law of Effect,** which states that if a response is followed by a pleasurable consequence it will tend to be repeated, and if a response is followed by an unpleasant consequence, it will tend to not be repeated. **B.F. Skinner** expanded on Thorndike's Law of Effect and coined the term operant conditioning for this type of learning. While classical conditioning focuses on what happens *before* the response, the key to operant conditioning is what happens *after* the response, or in other words, the consequence. **Reinforcement** is a consequence that is pleasurable and strengthens the response that came before it. **Punishment** is a consequence that is unpleasant and decreases the likelihood of the response that came before it. There are two types of reinforcers. **Primary reinforcers** satisfy basic needs and don't need to be learned. **Secondary reinforcers** get their reinforcing power through prior associations with a primary reinforcer and thus are learned. Reinforcement works by adding a pleasurable consequence after a response occurs (**positive reinforcement**) or removing something unpleasant after a response occurs (**negative reinforcement**). Both positive and negative reinforcement increase the likelihood that the response will occur again. **Shaping** involves the use of operant conditioning to reward successive approximations until the desired response is obtained. Operant conditioning has several parallels with classical conditioning such as **extinction,** which involves the removal of the reinforcement, and **spontaneous recovery** occurs when an organism attempts a previously learned response in order to receive a reward. In addition, a **discriminative stimulus** is defined as any stimulus that provides an organism with a signal or cue for making a certain response in order to get reinforcement. An important principle that Skinner discovered is that the timing of reinforcement can make a significant difference on how fast a response is learned. **Continuous reinforcement** occurs when a reinforcer is presented after every response. **Partial reinforcement** occurs when a reinforcer is given after some, but not all, of the correct responses. Partial reinforcement takes longer to go through extinction, or in other words, is more resistant to extinction. This is known as the **partial reinforcement effect**. The timing of partial reinforcement is referred to as the **schedule of reinforcement**. There are four different schedules of reinforcement: **fixed ratio**, **variable ratio**, **fixed interval**, and **variable interval**. A ratio schedule occurs when a reinforcer depends on the number of responses that are made. In an interval schedule, reinforcers are presented after a certain period of time has passed. If the reinforcers are always given after a set period of time or number of responses, the schedule is said to be fixed. If the reinforcer is given after varying periods of time or numbers of responses, the schedule is labeled as variable.

    The result of any of the above schedules of reinforcement is to increase a particular behavior. **Punishment**, on the other hand, always decreases the likelihood of a response. Punishment is any consequence of a response that causes that response to be less likely to happen again. While reinforcement strengthens a response that already exists, the goal of punishment is often to eliminate the response, which is usually a much harder task. Typically punishment only temporarily suppresses the response. **Punishment by application** describes the situation in which a response is followed by the addition of something unpleasant. Punishment by application is not the most effective way to modify behavior and has a number of serious drawbacks. **Punishment by removal** occurs when a response is followed by the removal of something pleasant. Punishment can be made more effective if it is administered immediately after the undesired behavior, is administered consistently, and is paired with reinforcement for the right behavior.

    The term **behavior modification** is used to describe the process of using operant conditioning to change behavior. A **token economy** involves the use of tokens to modify behavior. **Time-outs** are an example of punishment by removal where the child is removed from a situation where they could get attention from others. **Applied behavior analysis or ABA** uses shaping techniques to obtain a desired behavior and is particularly successful with children with disorders such as autism.

    Cognitive learning theorists focus on the mental processes (or cognitions) that occur during learning. **Edward Tolman** studied the phenomenon of **latent learning** in rats placed in a maze but not reinforced for finding their way out. He found that when the rats were subsequently reinforced, learning occurred much faster than for rats who had never been in the maze. **Martin Seligman** studied a phenomenon he called **learned helplessness** in dogs. He found that dogs classically conditioned to a tone followed by a painful shock would not later try to escape the shock when provided the opportunity. Seligman extended the concept of learned helplessness to humans in an attempt to explain depression. A third cognitive psychologist, **Wolfgang Köhler**, studied the phenomenon of **insight learning** in animals. Köhler believed insight learning involved a sudden perception of relationships that could not be gained through trial and error learning. All three theories of learning are related in that they focus on what's going on inside the learner's mind during the learning process as opposed to the external stimuli and rewards of classical and operant conditioning.

A third category of learning is that of **observational learning**, or the learning of a new behavior by observing someone else who is performing that behavior. **Albert Bandura** has been a major contributor to the study of observational learning and conducted a series of classic studies observing children's learned behaviors with a blow-up "Bobo" doll. Bandura concluded that four elements were needed for observational learning to occur; these elements are attention, memory, imitation and motivation.

KEY POINTS

- Explain what classical conditioning is, how it works, and how it was discovered.
- Describe the mechanisms of operant conditioning, its application in the real world and the researchers who contributed to our understanding of the process.
- Introduce cognitive learning theory.
- Define observational learning and describe Bandura's classic experiments in the area of observational learning.

KEY CONCEPTS

learning	Relatively permanent change in behavior due to experience or practice.
Ivan Pavlov	1849-1936. A Russian physiologist who first described the phenomenon now known as classical conditioning.
classical conditioning	Learning to make a reflex response to a stimulus other than the original, natural stimulus that normally produces the reflex.
unconditioned stimulus (UCS)	A naturally occurring stimulus that leads to an involuntary response.
unconditioned response (UCR)	An involuntary response to a naturally occurring or unconditioned stimulus.
neutral stimulus (NS)	Stimulus that has no effect on the desired response.
conditioned stimulus (CS)	Stimulus that becomes able to produce a learned reflex response by being paired with the original unconditioned stimulus.
conditioned response (CR)	Learned reflex response to a conditioned stimulus.

acquisition	In classical conditioning, the repeated pairing of a neutral stimulus with an unconditioned stimulus in order to produce a conditioned response.
stimulus generalization	The tendency to respond to a stimulus that is similar to the original conditioned stimulus with the conditioned response.
stimulus discrimination	The tendency to stop making a generalized response to a stimulus that is similar to the original conditioned stimulus because the similar stimulus is never paired with the unconditioned stimulus.
extinction	In classical conditioning, the disappearance or weakening of a learned response following the removal or absence of the unconditioned stimulus.
spontaneous recovery	The reappearance of a learned response after extinction has occurred.
higher order conditioning	Occurs when a strong conditioned stimulus is paired with a neutral stimulus, causing the neutral stimulus to become a second conditioned stimulus.
conditional emotional response	Emotional response that has become classically conditioned to occur to learned stimuli, such as a fear of dogs or the emotional reaction that occurs when seeing an attractive person.
vicarious conditioning	Classical conditioning of a reflex response or emotion by watching the reaction of another person.
conditioned taste aversions	Development of a nausea or aversive response to a particular taste because that taste was followed by a nausea reaction, occurring after only one association.
biological preparedness	Referring to the tendency of animals to learn certain associations, such as taste and nausea, with only one or few pairings due to the survival value of the learning.
stimulus substitution	Original theory in which Pavlov stated that classical conditioning occurred because the conditioned stimulus became a substitute for the unconditioned stimulus by being paired closely together.
expectancy	Modern theory in which classical conditioning is seen to occur because the conditioned stimulus provides information or an expectancy about the coming of the unconditioned stimulus.
operant conditioning	The learning of voluntary behavior through the effects of pleasant and unpleasant consequences to responses.
Edward Thorndike	1874-1949. Discovered the law of effect and laid the groundwork for operant conditioning through his work with puzzle boxes.

Law of Effect	Law stating that if a response is followed by a pleasurable consequence, it will tend to be repeated, and if followed by an unpleasant consequence, it will tend to not be repeated.
B.F. Skinner	1904-1990. Proponent of behaviorist perspective and pioneer in the field of operant conditioning.
reinforcement	The strengthening of a response that occurs when that response is followed by a pleasurable consequence.
reinforcer	Any event or object that, when following a response, increases the likelihood of that response occurring again.
primary reinforcers	Any reinforcer that is naturally reinforcing by meeting a basic biological need, such as hunger, thirst, or touch.
secondary reinforcers	Any reinforcer that becomes reinforcing after being paired with a primary reinforcer, such as praise, tokens, or gold stars.
positive reinforcement	The reinforcement of a response by the addition or experiencing of a pleasure stimulus.
negative reinforcement	The reinforcement of a response by the removal, escape from, or avoidance of an unpleasant stimulus.
shaping	The reinforcement of simple steps in behavior that lead to a desired, more complex behavior.
extinction	In operant conditioning, the disappearance or weakening of a learned response following the removal of a reinforcer.
spontaneous recovery	The reappearance of a learned response after extinction has occurred.
discriminative stimulus	Any stimulus, such as a stop sign or a doorknob, that provides the organism with a cue for making a certain response in order to obtain reinforcement.
continuous reinforcement	The reinforcement of each and every correct response.
partial reinforcement	The reinforcement of some, but not all, of the correct responses.
partial reinforcement effect	The tendency for a response that is reinforced after some, but not all, correct responses to be very resistant to extinction.
schedule of reinforcement	Timing of reinforcement for correct responses.
fixed ratio	Schedule of reinforcement in which the number of responses required for reinforcement is always the same.
variable ratio	Schedule of reinforcement in which the number of responses

required for reinforcement is different for each trial or event.

fixed interval	Schedule of reinforcement in which the interval of time that must pass before reinforcement becomes possible is always the same.
variable interval	Schedule of reinforcement in which the interval of time that must pass before reinforcement becomes possible is different for each trial or event.
punishment	Any event or object that, when following a response, makes that response less likely to happen again.
punishment by application	The punishment of a response by the addition or experiencing of an unpleasant stimulus.
punishment by removal	The punishment of a response by the removal of a pleasurable stimulus.
behavior modification	The use of operant conditioning techniques to bring about desired changes in behavior.
token economy	Type of behavior modification in which desired behavior is rewarded with tokens that can then be used to acquire items of value.
time-out	Behavior modification technique where the subject is removed from all sources of attention. An example of punishment by removal.
applied behavior analysis (ABA)	Modern term for a form of behavior modification that uses shaping techniques to mold a desired behavior or response.
cognitive learning	Learning model that focuses on the mental processes required for the acquisition of new behaviors.
Edward Tolman	1886-1959. Developed several theories of cognitive learning including the concept of latent learning.
latent learning	Learning that remains hidden until its application becomes useful.
Martin Seligman	1942-present. Cognitive learning theorists who conducted a series of studies on learned helplessness in dogs.
learned helplessness	The tendency to fail to act to escape from a situation because of a history of repeated failures in the past.
Wolfgang Köhler	1887-1967. Co-founder of Gestalt Psychology, studied problem-solving in animals and promoted the concept of insight learning.
insight learning	The sudden perception of relationships among various parts of a problem, such as an "a-ha" experience, allowing the solution to

the problem to come quickly.

| observational learning | Learning new behavior by watching a model perform that behavior. |
| Albert Bandura | 1925-present. Conducted a series of classic studies on how children model aggressive behavior towards an inflatable Bobo doll and developed the concept of observational learning. |

HINTS

1. Many students get confused with the terms of classical conditioning. There are four major components to this type of learning: unconditioned stimulus (UCS), conditioned stimulus (CS), unconditioned response (UCR) and conditioned response (CR). The best way to keep these terms straight is to ask yourself two questions.

   1. Is the event I am interested in a stimulus or a response?

   2. Is the stimulus/response something that was learned or something that occurs naturally, by instinct?

   The first question is the easiest way to break down the information. If an event is a stimulus, it will cause something else to happen. List some examples of stimuli here:

   _____

   You might have mentioned any number of stimuli including events such as a bright light, a puff of air, a loud siren, a soft whisper, a touch on your arm, the smell of cookies, or a written word. The list is quite large. A stimulus is any event that causes a response.

   Now that you have a good feeling for what stimuli are, try listing some examples of some possible responses.

   _____

   You might have mentioned events such as blinking your eyes, laughing, crying, jumping up, an increase in heart rate, feeling scared, raising your hand, or driving faster. A response is any behavior (inside or outside of your body) that can be observed.

   Once you determine if your event is a stimulus or response, the second question is fairly easy. Is the stimulus something the subject had to learn how to respond to? If so, then it would be a learned or conditioned stimulus. If the stimulus is something that causes the response automatically, then it is an unlearned or unconditioned stimulus. The same rule applies for the responses. If this is a response that does not occur by instinct, but instead has been learned through experience, then this is a learned or conditioned response. If the response happens the first time you encounter the stimulus, as an instinct, then it is an unlearned or unconditioned response. Now try some examples and see how you do.

A puff of air is aimed at your eye and you blink.
The event we are interested in is: <u>the blink</u>

Question 1: Is this a stimulus or a response?

_____

If you wrote response, then you are correct.
Blinking is a behavior that we can observe.

Question 2: Is this response learned or unlearned?

_____

If you wrote unlearned, then you are correct.
Blinking to a puff of air is an instinct.

Now you can fill in the blanks.
The first answer tells you this is a response, so it is either a CR or a UCR.
The second answer tells you this is unlearned or unconditioned, so it must be a UCR.

Now circle the right term:

	<u>Stimulus</u>	<u>Response</u>
<u>Learned</u>	CS	CR
<u>Unlearned</u>	UCS	UCR

Try some more on your own.

A picture of a piece of chocolate cake causes your mouth to water.
The event we are interested in is: <u>the picture of the cake</u>

Question 1: Is this a stimulus or a response?

_____

Question 2: Is this response learned or unlearned?

_____

Now circle the right term:

	<u>Stimulus</u>	<u>Response</u>
<u>Learned</u>	CS	CR
<u>Unlearned</u>	UCS	UCR

Your heart speeds up as you see a police car pull up behind you.
   The event we are interested in is: your heart speeding up

   Question 1: Is this a stimulus or a response?

   _____

   Question 2: Is this response learned or unlearned?

   _____

Now select the right term:

	Stimulus	Response
Learned	CS	CR
Unlearned	UCS	UCR

A loud noise causes someone to jump.
   The event we are interested in is: the loud noise

   Question 1: Is this a stimulus or a response?

   _____

   Question 2: Is this response learned or unlearned?

   _____

Now select the right term:

	Stimulus	Response
Learned	CS	CR
Unlearned	UCS	UCR

You should have selected the following
   blinking your eyes is a UCR
   the piece of cake is a CS
   your heart speeding up is a CR
   the loud noise is a UCS

2. A good way to learn the schedules of reinforcement in operant conditioning is to take one behavior and explain how it would be reinforced under each of the schedules. Remember that the fixed schedules always reinforce the behavior the same way—for example, after every third response. The variable schedules vary. For example, reinforcement is given after the third response, then after the first response, then after the sixth response, so that in the long run, it averages out to every third response. The other item to keep in mind is that ratio refers to the

number of responses or rate of responding (ratio=rate) and interval refers to the amount of time that has passed.

Now assume you have your own Skinner box with a hungry rat ready to push a lever and receive some food pellets as reinforcement. Explain what the rat would have to do to get her first four food pellets. Be sure to be specific; for example, press the lever 15 times or press the lever after a 10 minute interval.

Schedule of reinforcement	What the rat must do to receive food	Reinforcer	Description of this schedule
Fixed Ratio	1 *press the lever 15 times*	Food Pellet #1	
	2 _____	Food Pellet #2	
	3 _____	Food Pellet #3	
	4 _____	Food Pellet #4	
Variable Ratio	1 _____	Food Pellet #1	
	2 _____	Food Pellet #2	
	3 _____	Food Pellet #3	
	4 _____	Food Pellet #4	
Fixed Interval	1 _____	Food Pellet #1	
	2 _____	Food Pellet #2	
	3 _____	Food Pellet #3	
	4 _____	Food Pellet #4	
Variable Interval	1 _____	Food Pellet #1	
	2 _____	Food Pellet #2	
	3 _____	Food Pellet #3	
	4 _____	Food Pellet #4	

3. Both positive and negative reinforcement lead to an increase in behavior. In positive reinforcement, something good is given; in negative reinforcement, something bad is taken away. Sometimes it can be confusing because it depends on whose perspective you are using. For example, a child whining in the grocery store line until he gets the candy he wants can be viewed as either positive or negative reinforcement. Keep in mind that from both perspectives the behavior increases. Examine the following chart to see why

View Point	Behavior	Result/Reinforcer	Type of reinforcement
Child	whining	get candy	positive (something good is given)
Parent	give child candy	whining stops	negative (something bad—the whining—is taken away)

4. Negative reinforcement and punishment are often confused. In negative reinforcement, something bad is taken away. In punishment by removal, something good or desirable is taken away. Most people would enjoy being negatively reinforced but would be upset about being punished. Work through the following scenarios to determine whether the person is being negatively reinforced or punished. The first one has been completed for you.

Behavior	Consequence	Is something good or bad taken away?	Is this negative reinforcement or punishment?	Will the behavior increase or decrease
Taking an aspirin for a headache.	Headache goes away.	*bad*	*negative reinforcement*	*increase*
Running a red light.	Driver's license is taken away.			
Cleaning your room so that you are no longer grounded.	You are no longer grounded.			
Drinking coffee in the morning when you are very tired.	You no longer feel tired.			
Staying out past your curfew.	Your parents ground you.			
Getting in a fight with a friend.	Your friend will not talk to you anymore.			

103

Fastening your seatbelt when the buzzer is making a noise.	The buzzer stops.			
Driving your car until it runs out of gas.	You can't drive your car anymore.			
Your boyfriend nags you until you take him out to dinner.	The nagging stops.			

Suggested answers

Schedule of reinforcement	What the rat must do to receive food	Reinforcer	Description of this schedule
Fixed Ratio	*1. press lever 20 times*	*Food Pellet #1*	*This schedule produces a high rate of responding with significant pauses right after each reinforcer.*
	2. press lever 20 times	*Food Pellet #2*	
	3. press lever 20 times	*Food Pellet #3*	
	4. press lever 20 times	*Food Pellet #4*	
Variable Ratio	*1. press lever 15 times*	*Food Pellet #1*	*On average, the rat presses the lever 20 times. This schedule produces a high rate of responding with no pauses after the reinforcer.*
	2. press lever 35 times	*Food Pellet #2*	
	3. press lever 10 times	*Food Pellet #3*	
	4. press lever 20 times	*Food Pellet #4*	
Fixed Interval	*1. press lever after 5 minutes*	*Food Pellet #1*	*This schedule produces a lower rate of responding with pauses after each reinforcer.*
	2. press lever after 5 minutes	*Food Pellet #2*	
	3. press lever after 5 minutes	*Food Pellet #3*	
	4. press lever after 5 minutes	*Food Pellet #4*	
Variable Interval	*1. press lever after 2 minutes*	*Food Pellet #1*	*On average, the interval is 5 minutes. This schedule produces a lower rate of responding with a pause after each reinforcer.*
	2. press lever after 6 minutes	*Food Pellet #2*	
	3. press lever after 4 minutes	*Food Pellet #3*	
	4. press lever after 8 minutes	*Food Pellet #4*	

Behavior	Consequence	Is something good or bad taken away?	Is this negative reinforcement or punishment?	Will the behavior increase or decrease?
Taking an aspirin for a headache.	Headache goes away.	*bad*	*negative reinforcement*	*increase*
Running a red light.	Driver's license is taken away.	*good*	*punishment*	*decrease*
Cleaning your room so that you are no longer grounded.	You are no longer grounded.	*bad*	*negative reinforcement*	*increase*
Drinking coffee in the morning when you are very tired.	You no longer feel tired.	*bad*	*negative reinforcement*	*increase*
Staying out past your curfew.	Your parents ground you.	*good*	*punishment*	*decrease*
Getting in a fight with a friend.	Your friend will not talk to you anymore.	*good*	*punishment*	*decrease*
Fastening your seatbelt when the buzzer is making a noise.	The buzzer stops.	*bad*	*negative reinforcement*	*increase*
Driving your car until it runs out of gas.	You can't drive your car anymore.	*good*	*punishment*	*decrease*
Your boyfriend nags you until you take him out to dinner.	The nagging stops.	*bad*	*negative reinforcement*	*increase*

SAMPLE EXAM

For the following multiple choice questions, select the answer you feel best answers the question and explain the rationale or reason for your selection in the space provided.

Objective 5.1

1.   _____ is any relatively permanent change in behavior brought about by experience or practice.
   a) learning
   b) adaptation
   c) memory enhancement
   d) muscle memory

Rationale:
A is the correct answer. This is the definition of learning given in the textbook and restated in the summary.

Objective 5.2

2.   The researcher responsible for discovering classical conditioning was:
   a) Skinner
   b) Tolman
   c) Kohler
   d) Pavlov

Rationale:
D is the correct answer. Skinner developed the theory of operant conditioning and both Kohler and Tolman focused on cognitive learning.

3.   Which of the following correctly describes the process of classical conditioning?
   a) pairing a stimulus that naturally causes a certain response with a second stimulus that naturally causes the same response.
   b) pairing a stimulus that naturally causes a certain response with a second stimulus that does not naturally cause that response.
   c) presenting a pleasurable stimulus after the occurrence of a specific response.
   d) presenting an unpleasant stimulus after the occurrence of a specific response.

Rationale:

_____

_____

4. When Pavlov placed meat powder or other food in the mouths of canine subjects, they began to salivate. The salivation was a/an:
    a) unconditioned response.
    b) unconditioned stimulus.
    c) conditioned response.
    d) conditioned stimulus.

    Rationale:

    _____

    _____

5. Judy would sometimes discipline her puppy by swatting its nose with a rolled-up newspaper. One day she brought the newspaper into the house still rolled up, and her puppy ran from her in fear. By pairing the rolled paper with the swat, Judy's puppy had developed a(n) _____ response to the rolled-up paper.
    a) generalized
    b) conditioned
    c) unconditioned
    d) discriminative

    Rationale:

    _____

    _____

6. You decide you want to try to classically condition your pet dog. What is the correct order that you should use to present the stimuli to your dog?
    a) unconditioned stimulus – neutral stimulus
    b) neutral stimulus – neutral stimulus
    c) neutral stimulus – unconditioned stimulus
    d) present the unconditioned stimulus only

    Rationale:

    _____

    _____

7. After you successfully classically conditioned your pet dog, you repeatedly presented the conditioned stimulus without ever pairing it with the unconditioned stimulus. Over time, your dog stops performing the conditioned response. What has happened?
    a) extinction
    b) spontaneous recovery
    c) generalization
    d) stimulus discrimination

    Rationale:

    _____

    _____

8. John Watson and his colleague, Rosalie Rayner, offered a live, white rat to Little Albert and then made a loud noise behind his head by striking a steel bar with a hammer. The white rat served as the _____ in their study.
    a) discriminative stimulus
    b) counterconditioning stimulus
    c) conditioned stimulus
    d) unconditioned stimulus

Rationale:

_____

_____

Objective 5.4

9. Pavlov discovered classical conditioning through his study of
    a) cats escaping from a puzzle box.
    b) primate research into problem solving.
    c) digestive secretions in dogs.
    d) lever pressing responses of rats.

Rationale:

_____

_____

Objective 5.5

10. Television advertisers have taken advantage of the fact that most people experience positive emotions when they see an attractive, smiling person. This association is an example of
    a) operant conditioning.
    b) a conditioned emotional response.
    c) negative reinforcement.
    d) Punishment.
    Rationale:

_____

_____

Objective 5.6

11. The current view of why classical conditioning works the way it does by cognitive theorists such as Rescorla, adds the concept of _____to the conditioning process.
    a) generalization
    b) habituation
    c) memory loss
    d) expectancy

Rationale:

_____

_____

12. "If a response is followed by a pleasurable consequence, it will tend to be repeated. If a response is followed by an unpleasant consequence, it will tend not to be repeated." This is a statement of
_____.

    a) The law of positive reinforcement
    b) Rescorla's Cognitive perspective
    c) Thorndike's Law of Effect
    d) Garcia's Conditional Emotional Response

Rationale:

_____

_____

13. Kenra has a new pet cat and decides to modify her cat's behavior by administering pleasant and unpleasant consequences after her cat's behaviors. Kenra is using the principles of

    a) observational learning.
    b) operant conditioning.
    c) classical conditioning.
    d) insight learning.

Rationale:

_____

_____

Objective 5.8

14. A box used in operant conditioning of animals, which limits the available responses and thus increases the likelihood that the desired response will occur, is called a _____.
    a) trial box
    b) response box
    c) Watson box
    d) Skinner box

Rationale:

_____

_____

15. A negative reinforcer is a stimulus that is _____ and thus _____ the probability of a response.
    - a) removed; increases
    - b) removed; decreases
    - c) presented; increases
    - d) presented; decreases

    Rationale:

    _____

    _____

16. The partial reinforcement effect refers to the fact that a response that is reinforced after some, but not all, correct responses _____
    - a) will be more resistant to extinction than a response that receives continuous reinforcement (a reinforcer for each and every correct response).
    - b) will be less resistant to extinction than a response that receives continuous reinforcement (a reinforcer for each and every correct response).
    - c) more variable in its resistance to extinction than a response that receives continuous reinforcement (a reinforcer for each and every correct response).
    - d) totally resistant to extinction unlike a response that receives continuous reinforcement (a reinforcer for each and every correct response).

    Rationale:

    _____

    _____

Objective 5.10

17. Which example best describes the fixed interval schedule of reinforcement?
    - a) receiving a paycheck after two weeks of work.
    - b) receiving a bonus after selling 20 cell phones.
    - c) giving your dog a treat every time he comes when you call him.
    - d) giving your dog a treat every third time he comes when you call him.

    Rationale:

    _____

    _____

18. Which schedule of reinforcement should you select if you would like to produce the highest number of responses with the least number of pauses between the responses?
    - a) fixed ratio
    - b) variable ratio
    - c) fixed interval
    - d) variable interval

    Rationale:

    _____

    _____

Objective 5.11

19. When a stimulus is removed from a person or animal and it decreases the probability of response, it is known as _____.
  a) positive punishment
  b) punishment by removal
  c) negative reinforcement
  d) negative punishment

Rationale:

_____

_____

20. Your child has begun drawing on the walls of your house and you would like this activity to stop. Which of the following actions would, at least temporarily, decrease the occurrence of the behavior in your child?
  a) use insight learning to get your child to stop drawing on the wall
  b) use classical conditioning to create a positive association with drawing on the wall
  c) negatively reinforce your child after she draws on the wall
  d) punish your child after she draws on the wall

Rationale:

_____

_____

Objective 5.12

21. An example of a discriminative stimulus might be a:
  a) stop sign
  b) the stimulus that acts as a UCS in classical conditioning
  c) the white rat in Watson's Little Albert study of producing phobias
  d) none of these

Rationale:

_____

_____

22. In their 1961 paper on instinctive drift, the Brelands determined that three assumptions most Skinnerian behaviorists believed in were not actually true. Which is one of the assumptions that were **NOT** true?
     a) The animal comes to the laboratory a tabula rasa, or "blank slate," and can therefore be taught anything with the right conditioning.
     b) Differences between species of animals are insignificant.
     c) All responses are equally able to be conditioned to any stimulus.
     d) All of these were not true.

     Rationale:

     _____

     _____

Objective 5.14

23. Applied behavior analysis or ABA has been used with autistic children. The basic principle of this form of behavior modification is _____.
     a) partial reinforcement
     b) classical conditioning
     c) negative punishment
     d) shaping

     Rationale:

     _____

     _____

Objective 5.15

24. Biofeedback is an application of _____.
     a) classical conditioning
     b) operant conditioning
     c) social learning
     d) preparedness

     Rationale:

     _____

     _____

25.   Cognition refers to

       a)   behavior that is observable and external.
       b)   behavior that is directly measurable.
       c)   the mental events that take place while a person is behaving.
       d)   memories.

Rationale:

_____

_____

Objective 5.17

26.   The idea that learning occurs, and is stored up, even when behaviors are not reinforced is called _____.

       a)   insight
       b)   latent learning
       c)   placebo learning
       d)   innate learning

Rationale:

_____

_____

Objective 5.18

27.   A researcher places dogs in a cage with metal bars on the floor. The dogs are randomly given electric shocks and can do nothing to prevent them or stop them. Later, the same dogs are placed in a cage where they can escape the shocks by jumping over a low hurdle. When the shocks are given, the dogs do not even try to escape. They just sit and cower. This is an example of

_____.

       a)   learned helplessness
       b)   stimulus discrimination
       c)   aversive conditioning
       d)   vicarious learning

Rationale:

_____

_____

Objective 5.19

28.   The "a-ha!" experience is known as
        a)   latent learning.
        b)   insight learning.
        c)   thoughtful learning.
        d)   serial enumeration.

Rationale:

_____

_____

Objective 5.20

29.   If you learn how to fix your car by watching someone on TV demonstrate the technique, you are acquiring that knowledge through
        a)   latent learning.
        b)   operant conditioning.
        c)   classical conditioning.
        d)   observational learning.

Rationale:

_____

_____

Objective 5.21

30.   In Bandura's study with the Bobo doll, the children in the group who saw the model punished did not imitate the model at first. They would only imitate the model if given a reward for doing so. The fact that these children had obviously learned the behavior without actually performing it is an example of
        a)   latent learning.
        b)   operant conditioning.
        c)   classical conditioning.
        d)   insight learning.

Rationale:

_____

_____

31. In Bandura's study of observational learning, what does the abbreviation AMIM stand for?
    a) attention, memory, imitation, motivation
    b) alertness, motivation, intent, monetary reward
    c) achievement, momentum, initiative, memory
    d) achievement, motivation, intellectual capacity, memory

Rationale:

_____

_____

SAMPLE EXAM ANSWERS & RATIONALES

1. a   This is the definition of learning given in the textbook and restated in the summary.
2. d   Skinner developed the theory of operant conditioning and both Kohler and Tolman focused on cognitive learning.
3. b   Classical conditioning occurs when you pair a neutral stimulus (NS) with an unconditioned stimulus (UCS). After repeated pairings, the NS now causes a response similar to the naturally occurring response. The stimulus is now called a conditioned stimulus and the response is the conditioned response.
4. a   An unconditioned response is a response that occurs naturally and does not have to be learned. When food is placed in a dog's mouth, the dog will naturally begin to salivate.
5. b   A conditioned response is a response that has been learned through association. Originally, the rolled up newspaper did not cause a response of fear in the puppy but after repeated pairings with a swat, it now causes the fear response.
6. c   For classical conditioning to occur, the neutral stimulus must be repeated paired with an unconditioned stimulus. In addition, the neutral stimulus must be presented *before* the unconditioned stimulus.
7. a   Extinction occurs when the CS is continuously presented without the UCS.
8. c   First, decide if the rat is a stimulus or a response. Obviously, the rat is a stimulus. Then figure out if the rat naturally or instinctively will cause the response of fear or if the response needs to be learned. If it needs to be learned, then the stimulus is a conditioned stimulus.
9. c   Pavlov was a Russian physiologist who won a Nobel prize for his study of the digestive system in dogs. It was during this research that he observed the phenomenon of classical conditioning and devoted the rest of his years in research to the study of classical conditioning.
10. b   The association between attractive people and feelings of happiness is learned through classical conditioning and is specifically referred to as a conditioned emotional response since it deals with a response of emotion. Notice that all the other choices were related to operant conditioning.
11. d   Expectancy is the idea that the conditioned stimulus has to provide some information about the upcoming unconditioned stimulus, so that we are *expecting* the UCS to occur.
12. c   Thorndike developed this principle through his study of animals escaping from puzzle boxes.
13. b   This is a modified form of the definition of operant conditioning.
14. d   The Skinner box was designed by B.F. Skinner and typically included an apparatus for the animal to move (such as a lever to press) and a mechanism for delivering a reward to the animal.
15. a   Always start with the fact that reinforcement always increases the response. This immediately eliminates options "b" and "d." Negative reinforcement occurs when an unpleasant stimulus is removed, making "a" the correct choice.
16. a   If a response is resistant to extinction, that means that the person will continue making that response even when it is not followed by a reinforcer.
17. a   Fixed means that the reinforcement will always be presented after the same period of time or number of responses. Interval means that you are dealing with the passage of time.
18. b   The ratio schedule produces the most rapid responses since the reward depends on making a certain number of responses. The variable schedule reduces the pauses

after receiving the reinforcer because the next reward could be given at any time.

19.   b   Remember that punishment decreases behavior and reinforcement increases behavior; because the question is asking about a behavior decrease, they must be talking about punishment. Removing a stimulus is described as punishment by removal.

20.   d   Once again, you would like the behavior to decrease, so you should select punishment.

21.   a   A discriminative stimulus is defined as a stimulus that provides a cue that a response might lead to reinforcement. It is a term used with operant conditioning.

22.   d   The Brelands questioned all three of these assumptions.

23.   d   ABA rewards closer and closer approximations to the desired behavior; this is the definition of shaping.

24.   b   The change in physiological state is the response and the light or tone serves as the reinforcement.

25.   c   Cognitive psychologists focus on our thought process and mental activities.

26.   b   The word latent means something that's present but not visible.

27.   a   Learned helplessness was studied by Seligman as a potential animal model of depression.

28.   b   With this type of learning, you have a sudden realization or "insight."

29.   d   Observational learning occurs when you learn a new behavior or new knowledge through the observation of a model.

30.   a   Latent learning occurs when a new behavior has been acquired but the behavior is not performed, as the children in Bandura's experiment did not imitate the model until they were encouraged and rewarded to do so.

31.   a   Since all the selections match the abbreviation, try to think about what skills would be needed to learn by observation. First of all, you need to watch the person you are trying to learn from. Choices c and d can be eliminated because they don't list any skill that would assist with the observation. Choice b can then be eliminated if you realize that observational learning can occur without any rewards being offered.

APPLY IT

For this challenge, try applying the concepts of operant conditioning to shape your own behavior. Think of a study pattern that you would like to develop. For instance, would you like to be able to sit down and study for 50 minutes without being distracted? Or would you like to be able to finish your homework right when you get home so you can relax the rest of the evening? Now you can use the techniques of shaping with positive reinforcement to bring about the desired behavior in yourself. Follow these simple steps.

Step 1: Identify the behavior you would like to shape. This should be a specific behavior that can be easily identified. For example, "working for 50 minutes uninterrupted on school work" or "getting up by 7:00 am each morning" or "working out for 30 minutes each day."

Write your behavior here:

Step 2: Identify a reinforcer that works for you. Be careful with your selection. You need to pick a simple reinforcer that you can give to yourself as soon as you perform the behavior. It should not be complicated or hard to administer (for example, "going to the store and getting a cup of coffee" would be too complicated of a reward). Think about the things you find rewarding. It can be something as simple as giving yourself a small piece of candy, showing yourself a picture of a good friend, putting a sticker of a star on a sheet of paper on the fridge. Don't underestimate the power of these simple rewards. Whatever you pick, make sure it can be administered immediately after the response and that it does not require any additional work from you to administer.

Write your reinforcer here:

Step 3: Now you will need to shape the behavior. Start out rewarding yourself for completing a small portion of the desired behavior and slowly keep increasing the behavior required for achieving the goal. For example, if your goal is to work out for 30 minutes each day, start giving yourself a reward for working out at least 5 minutes each day. After a week, give yourself a reward for working out at least 10 minutes each day and so on. Write out your shaping schedule here:

Level 1: _____

Level 2: _____

Level 3: _____

Level 4: _____

Step 4: Do it! See how it works; you might be surprised at how effective the shaping technique can be. When you are done, write a brief summary of the results below.

CHAPTER 6 LEARNING OBJECTIVES

SUMMARY

Memory can be thought of as an active system that receives information from the senses, organizes and alters it as it stores it, and then retrieves information from storage. All the current models of memory involve the three processes of **encoding**, **storage**, and **retrieval**.

Three models or theories about memory are discussed in the text. One is the **levels of processing model**, which proposes that how long a memory will be remembered depends on the depth to which it was processed. A second model is the **parallel distributed processing model,** which proposes that memories are created and stored across a network of neural circuits simultaneously, or, in other words, in a parallel fashion. The third and currently most accepted model of memory is the **information processing model,** which proposes that memory is divided into three components – **sensory**, **short-term**, and **long-term**. Sensory memory is the first stage of memory and involves information from our sensory systems. Visual sensory memory is called **iconic memory** and was studied extensively by **George Sperling** through the use of the **partial report method**. The capacity of iconic memory is everything that can be seen at one time, and the duration is around half a second. **Eidetic imagery**, also known as photographic memory, is the ability to access visual sensory memory over a long period of time. Iconic memory is useful for allowing the visual system to view the surroundings as continuous and stable. **Echoic memory** is the memory of auditory information and has the capacity of what can be heard at any one moment and a duration of about two seconds.

The information processing model proposes that information moves from sensory memory to short-term memory through the process of **selective attention**. This process explains the phenomenon of the **cocktail party effect**, when you are at a party and hear your name in a conversation across the room. Another name for short-term memory is **working memory,** and some researchers propose that short-term memory consists of a central control process along with a visual "sketch pad" and auditory "recorder." **George Miller** studied the capacity of short-term memory using the **digit-span memory test** and discovered that people can store an average of seven chunks of information (plus or minus two) in their short term memory. **Chunking** is the process of reorganizing the information into meaningful units. The duration of short term memory is between 10-30 seconds without rehearsal. **Maintenance rehearsal** describes the process of continuing to pay attention to a piece of information, such as reciting a name over and over again in your head.

Long-term memory is the third stage of memory proposed by the information processing theory and has an essentially unlimited capacity and duration. Information may be encoded into long-term memory through **elaborative rehearsal**, a way of transferring information by making it meaningful. Long-term memories can be divided into two types, procedural and declarative. **Procedural, or non-declarative, memories** are memories for skill and habits, in other words, memories for things people can *do*.

Declarative memories are memories of fact, or things people can *know*. There are two types of declarative memories: semantic and episodic. **Semantic memory** is memory for the meanings of words and concepts, while **episodic memory** is the memory of events or "episodes." Procedural memories appear to be stored in the cerebellum and amygdala and are sometimes referred to as **implicit memory,** while declarative memory can be thought of as **explicit memory**. Explicit memories are easily verbalized, while implicit memories are nearly impossible to state in words. It is not entirely clear how the brain organizes information in long-term memory. One suggestion is that long-term memory consists of a **semantic network** with information being processed along parallel lines.

    Retrieval describes the process of pulling memories out of long-term memory. A **retrieval cue** is a stimulus that aids in the process of remembering. When the environment in which you learned an item serves as a retrieval cue, it is referred to as **encoding specificity**. If an emotional state serves as a retrieval cue, it is called **state dependent learning**. Information can be retrieved through the process of **recall**, such as filling in the blanks, or **recognition**, such as multiple choice questions in which the correct answer only needs to be "recognized." Not all information can be recalled equally well. The **serial position effect** describes the finding that information at the beginning and end of a list is more likely to be remembered than the information in the middle. The **primacy effect** proposes that the information at the beginning of the list is remembered due to rehearsal, while the **recency effect** proposes that the information at the end of the list is remembered due to the fact that it is still in short-term memory. Recognition is usually a much easier task than recall since the retrieval cue is the actual piece of information you are trying to remember, yet retrieval errors are still made when using recognition. A **false positive** occurs when someone recognizes a piece of information as a memory even though it did not happen. For example, a witness says they saw broken glass at the scene of an accident, when there was no glass broken in the accident. **Elizabeth Loftus** has spent over 30 years investigating the reliability of eyewitness memories and has found that what people see and hear about an event after the fact can affect the accuracy of their memories for that event. **Automatic encoding** is a term used to describe the memory process when we aren't actively paying attention to the information. A **flashbulb memory** is a specific type of automatic encoding that occurs when an unexpected and often emotional event occurs. Flashbulb memories typically contain a great deal of information including many details but might not be as accurate as they appear.

    The retrieval of memories is a much more **constructive process** than most people assume. Several factors affect the accuracy of information retrieval. One factor is the **misinformation effect,** in which false information presented after an event influences the memory of that event. When suggestions from others create inaccurate or false memories, this is referred to as the **false memory syndrome**. The false memory syndrome has frequently been observed while people are under hypnosis. Research by Loftus has suggested that in order for an individual to interpret a false event as a true memory, the event must seem plausible and the individual should be given information that supports the belief that the event could have happened to them personally. **Hindsight bias** is the tendency of people to falsely believe that they would have been able to accurately predict a result.

    Herman Ebbinghaus was one of the first scientists to systematically study the process of forgetting. Using lists of **nonsense syllables**, he discovered that most forgetting occurs in the initial hour after the material is learned. He presented his findings in a visual graph called the **curve of forgetting**. There are at least four different causes for forgetting. **Encoding failure** occurs when the information does not make it past the initial encoding process and never really becomes a memory. Another possible cause of forgetting is the **decay** of the memory trace in short-term memory or the disuse of the information in long-term memory. The final two causes of forgetting discussed in the textbook have to do with interference. **Proactive interference** occurs when information from the past disrupts newly learned information. **Retroactive interference** occurs when the newly learned information interferes with the memories of the information from the past.

    It is still unclear exactly how memories are physically stored in the brain. The concept of the physical change that takes place in the brain when memories are formed is called the **engram,** and scientists continue their search for it. In general, there is strong evidence to suggest that long-term procedural memories are stored in the cerebellum, while long-term declarative memories are stored in the frontal and temporal lobes. Storage of short-term memories has been associated with the prefrontal cortex and the temporal lobe. The process of physically storing a memory in your brain is called **consolidation** and could consist of a number of changes, including an increase in receptor sties, increased sensitivity at the synapse, changes on the dendrites or changes in proteins in the neuron. The hippocampus has been found to play an important role in the formation of new memories. This fact was mainly discovered by observing patients with damage to the hippocampus and noting their inability to form any new memories. A man named **H.M.** is the most famous of these patients. H.M.'s hippocampi were removed during a surgical procedure to reduce the severity of his epileptic seizures. After the surgery, H.M. could not form any new declarative memories. H.M. could, however, still form new procedural memories. **Amnesia** is a disorder that is characterized by severe memory loss, such as that of H.M.'s, and can take one of two forms. **Retrograde amnesia** is an inability to retrieve memories from the past, while **anterograde amnesia** is an inability to form any new memories. An inability to remember events from the first few years of life has been described as **infantile amnesia** and may be due to the implicit, or non-verbal, nature of those memories.

Alzheimer's disease is one type of dementia that is associated with severe memory loss. Currently there is no cure for Alzheimer's disease, but researchers are working hard to find one. Several possibilities include drugs that block the breakdown of acetylcholine, chemicals within the gingko biloba herb, drugs that stimulate nerve growth, and statins or drugs that lower cholesterol.

KEY POINTS

- Introduce the study of memory, including the basic processes of encoding, storage and retrieval as well as current theories of how memory works.
- Discuss the information processing theory of memory in detail, including the concepts of sensory, short-term and long-term memory.
- Identify the basic steps in the retrieval of information.
- Describe Ebbinghaus's work on forgetting and proposed explanations for forgetting.
- Explain the biological processes thought to underlie memory.

KEY CONCEPTS

memory	An active system that receives information from the senses, organizes and alters it as it stores it away, and then retrieves the information from storage.
encoding	The set of mental operations that people perform on sensory information to convert that information into a form that is usable in the brain's storage systems.
storage	Holding onto information for some period of time.
retrieval	Getting information that is in storage into a form that can be used.
levels of processing model	Model of memory that assumes information that is more "deeply processed," or processed according to its meaning rather than just the sound or physical characteristics of the word or words, will be remembered more efficiently and for a longer period of time.
parallel distributed processing model	A model of memory in which memory processes are proposed to take place at the same time, over a large network of neural

connections.

information processing model	Model of memory that assumes the processing of information for memory storage is similar to the way a computer processes memory, in a series of three stages.
sensory memory	The very first stage of memory, the point at which information enters the nervous system through the sensory systems.
short-term (working) memory	The memory system in which information is held for brief periods of time while being used.
long-term memory	The system of memory into which all the information is placed to be kept more or less permanently.
iconic memory	Visual sensory memory, lasting only a fraction of a second.
eidetic imagery	The ability to access a visual memory for 30 seconds or more.
echoic memory	The brief memory of something a person has just heard.
George Sperling	Psychologist who first studied iconic memory and discovered the duration of iconic memory is around half a second.
partial report method	Method used to study short term memory by having a subject report one row of letters at a precious time following the presentation.
selective attention	The ability to focus on only one stimulus from among all sensory input.
cocktail party effect	The ability to focus our listening attention on a single conversation among a large amount of background noise.
George Miller	1920-present. Published a paper in 1956 called "The magical number seven plus or minus two," which described the capacity of short term memory without rehearsal.
digit-span memory test	Test used by George Miller to determine the capacity of short-term memory. Subjects were asked to recall longer and longer lists of digits.
chunking	The process of regrouping material in memory in order to combine smaller pieces into one larger unit.
maintenance rehearsal	Practice of saying some information to be remembered over and over in one's head in order to maintain it in short-term memory.
elaborative rehearsal	A method of transferring information from STM into LTM by making that information meaningful in some way.

procedural (non-declarative) memory	Type of long-term memory including memory for skills, procedures, habits, and conditioned responses. These memories are not conscious but are implied to exist because they affect conscious behavior.
declarative memory	Type of long-term memory containing information that is conscious and known.
semantic memory	Type of declarative memory containing general knowledge, such as knowledge of language and information learned in formal education.
episodic memory	Type of declarative memory containing personal information not readily available to others, such as daily activities and events.
implicit memory	Memory that is not easily brought into conscious awareness, such as procedural memory.
explicit memory	Memory that is consciously known, such as declarative memory.
semantic network model	Model of memory organization which assumes that information is stored in the brain in an connected fashion, with concepts that are related to each other stored physically closer to each other than concepts that are not highly related.
retrieval cue	A stimulus for remembering.
encoding specificity	The tendency for memory of information to be improved if related information (such as surroundings or physiological state) available when the memory is first formed is also available when the memory is being retrieved.
state dependent learning	The ability to retrieve information more readily when a person is in the same emotional state they were in when the information was learned.
recall	Type of memory retrieval in which the information to be retrieved must be "pulled" from memory with very external few cues.
recognition	The ability to match a piece of information or a stimulus to a stored image or fact.
serial position effect	Tendency of information at the beginning and end of a body of information to be remembered more accurately than information in the middle of the body of information.
primacy effect	Tendency to remember information at the beginning of a body of information better than the information that follows.
recency effect	Tendency to remember information at the end of a body of information better than the information ahead of it.

| false positive | Error of recognition in which people think that they recognize some stimulus that is not actually in memory. |

false positive — Error of recognition in which people think that they recognize some stimulus that is not actually in memory.

Elizabeth Loftus — Psychologist working on memory and how it can be influenced; she is known for her work with false memories.

automatic encoding — Tendency of certain kinds of information to enter long-term memory with little or no effortful encoding.

flashbulb memory — Type of automatic encoding that occurs because an unexpected event has strong emotional associations for the person remembering it.

constructive processing — Referring to the retrieval of memories in which those memories are altered, revised, or influenced by newer information.

misinformation effect — The tendency of misleading information presented after an event to alter the memories of the event itself.

false memory syndrome — A condition in which a person has a memory that is objectively false but strongly believed to be true.

hindsight bias — The tendency to falsely believe, through revision of older memories to include newer information, that one could have correctly predicted the outcome of an event.

Herman Ebbinghaus — German psychologist who was a pioneer in the study of human memory. Made extensive use of nonsense syllables in his studies.

nonsense syllables — Consonant-vowel-consonant combinations that can be pronounced but have no semantic meaning.

curve of forgetting — A graph showing a distinct pattern in which forgetting is very fast within the first hour after learning a list and then tapers off gradually.

encoding failure — Failure to process information into memory.

decay — Loss of memory due to the passage of time, during which the memory trace is not used.

proactive interference — Memory retrieval problem that occurs when older information prevents or interferes with the retrieval of newer information.

retroactive interference — Memory retrieval problem that occurs when newer information prevents or interferes with the retrieval of older information.

memory trace or engram — Physical change in the brain that occurs when a memory is formed.

consolidation	The changes that take place in the structure and functioning of neurons when an engram is formed.
H.M.	Famous patient who lost the ability to form new memories after surgical removal of his hippocampi.
amnesia	Disorder characterized by severe memory loss.
retrograde amnesia	Loss of memory from the point of some injury or trauma backwards, or loss of memory for the past.
anterograde amnesia	Loss of memory from the point of injury or trauma forward, or the inability to form new long-term memories.
infantile amnesia	The inability to retrieve memories from much before the age of three.
Alzheimer's disease	The most common form of dementia in elderly people; leads to severe cognitive loss due to the deterioration of brain tissue.

HINTS

1. Two of the most important concepts presented in this chapter consist of a three-part model. One concept is the basic processes involved in memory – encoding, storage, and retrieval. The other concept is the information processing model of memory, which consists of sensory, short-term, and long-term memory. Students often get these ideas confused. To help you clarify the concepts, correctly identify the components of the information processing model in the diagram below. Remember that encoding, storage, and retrieval can happen at each of these stages. List an example of encoding, storage and retrieval for each stage.

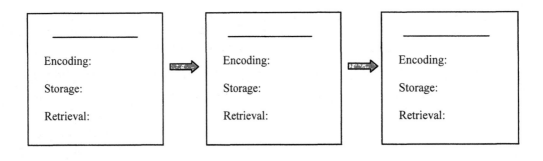

2. Long term memory can be divided into two basic types of memory – procedural and declarative. Declarative memories can be further broken down into episodic and semantic. To help you understand the difference between these types of memories, come up with a specific memory from your own life and write it in the appropriate box.

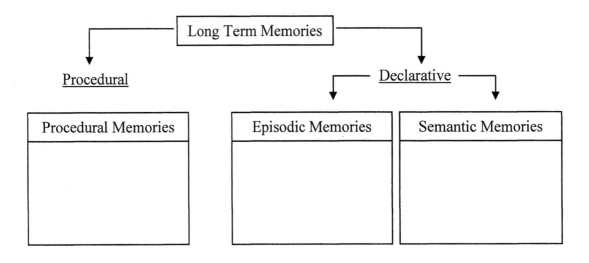

3. It is important to understand the difference between retroactive and proactive interference. In retroactive interference, newly learned information interferes with information learned in the past. In proactive interference, information learned in the past interferes with newly learned information. The best way to identify the type of interference is to identify when the information was learned and which information is causing the error. Try filling in the following table for some samples of retroactive and proactive interference. The first one is completed as a sample.

If the interference goes from past to present, it is proactive.
If the interference goes from present to past, it is retroactive.
It might help to draw an arrow for the information that is causing the error. If the arrow goes left to right it is proactive interference and if it goes right to left it is retroactive.

Example 1: John studied for his biology exam and then studied for his psychology exam. Now he keeps writing down psychology terms on his biology test.

Info learned in past	Info learned in present	Type of interference
Biology ←	*Psychology*	*Retroactive – because the present is interfering with the old information*

Example 2: Sophia keeps getting herself in trouble by calling her new boyfriend "Stan" (the name of her old boyfriend) instead of Matt.

Info learned in past	Info learned in present	Type of interference

Example 3: Julio taught himself to play the guitar and then decided to take some lessons. His instructor has taught him the correct way to play the chords but he keeps forgetting and playing the way he originally learned.

Info learned in past	Info learned in present	Type of interference

Example 4: Alice worked hard to become fluent in Spanish, and once she accomplished that she decided to take a class to learn Portuguese. Now when she is trying to speak Spanish with her friends she finds herself inserting words in Portuguese instead of Spanish.

Info learned in past	Info learned in present	Type of interference

Suggested answers for Study Hint 1

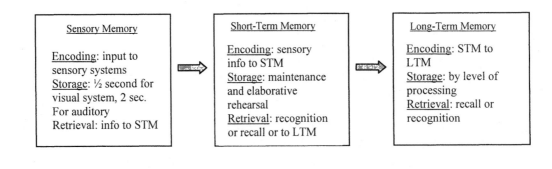

Sensory Memory		Short-Term Memory		Long-Term Memory
Encoding: input to sensory systems Storage: ½ second for visual system, 2 sec. For auditory Retrieval: info to STM	⟹	Encoding: sensory info to STM Storage: maintenance and elaborative rehearsal Retrieval: recognition or recall or to LTM	⟹	Encoding: STM to LTM Storage: by level of processing Retrieval: recall or recognition

Suggested answers for Study Hint 2

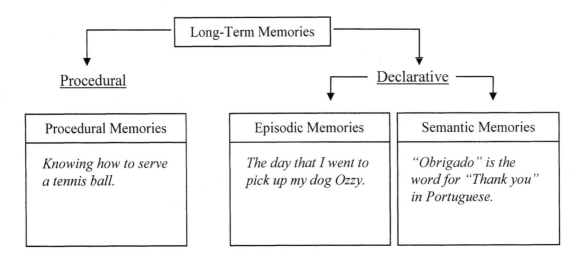

Long-Term Memories

Procedural

Declarative

Procedural Memories	Episodic Memories	Semantic Memories
Knowing how to serve a tennis ball.	*The day that I went to pick up my dog Ozzy.*	*"Obrigado" is the word for "Thank you" in Portuguese.*

Answers for Study Hint 3

Example 2: Sophia keeps getting herself in trouble by calling her new boyfriend "Stan" (the name of her old boyfriend) instead of Matt.

Info learned in past	Info learned in present	Type of interference
old boyfriend's name was "Stan" ———→	*new boyfriend's name is "Matt"*	*Proactive – because the past is interfering with the new information*

Example 3: Julio taught himself to play the guitar and then decided to take some lessons. His instructor has taught him the correct way to play the chords but he keeps forgetting and playing the way he originally learned.

Info learned in past	Info learned in present	Type of interference
self taught chords ———→	*correct method for chords*	*Proactive – because the past is interfering with the new information*

Example 4: Alice worked hard to become fluent in Spanish, and once she accomplished that she decided to take a class to learn Portuguese. Now when she is trying to speak Spanish with her friends she finds herself inserting words in Portuguese instead of Spanish.

Info learned in past	Info learned in present	Type of interference
Spanish ←———	*Portuguese*	*Retroactive – because the present is interfering with the old information*

SAMPLE EXAM

For the following multiple choice questions, select the answer you feel best answers the question and explain the rationale or reason for your selection in the space provided.

Objective 6.1

1. _____ is defined as an active system that receives information from the senses, organizes and alters it as it stores it away, and then retrieves the information from storage.
    a) Classical Conditioning
    b) Operant Conditioning
    c) Learning
    d) Memory

    Rationale:
    D is the correct answer. Memory involves the three processes of encoding, storage and retrieval. All three other choices deal with the process of learning.

Objective 6.2

2. The first step in the memory process is _____ information in a form that the memory system can use.
    a) encoding
    b) storing
    c) retrieving
    d) evaluating

    Rationale:

    _____

    _____

3. The "levels-of-processing" theory suggests that which of the following questions would lead to better memory of the word "frog?"
    a) "Does it rhyme with "blog?"
    b) "Is it in capital letters?"
    c) "Is it written in cursive?"
    d) "Would it be found in a pond?"

    Rationale:

    _____

    _____

4.	Which memory system provides us with a very brief representation of all the stimuli present at a particular moment?
	a) primary memory
	b) sensory memory
	c) long-term memory
	d) short-term memory
	Rationale:

	_____

	_____

5.	Your friend asks you a question and just as you say "What?" you realize what the person said. Which part of your memory was maintaining your friend's words?
	a) iconic sensory memory
	b) echoic sensory memory
	c) short-term memory
	d) long-term memory
	Rationale:

	_____

	_____

Objective 6.4

6.	_____ is synonymous with short-term memory.
	a) Shadow memory
	b) Working memory
	c) Secondary memory
	d) Sensory registers
	Rationale:

	_____

	_____

7.	Your professor asks you to get up in front of the class and repeat a long list of numbers that she reads to you. If you are not given a chance to repeat the numbers to yourself as she reads them, what is the longest list of numbers you will most likely to be able to remember?
	a) 2
	b) 7
	c) 12
	d) 25
	Rationale:

	_____

	_____

8. You try to remember a phone number by repeating it over and over to yourself. What type of rehearsal are you using?
    a) condensed
    b) permanent
    c) elaborative
    d) maintenance

    Rationale:

    _____

    _____

9. The best analogy for the way long-term memory is conceptualized would be _____.
    a) a revolving door
    b) a filing cabinet
    c) a desk top
    d) a computer keyboard

    Rationale:

    _____

    _____

Objective 6.6

10. Procedural memories are to _____ memories as declarative memories are to _____ memories.
    a) implicit; explicit
    b) explicit; implicit
    c) general knowledge; personal facts
    d) personal facts; general knowledge

    Rationale:

    _____

    _____

11. Which of the following types of LTM are forms of explicit memory?
    a) procedural
    b) semantic
    c) episodic
    d) both (b) and (c)

    Rationale:

    _____

    _____

12. As a young child, you spent hours on your skateboard. After several years of not skating, you jump on your board as if you never missed a day. The long-term memory of how to skate is an example of what type of memory?
    a) explicit
    b) episodic
    c) semantic
    d) procedural

    Rationale:

    _____

    _____

13. As you are skating down the street on your skateboard, you think back to the day you accidentally skated into a parked car and had to go the hospital to get stitches. The memory of this event would be described as a(n) _____ memory.
    a) procedural
    b) implicit
    c) episodic
    d) semantic

    Rationale:

    _____

    _____

Objective 6.7

14. According to the semantic network model, it would take more time to answer "true" to which sentence?
    a) "A salmon is an animal."
    b) "A salmon is a fish."
    c) "A canary is a bird."
    d) All of these would take the same time.

    Rationale:

    _____

    _____

Objective 6.8

15. If memory was like the sea, we could say that _____ is long-term memory, _____ are the memories, and _____ are retrieval cues.
    a) the sea, fish, hooks
    b) a boat, worms, fish
    c) a boat, hooks, worms
    d) an island, worms, fishing poles

    Rationale:

    _____

    _____

133

16. Which of the following concepts describes why it is best to take a test in the same room in which you learned the material?
    a) state dependent learning
    b) encoding specificity
    c) tip of the tongue phenomenon
    d) cocktail party effect

    Rationale:

    _____

    _____

17. While you were studying for your history final, you were very angry at your roommate for playing her music too loud. If you wanted to maximize your ability to remember the information on the final, what mood should you be in while you are taking the final?
    a) happy
    b) sad
    c) angry
    d) surprised

    Rationale:

    _____

    _____

Objective 6.9

18. The test you are taking right now requires which type of memory retrieval process?

    a) recall
    b) recognition
    c) encoding
    d) echoic
    Rationale:

    _____

    _____

19. False positives occur when a person incorrectly "matches" a stimulus that is merely similar to a real memory. One major problem with eye witness testimony is that

    _____.
    a) extinction of auditory memories causes the witness to forget what was said.
    b) witnesses are prone to habituate to the courtroom and forget what happened.
    c) false positives can cause eyewitness testimony to be quite inaccurate.
    d) none of these are true
    Rationale:

    _____

    _____

20.   For more than 30 years, the most influential researcher into eyewitness memory has been
_____.

       a)   Broadbent
       b)   Sperling
       c)   Loftus
       d)   Treisman

Rationale:

_____

_____

Objective 6.11

21.   Flashbulb memories _____.

       a)   are not subject to periodic revision
       b)   usually concern events that are emotionally charged
       c)   are almost always highly accurate
       d)   usually concern events from early childhood

Rationale:

_____

_____

Objective 6.12

22.   In this view, memories are literally "built" from the pieces stored away at encoding. This
view is called _____.

       a)   constructive processing
       b)   hindsight bias
       c)   adaptation of memory traces
       d)   flashbulb integration

Rationale:

_____

_____

23. Which of the following phenomena provides support for the concept that memories are reconstructed as they are retrieved or remembered?
   a) tip of the tongue
   b) hindsight bias
   c) cocktail party effect
   d) retrograde amnesia

Rationale:

_____

_____

Objective 6.13

24. Which of the following is an example of the misinformation effect?
   a) Forgetting where you left your keys.
   b) Falsely remembering that a friend was wearing a jacket after being asked what color your friend's jacket was.
   c) Remembering a traumatic event from childhood.
   d) Telling someone a lie.

Rationale:

_____

_____

Objective 6.14

25. Which of the following statements about hypnosis is **NOT** true?
   a) Subjects cannot always distinguish between memories they have always had and new "memories" recently recovered under hypnosis.
   b) Hypnotic age regression appears to increase the accuracy of childhood recall.
   c) The impact of hypnosis on the reliability of later memory depends on the type of question asked. Open-ended questions cause less memory "contamination" than closed-ended, leading questions.
   d) Some pseudomemories (false memories) suggested by hypnosis do not persist after the hypnosis.

Rationale:

_____

_____

26. Which of the following techniques are used by therapists to implant a false memory?
    a) hypnosis, drugs, and suggestion
    b) partial reinforcement, rewards and punishments
    c) presentations of images of the person's problems, presented in a subliminal fashion
    d) all of these are used

Rationale:

_____

_____

27. Which of these is viewed as the major problem in the repressed-memory controversy?
    a) guaranteeing the right to sue alleged abusers
    b) therapists' unwillingness to help recover memories
    c) deliberate deception on the part of those who claim abuse
    d) distinguishing true repressed memories from false memories

Rationale:

_____

_____

Objective 6.15

28. Ebbinghaus found that information is forgotten _____
    a) more rapidly as time goes by.
    b) gradually at first, then increasing in speed of forgetting.
    c) quickly at first, then tapering off gradually.
    d) most quickly one day after learning.

Rationale:

_____

_____

29. Shalissa has two exams today. One is in French and the other is in history. Last night she studied French before history. When she gets to her history test, all she can remember is French! Shalissa's memory is suffering from _____.
    a) cue-dependent forgetting
    b) proactive interference
    c) decay
    d) retroactive interference

Rationale:

_____

_____

Objective 6.16

30. In the famous case of H. M., after having part of his brain removed, he could no longer _____.
    a) pay attention to specific stimuli
    b) retrieve memories
    c) form new memories
    d) make sense of memories

Rationale:

_____

_____

31. The physical processes that occur when a memory is formed are called

    a) consolidation
    b) actuation
    c) potentiation
    d) depolarization

Rationale:

_____

_____

32.   Which of these is an example of what has been called infantile amnesia?

      a)   At age 25, Betty can recall only good memories of what happened when she was 4 to 5 years old.

      b)   When he is ten years old, John has no memory of a family vacation that occurred when he was 2 years old.

      c)   When faced with a horrible stressor, some people return to an earlier stage of development such as infancy for the comfort that it provides.

      d)   Despite the fact that Alice began to learn how to play the violin when she was three, she has very little skill now that she is in her 30s.

Rationale:

_____

_____

Objective 6.18

33.   There currently is a cure for Alzheimer's Disease.

      a)   True

      b)   False

Rationale:

_____

_____

SAMPLE EXAM ANSWERS & RATIONALES

1.   d   Memory involves the three processes of encoding, storage and retrieval. All three other choices deal with the process of learning.

2.   a   The memory process involves the three steps of encoding, storage, and retrieval. The first of these steps is encoding.

3.   d   The levels-of-processing model proposes that the "deeper" the level of processing, the more likely it is to be remembered. This means that the more meaning or significance you can give to a piece of information, the better you remember it. Associating a frog with the place it lives is the most meaningful association of all the four choices.

4.   b   Sensory memory is the briefest of all the memory stages proposed by the information processing model. Visual sensory memory lasts only about one-half a second.

5.   b   Echoic memory is the memory of sounds. It should be easy to remember if you just think of an "echo" for echoic.

6.   b   Short-term memory is thought to be the place where memories either enter long-term memory or disappear. The idea is that if we work with the information, using memory techniques or rehearsal strategies, then the information will be retained in long-term memory.

7.   b   The amount of information we can retain in short-term memory was studied by George Miller and presented in a paper called "The magic number 7 plus or minus two."

8.   d   Maintenance rehearsal is one of the most basic methods to remember something and involves simply repeating the information over and over. Elaborative rehearsal is more complex and involves forming an association with the information.

9.   b   Long-term memory is where information is stored for an indefinite amount of time. If you look at the choices for this question, the only item that accommodates the storage of anything for a long period of time is a filing cabinet.

10.   a   Procedural memories (such as how to ride a bike) are hard to verbalize, just as implicit memories are hard to verbalize. If something is explicit, that means it is very clear and obvious, just as declarative memories (like the memory of your first kiss) are very easy to identify.

11.   d   Semantic memories are memories of facts, such as the capitol of the United States. Episodic memories are memories of episodes, such as your last birthday celebration.

12.   d   Procedural memories are memories for procedures (or habits and skills).

13.   c   This is a memory of a specific episode.

14.   a   In selection A, you have to move across two categories – salmon to fish to animal, whereas in selections B and C, you only move across one category – salmon to fish and canary to bird.

15.   a   Try to consider the most important aspects of long-term memory, memories and retrieval cues. Long-term memory can hold a large amount of information like the sea, a boat or an island. The memories are what are found in long-term memory. We find fish in the sea but we don't typically store a large number of worms or hooks in a boat or worms in an island. Retrieval cues are used to pull out the memories, hooks can pull out worms none of the other options make sense (fish don't pull out worms, worms don't pull out hooks, and fishing poles don't pull out worms). So the correct choice is A.

16.   b   Encoding specificity refers to your physical surroundings and how they can act as retrieval cues for information.

17.   c   State dependent learning refers to your emotional state and how being in the same

mood during retrieval as you were during the encoding process can help you remember more information.

18. b   You are given the right answer and you simply have to select it from choices A-D.

19. c   The work of Elizabeth Loftus has demonstrated that false positives among eyewitnesses are more frequent than we used to believe.

20. c   Elizabeth Loftus is one of the most influential researchers into false memories.

21. b   Flashbulb memories can be altered over time.

22. a   Constructive processing assumes that all the pieces of a memory are stored in different locations and "reassembled" every time the memory is retrieved.

23. b   In hindsight bias, our memory of a past event is influenced by new information.

24. b   The misinformation effect occurs when a leading question or statement actually alters your memory of an event.

25. b   Studies on memories retrieved under hypnosis have failed to find an increase in accuracy for recalling childhood events.

26. a   Therapists have mainly used hypnosis, drugs, or suggestion to implant false memories.

27. d   Often an individual cannot distinguish between their own true memories and false memories.

28. c   Most forgetting occurs within the first hour after the material is learned.

29. b   Proactive interference occurs with the already learned material interferes with the new information.

30. c   After H.M's hippocampus was removed, he lost the ability to move memories from short term to long term memory.

31. a   The term consolidation refers to the physical basis of memories. Researchers are still working to determine the precise details of consolidation.

32. b   Infantile amnesia refers to the inability to remember events that occurred during the first one to two years of life.

33. b   Although researchers have made a tremendous amount of progressive toward our understanding of Alzheimer's disease, there still is no cure for the disease.

APPLY IT

This section will help you use the concepts you are learning in this class to improve your study skills.

In this chapter you learned about two factors that affect your ability to retrieve information – encoding specificity and state dependent learning. Encoding specificity states that your physical environment can serve as retrieval cues when it resembles the environment in which the material was learned, while state dependent learning states that your emotional "environment" can also serve as a retrieval cue.

For this study challenge, you will select a physical or emotional cue that you will use to help you retrieve the information during the exam. It will work best if you choose a cue that is distinct. Here are some examples that students have chosen in the past (you will probably find that it will be much easier to manipulate some aspect of your physical environment rather than your emotional state):

- *Watermelon bubble gum*
- *Ginger green tea*
- *A pink neon bracelet*
- *An ugly bright orange shirt*
- *A pencil with a fuzzy ball on the end*
- *A pair of big clunky work boots*

Stop for a minute and think about what you would need to do in order to create your own personal instance of encoding specificity.

Okay, hopefully you figured out that it is not that complicated. You simply need to pick an environmental cue, study with that cue present and then take the test with that cue present as well. Be sure to pick a cue that you will be able to take in to the exam room with you. And that's it. You can lay out your game plan in the space below.

List your environmental cue here: _____

Try to study with the cue as many times as possible. For example, every time you are in class or are studying for the exam, be sure you are chewing watermelon bubble gum, or drinking ginger green tea (only if drinks are allowed in your classroom). Also, be sure that you do not have the cue present when you are studying for other tests or are attending other classes. You want to avoid the possibility of interference.

List the number of times you studied with the cue here: _____

Now, take the cue with you to the test. You will probably be surprised at how much it helps you to retrieve the learned information. Write a brief summary of your findings in the space below.

CHAPTER 7 LEARNING OBJECTIVES

7.1   What are some of the special research methods used to study development?

7.2   What is the relationship between heredity and environmental factors in determining development?

7.3   How do chromosomes, genes, and DNA determine a person's characteristics or disorders?

7.4   How do twins develop during pregnancy?

7.5   How do conjoined twins adjust to being connected to each other?

7.6   What happens during the germinal, embryonic, and fetal periods of pregnancy and what are some hazards in prenatal development?

7.7   What kind of physical changes take place in infancy and childhood?

7.8   What are the facts and the myths concerning infant immunizations?

7.9   What are three ways of looking at cognitive development?

7.10   How does language develop?

7.11   How do infants and children develop personalities and form relationships with others?

7.12   What happens in Erikson's first four stages of psychosocial development?

7.13   How do children learn about gender?

7.14   What are the changes that occur in puberty?

7.15   How do adolescents develop formal operations and moral thinking?

7.16   What happens during the adolescent's search for identity?

7.17   What are the physical and cognitive changes that occur during adulthood and aging?

7.18   How do adults deal with the issues of work, relationships, parenting, and death?

7.19   What are the theories of why aging occurs?

7.20   What are the stages of death and dying?

7.21   How does attention deficit-hyperactivity disorder affect adults?

SUMMARY

Human development is the scientific study of the changes that occur in people as they age from conception to death. Since age cannot be directly manipulated by a researcher, developmental psychologists have had to develop alternative methods to investigate the effects of aging on psychological processes. Three common methods used are **longitudinal**, **cross-sectional** and **cross-sequential** studies. Longitudinal studies have the advantage of following the same subject across time but are limited due to the amount of time and money required to complete the study and the problem of attrition. Cross-sectional studies are cheaper, faster, and easier to conduct since they gather information from different age groups at one particular period of time; however, results from these studies may be confounded due to individual and history differences. Cross-sequential studies are a combination of longitudinal and cross-sectional techniques and often represent an ideal compromise. One of the biggest debates among developmental psychologists is the question of **nature** versus **nurture**. Nature refers to the influence of everything you inherited genetically from your biological parents, and nurture refers to the influence your environment has had on your development. More recently, the question of interest has switched from nature *versus* nurture to the interaction of nature and nurture. Behavioral genetics is the field of science that studies the interactions of nature, or genes, and nurture, or the environment.

Genetics is the science of heredity and involves the study of DNA, genes and chromosomes. **DNA** is the smallest unit of the three and are strands of molecules linked together like a twisted ladder. The links are made up of amines, and their names are abbreviated with the letters A, T, G, and C. The next largest unit is the **genes,** which are sections of the ladder containing instructions on how to make a specific protein. One way to think of genes is individual recipes for proteins. The biggest units are the **chromosomes,** which are long strands of DNA twisted together and wound up in coils. The chromosomes are found in the nucleus of all the cells of your body except red blood cells. Humans have a total of 46 chromosomes, 23 from the mother's egg and 23 from the father's sperm. Each chromosome from the mother matches a chromosome from the father to form 23 pairs. Both chromosomes in the pair have the same genes (for example, each chromosome contains a gene for hair color). Even though they contain the same gene, the instructions on that gene might be slightly different; for example, one of the genes has the instructions for blonde hair, while the other gene contains the instructions for brown hair. The first 22 pairs of chromosomes are called autosomes, and the last pair (the twenty third) pair contains the instructions for determining sex and are called the sex chromosomes. **Dominant genes** are the genes that are more likely to influence the trait. **Recessive genes** are not as strong and will only get their instructions carried out if the other chromosome in the pair also contains a recessive gene. In reality, almost all traits are determined by multiple gene pairs. This is called **polygenic inheritance**. Some diseases result from problems with recessive genes and are only expressed when both parents have the recessive gene. Some of these diseases include cystic fibrosis, sickle cell anemia, Tay-Sachs disorder and PKU. Some disorders result from the fact that there are the wrong number of chromosomes in the fertilizing egg or sperm. Down's syndrome results from having 3 chromosomes in the twenty first pair. Klinefelter's syndrome results from an extra chromosome in the twenty third pair. Turner's syndrome results from females that are missing an X chromosome in the twenty third pair.

Many people believe that **conception** represents the beginning of life. **Fertilization** occurs when the sperm penetrates the egg (or **ovum**). The result is a single cell with 46 chromosomes (23 from the sperm and 23 from the egg). This cell is called a **zygote**. **Monozygotic (or identical) twins** result from the zygote splitting into two separate masses early in the division process. **Dizygotic (or fraternal) twins** result from two eggs being fertilized by two separate sperm. Siamese twins are more properly referred to as **conjoined twins** and result from an incomplete separation of the zygotic mass. Britty and Abby Hensel are an example of conjoined twins. The **germinal period** of pregnancy is the first two weeks after fertilization during which the zygote migrates down to the uterus and attaches to the uterine wall. The placenta and umbilical cord both begin to develop during this period. The **embryonic period** lasts from about Week 2 to Week 8, after which the **embryo** is about one inch long with primitive eyes, nose, lips, teeth, arms and legs. **Critical periods** are times in development during which an environmental influence can impact the development of the fetus. Different organs and structures have different critical periods. The environmental influences that can impact the development of the fetus are called **teratogens**. The **fetal period** lasts from the eighth week after conception to the end of the pregnancy. Tremendous growth of the fetus occurs during this time. A baby born before the thirty eighth week of pregnancy is considered preterm and is at risk for survival, especially if he or she weighs less than five and a half pounds. Most miscarriages, also called spontaneous abortions, occur in the first three months of a pregnancy.

Infants have a large number of capabilities even immediately after birth. Most infants are able to perform five innate reflexes. Touch is the most well-developed sense, followed by smell and taste. Vision is the least functional of the senses. The rods are developed at birth, but cones must develop over a six month time period. At birth, an infant's vision is most clear seven to ten inches from their face. Also, infants appear to show a preference for the human voice and human faces. Due to a recent trend of many parents choosing not to give immunization shots to their children, there is a growing concern over the possibility of widespread epidemics. Most immunizations are made from the dead virus and cannot cause an infection in the recipient. A few immunizations are made from weakened versions of the virus but still pose only a very small risk of infection. Immunizations have been found to be 85-99% effective in preventing the disease, with the most common reactions being redness and swelling where the shot was given, along with fever and a rash. No link has been found between autism and immunization.

The brain triples in weight during the first two years of life, with the increase being caused by the expansion of existing cells, not the growth of new ones. **Jean Piaget** believed that the primary factor in the development of a child's cognitive abilities was the child's interactions with objects in the environment. He proposed four stages of **cognitive development** from infancy to adolescence. The **sensorimotor stage**, lasting from infancy to age two, involves the use of the senses and muscles to learn about the environment and includes the development of **object permanence** and symbolic thought. The **preoperational stage** lasts from age two to seven and involves language and concept development through the process of asking questions. Children in this stage display the ability of symbolic thought through make-believe play and also display characteristics of **egocentrism**, **centration** and **irreversibility**. The **concrete operational** stage lasts from age seven to twelve and includes the development of concepts such as **conservation** and reversible thinking. However, children in this stage are still unable to deal with abstract concepts such as freedom or love. The **formal operational stage** is the final stage of cognitive development, according to Piaget, and lasts from the age of twelve on. During this stage abstract, hypothetical thinking develops. Research suggests that about one-half of the adults in the U.S. reach this stage of cognitive development. Piaget's concepts have been successfully applied in schools but have also been criticized for their emphasis on distinct stages of development, over-emphasis on egocentrism and failure to mention the role of the family or social environment in the child's development.

Lev Vygotsky was a Russian psychologist who felt the primary factor in development was the social environment. He proposed a concept called **scaffolding** in which a more highly skilled person gives the learner help and then stops as the learner develops on his own. Vygotsky believed that each child has a **zone of proximal development** or ZPD, which is the difference between what a child can do alone and what he or she can do with the help of a teacher. Vygotscky's principles have been applied in the classroom through the use of cooperative learning and reciprocal teaching.

Psychologists interested in information processing theory have investigated the memory capabilities of the developing infant and have found that infants demonstrate memory from birth, four to five year olds appear to be able to store about three items in their short term memory and have both episodic and procedural memories in long term memory. Language development appears to be an important step in cognitive development and facilitates the development of symbolic thinking. The stages of language development experienced by all speakers includes cooing around two months of age, babbling at six months of age, one-word speech or **holophrases** around one year of age, **telegraphic speech** at around one and a half years, and then whole sentences.

Temperament refers to the behavioral and emotional characteristics observed in infancy. Several researchers have suggested the existence of three types of temperaments: easy, difficult, and slow to warm up. **Attachment** is the emotional bond between an infant and caregiver. Mary Ainsworth and others studied attachment using the Strange Situation and observed four attachment styles: secure, avoidant, ambivalent and disorganized/disoriented. Harry Harlow studied the nature of attachment behaviors by observing Rhesus monkeys interact with two different "surrogate" mothers. He found that **contact comfort** was an important factor in attachment.

Erik Erikson, who originally trained as a Freudian psychoanalyst, proposed an eight-stage theory of development that occurrs over the entire lifespan. Each stage involves an emotional crisis in the individual's social interactions. The first four stages occur during infancy and childhood and consist of the crises of **trust versus mistrust**, **autonomy versus shame and doubt**, **initiation versus guilt**, and **industry versus inferiority**.

Adolescence is the period of time from around age 14 to the early 20s and is most clearly identified by the physical changes that occur in **puberty**. Mentally, many adolescents are moving into Piaget's formal operational stage of development, which includes the ability to think in the abstract and to consider hypothetical situations. At the same time, adolescents still demonstrate a considerable amount of egocentric thinking as can be seen in the thought processes of the **personal fable**, in which the adolescent feels they are different from all others and the **imaginary audience**, where the adolescent is convinced that everyone is looking at them.

Lawrence Kohlberg proposed a theory about the development of moral thinking and divided the development into three levels: **pre-conventional**,during which the individual conforms to social norms, **conventional,** during which time the consequences determine morality and **post-conventional,** during which a person's individual moral principles determine right and wrong. The social crisis proposed by Erikson for the period of adolescence is that of **identity versus role confusion**.

Adulthood can be roughly identified as the time period from the early 20s until death. Middle age is often associated with an increase in health problems and includes the events of **menopause** for women and **andropause** for men. Cognitive abilities do not decline overall, but the speed of processing does appear to slow down and people tend to have a harder time retrieving specific information from their memory. Erikson proposed three psycho-social developmental stages for adulthood. The stages are **intimacy versus isolation**, **generativity versus stagnation**, and **ego integrity versus despair**.

There are a number of theories as to why our bodies physically age. The cellular clock theory suggests that cells are limited in the number of times they can reproduce. The wear and tear theory proposes that aging is a result of outside stressors such as physical exertion and bodily damage. The free radical theory states that as people get older, more and more free radicals accumulate in their bodies.

Elizabeth Kubler-Ross proposed a well-known theory of the dying process. Based on her work with dying patients, Kubler-Ross felt that people experienced a series of five different emotions including denial, anger, bargaining, depression and acceptance. Others see dying as more of a process rather than a series of stages.

In the last few decades, researchers have begun to realize that **attention deficit hyperactivity disorder (ADHD)** often persists into adulthood. Many treatments are currently available for adult ADHD.

KEY POINTS

- Introduce the research methods and major issues in developmental psychology.
- Describe the stages of prenatal development.
- Discuss the theories of Piaget and Vygotsky with regards to cognitive development.
- Describe the process of language development.
- Explain the concept of personality, including the idea of temperament, attachment theory and Erikson's social crisis model.
- Identify the major stages of development in adolescence and adulthood.
- Discuss three theories of aging and Kubler-Ross's stages of dying.

KEY CONCEPTS

human development	The scientific study of the changes that occur in people as they age, from conception until death.
longitudinal design	Research design in which one participant or group of participants is studied over a long period of time.
cross-sectional design	Research design in which several different age groups of participants are studied at one particular point in time.
cross-sequential design	Research design in which participants are first studied by means of a cross-sectional design, but also followed and assessed for a period of no more than six years.
nature	The influence of our inherited characteristics on our personality, physical growth, intellectual growth, and social interactions.
nurture	The influence of the environment on personality, physical growth, intellectual growth, and social interactions.
Genetics	The science of inherited traits.
DNA (deoxyribonucleic acid)	Special molecule that contains the genetic material of the organism.
gene	Section of DNA having the same arrangement of chemical

	elements.
chromosome	Tightly wound strand of genetic material (or DNA).
dominant gene	Refers to a gene that actively controls the expression of a trait.
recessive gene	Refers to a gene that only influences the expression of a trait when paired with an identical gene.
polygenic inheritance	A trait or characteristic that is determined by more than one gene pair.
conception	The moment at which a female becomes pregnant.
fertilization	The union of the ovum and sperm.
ovum	The female sex cell, or egg.
zygote	Cell resulting from the uniting of the ovum and sperm.
germinal period	First 2 weeks after fertilization, during which the zygote moves down to the uterus and begins to implant in the lining.
monozygotic twins	Identical twins formed when one zygote splits into two separate masses of cells, each of which develops into a separate embryo.
dizygotic twins	Often called fraternal twins, occurring when two eggs each get fertilized by two different sperm, resulting in two zygotes in the uterus at the same time.
conjoined twins	Often called Siamese twins, occurring from an incomplete separation of the zygotic cells.
embryo	Name for the developing organism from 2 weeks to 8 weeks after fertilization.
embryonic period	The period from 2 to 8 weeks after fertilization, during which the major organs and structures of the organism develop.
critical periods	Times during which some environmental influence can have an impact on the development of the infant.
teratogen	Any factor that can cause a birth defect.
fetal period	The time from about 8 weeks until the birth of the child.
fetus	Name for the developing organism from 8 weeks after fertilization to the birth of the baby.
Jean Piaget	1896–1980. Swiss developmental psychologist who proposed a

147

four-stage theory of cognitive development based on the concept of mental operations.

cognitive development	The development of thinking, problem-solving, and memory.
sensorimotor stage	Piaget's first stage of cognitive development in which the infant uses its senses and motor abilities to interact with objects in the environment.
object permanence	The knowledge that an object exists even when it is not in sight.
preoperational stage	Piaget's second stage of cognitive development in which the preschool child learns to use language as a means of exploring the world.
egocentrism	The inability to see the world through anyone else's eyes.
centration	In Piaget's theory, the tendency of a young child to focus only one feature of an object while ignoring other, relevant features.
irreversibility	In Piaget's theory, the inability of the young child to mentally reverse an action.
concrete operational stage	Third stage of cognitive development in which the school-age child becomes capable of logical thought processes, but is not yet capable of abstract thinking.
conservation	In Piaget's theory, the ability to understand that simply changing the appearance of an object does not change the object's nature.
formal operational stage	Piaget's last stage of cognitive development in which the adolescent becomes capable of abstract thinking.
Lev Vygotsky	1896–1934. Russian developmental psychologist who emphasized the role of the social environment on cognitive development and proposed the idea of zones of proximal development.
scaffolding	Process in which a more skilled learner gives help to a less skilled learner, reducing the amount of help as the less skilled learner becomes more capable.
zone of proximal development (ZPD)	Vygotsky's concept of the difference between what a child can do alone and what that child can do with the help of a more skilled teacher.
holophrases	Single word utterances seen universally in the stages of language development.
telegraphic speech	Type of speech in which words are left out of a sentence, but the meaning of the sentence remains, such as "want cookie" to mean "I would like a cookie."

temperament	The behavioral characteristics that are fairly well established at birth, such as easy, difficult, and slow to warm up.
attachment	The emotional bond between an infant and the primary caregiver.
contact comfort	Variable of tactile sensation that was proposed by Harry Harlow to be an important component in the formation of attachment.
Erik Erikson	1902–1994. Developmental psychologist trained in the methods of psychoanalysis who proposed a theory of personality development based on a series of emotional crises.
trust versus mistrust	First stage of personality development in which the infant's basic sense of trust or mistrust develops as a result of consistent or inconsistent care.
autonomy versus shame and doubt	Second stage of personality development in which the toddler strives for physical independence.
initiative versus guilt	Third stage of personality development in which the preschool-aged child strives for emotional and psychological independence, and attempts to satisfy curiosity about the world.
industry versus inferiority	Fourth stage of personality development in which the grade school-aged child strives for a sense of competence and self-esteem.
adolescence	The period of life from about age 13 to the early twenties during which a young person is no longer physically a child but is not yet an independent, self-supporting adult.
puberty	The physical changes that occur in the body as sexual development reaches its peak.
personal fable	Type of thought common to adolescents in which young people believe themselves to be unique and protected from harm.
imaginary audience	Type of thought common to adolescents in which young people believe that other people are just as concerned about the adolescent's thoughts and characteristics as they themselves are.
Lawrence Kohlberg	1927–1987. Developmental psychologist known for his theory on the development of moral reasoning.
pre-conventional morality	First level of Kohlberg's stages of moral development in which the child's behavior is governed by the consequences of the behavior.
conventional morality	Second level of Kohlberg's stages of moral development in which

	the child's behavior is governed by conforming to the society's norms of behavior.
post-conventional morality	Third level of Kohlberg's stages of moral development in which the person's behavior is governed by moral principles that have been decided upon by the individual and which may be in disagreement with accepted social norms.
identity versus role confusion	Fifth stage of personality development in which the adolescent must find a consistent sense of self.
menopause	The cessation of ovulation and menstrual cycles and the end of a woman's reproductive capability.
andropause	Gradual changes in the sexual hormones and reproductive system of males.
intimacy versus isolation	Sixth stage of Erikson's model of personality development in which an emotional and psychological closeness that is based on the ability to trust, share and care, while still maintaining one's sense of self is developed.
generativity versus stagnation	Seventh stage of Erikson's model of personality development in which the crisis involves providing guidance to one's children or the next generation, contributing to the well-being of the next generation through career or volunteer work or developing a sense of stagnation.
ego integrity versus despair	Eighth and final stage of Erikson's model of development in which the goal is to develop a sense of wholeness that comes from having lived a full life and the ability to let go of regrets; the final completion of the ego.
Elizabeth Kubler-Ross	1926-2004. Swiss psychiatrist known for her work with dying patients and her proposed theory of five stages of dying.
attention deficit hyperactivity disorder (ADHD)	Disorder characterized by lack of impulse control, inability to concentrate and hyperactivity.

HINTS

1. Students often get mixed up on the relationship of DNA to genes to chromosomes. It might be helpful to look at the terms visually. Remember, chromosomes are the largest unit. Chromosomes can be made up of genes and genes can be broken down into DNA. Try labeling the following diagram correctly.

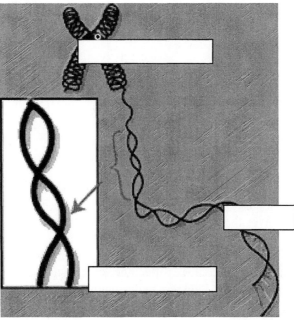

2. Perhaps the most influential theory on cognitive development is Jean Piaget's theory. He proposed four stages of cognitive development. To enhance your learning of these stages, fill in the chart below. Try to fill it in as much as possible without going back to your notes and/or the textbook. The first stage has been filled in as an example.

Stage	Age	Characteristics	How would you test to see if someone is in this stage?
Sensorimotor	*0-2 years*	• Children explore using their sensory and motor systems. • Develop object permanence.	*Hide a toy under a blanket and see if the child looks under the blanket for the toy.*

3. Another major theory of development is proposed by Erik Erikson. Erikson's theory focuses on the development of personality, with each stage marked by a crisis that needs to be resolved. The crisis typically involves the social interactions of the individual and is represented by the two extremes of the possible outcomes (for example, industry versus inferiority). One way to keep track of these stages is to realize that the labels follow a pattern of "desirable outcome versus undesirable outcome." Also, they reflect the social activities that are typically going on at that age. Fill in the chart below to help you understand Erikson's theory of development.

Age	Social Activities	Desirable Outcome	Undesirable Outcome
0-1 years	*being fed, taken care of by someone else*	*sense of trust*	*sense of mistrust*

Some suggested answers for Study Hint 2:

Stage	Age	Characteristics	How would you test to see if someone is in this stage?
Sensorimotor	*0-2 years*	• *Children explore using their sensory and motor systems.* • *Develop object permanence.*	*Hide a toy under a blanket and see if the child looks under the blanket for the toy.*
Preoperational	*2-7 years*	• *A lot of egocentric thinking.* • *Children can represent objects mentally.* • *Engage in make-believe play.* • *Do not understand concepts of conservation.* • *Tend to focus on one aspect of an object.*	*Ask the child if they would rather have two quarters or five pennies (they will probably want the five pennies).* *See if the child can play a make-believe game.*
Concrete Operational	*7-12 years*	• *Show an understanding for the principles of conservation.* • *Demonstrate logical thinking and can solve analogies.* • *Focus mostly on concrete objects and ideas.*	*Divide a string of clay into five pieces and see if the child thinks there is as much clay in the five pieces as there was in the one string.*
Formal Operational	*12 years and on*	• *Can use abstract reasoning to solve problems.* • *Able to consider hypothetical situations.*	*Ask the child an abstract question and see how they respond. An example of a question could be "What if snow were black?"*

Some suggested answers for Study Hint 3:

Age	Social Activities	Desirable Outcome	Undesirable Outcome
0-1 years	*being fed, taken care of by someone else*	*sense of <u>trust</u>*	*sense of <u>mistrust</u>*
1-3 years	*Learning to walk, talk, dress yourself, etc.*	*sense of <u>autonomy</u> (feeling that you are in control of your own body)*	*sense of <u>shame</u> and doubt*
3-5 years	*Going to preschool, being responsible to obey family rules, learning your role as a member of a family*	*sense of <u>initiative</u>*	*sense of <u>guilt</u> or irresponsibility*
5-12 years	*Going to school, completing school assignments, participating in social activities with peers*	*sense of <u>industry</u> (feeling capable of completing your work)*	*sense of <u>inferiority</u> or incompetence*
12-18 years	*Deciding "what you want to be when you grow up," choosing a career path, selecting your own group of friends*	*sense of <u>identity</u>*	*feeling of <u>role confusion</u>, unsure of who you are*
18-40 years	*Finding a partner to form a life-long commitment, succeeding in a career*	*sense of <u>intimacy</u>, feeling comfortable forming close relationships*	*sense of <u>isolation</u>, inability to form close ties with others*
40-60 years	*Focus on career and family. Perhaps grandchildren begin to enter the picture. Begin thinking of the legacy that you will leave for your children and/or the future generation.*	*sense of <u>generativity</u>, or succeeding in creating something that will benefit others in the future*	*sense of <u>stagnation</u>, or feeling that you have done nothing for the next generation*
60 years and on	*Dealing with retirement from your career. Ffamily might be more involved in their own lives. Facing the fact of death among those in your social group.*	*sense of <u>ego integrity</u>, or a sense of acceptance of your life and acceptance of death.*	*sense of <u>despair</u> about your life and a fear of your inevitable death.*

SAMPLE EXAM

For the following multiple choice questions, select the answer you feel best answers the question and explain the rationale or reason for your selection in the space provided.

Objective 7.1

1.   A researcher who selects a sample of people of varying ages and studies them at one point in time is, by definition, using the _____ method.
    a)   cohort design
    b)   longitudinal design
    c)   behavior genetics design
    d)   cross-sectional design

Rationale:
D is correct because cross-sectional design studies several different age groups at the same time.

2.   Which of the following is an example of a longitudinal study?
    a)   observing three groups of children (ages 2, 6, and 12) for a two-hour period.
    b)   observing three groups of children (ages 2, 6, and 12) for a two-week period.
         observing a group of 30 children at age 2 and again at age 6 and once more when the
    c)   children turn 12 years old.
    d)   surveying a group of middle-aged adults, half male and half female.

Rationale:
B is correct because a longitudinal study involves the study of a group of individuals at two or more points in their lives. It may be helpful to remember that a <u>longitudinal</u> study takes a <u>long</u> time to complete.

Objective 7.2

3.   What relatively new field investigates the influence of genes and heredity on behavior?
    a)   psychobiology
    b)   neuropsychology
    c)   behavioral genetics
    d)   psychoanalysis

Rationale:

_____

_____

4.   When a researcher discusses the contributions of "nature" on development, she is referring to the effects of your
    a)   environment.
    b)   heredity.
    c)   social interactions.
    d)   teratogens.

Rationale:

_____

_____

5.   Which of the following is a special molecule that contains the genetic material of the organism?
        a) DNA
        b) gene
        c) chromosomes
        d) amines

        Rationale:

        _____

        _____

6.   Which of the following is essentially a "recipe" or set of instructions for making a protein?
        a) DNA
        b) a chromosome
        c) a gene
        d) an enzyme

        Rationale:

        _____

        _____

7.   Why are males more likely than females to exhibit sex-linked traits?
        a) Males' X chromosome may not have a necessary dominant gene.
        b) Females are actually the stronger sex.
        c) Females have a protective enzyme in their sex hormones.
        d) Males' Y chromosome may not have a necessary dominant gene.

        Rationale:

        _____

        _____

Objective 7.4

8.   Dizygotic twins are formed from one egg and two sperms.
        a) True
        b) False

        Rationale:

        _____

        _____

9.   Monozygotic twins _____.
        a) are genetically identical.
        b) are genetically different.
        c) will be of a different sex.
        d) is more likely to occur when a woman is taking fertility drugs.

Rationale:

_____

_____

Objective 7.5

10.   Britty and Abby Hensel are a type of twin referred to as_____.
        a) non-identical
        b) dizygotic
        c) fraternal
        d) conjoined

Rationale:

_____

_____

Objective 7.6

11.   What are some of the common consequences to a child if the mother smoked while pregnant?
        a) increased birth weight and lethargy
        b) lower birth weight and short stature
        c) severe hearing loss and heart defects
        d) severely deformed limbs and muscle spasms

Rationale:

_____

_____

12.   The longest prenatal period during which tremendous growth occurs and the organs continue to develop and become functional is called_____.
        a) germinal
        b) embryonic
        c) fetal
        d) gestational

Rationale:

_____

_____

Objective 7.7

13. In the _____ reflex, the baby moves its head toward any light touch to its face.
     a) sucking
     b) startle
     c) rooting
     d) grasping

     Rationale:

     _____

     _____

14. Which sense is the most well developed at birth?
     a) taste
     b) touch
     c) sight
     d) hearing

     Rationale:

     _____

     _____

Objective 7.8

15. Which of the following statements about immunizations is true?
     a) Children who are given an immunization are fairly likely to get the disease itself.
     b) Immunizations almost always cause bad reactions.
     c) Immunizations are needed even if the disease has been eliminated.
     d) Some immunizations cause autism in children.

     Rationale:

     _____

     _____

Objective 7.9

16. Your little sister picks up objects, feels every part of them, and then puts them in her mouth. What stage of Jean Piaget's model of cognitive development does this behavior suggest?
     a) concrete operations
     b) sensorimotor
     c) preoperational
     d) formal operations

     Rationale:

     _____

     _____

17.   A theory that looks at the way people deal with the information that comes in through the senses is called_____.
        a)   information processing theory
        b)   sensorimotor intelligence
        c)   habituation
        d)   metamemory

Rationale:

_____

_____

18.   Which of the following would a child in Piaget's preoperational stage of cognitive development NOT be able to do?
        a)   mentally represent an object
        b)   play make-believe
        c)   see the world from someone else's perspective
        d)   use symbolic thought

Rationale:

_____

_____

19.   Vygotsky's idea that children develop cognitively when someone else helps them by asking leading questions and providing examples is called
        a)   scaffolding
        b)   centration
        c)   conservation
        d)   metamemory

Rationale:

_____

_____

Objective 7.10

20.   The first noticeable signs of language development in infants is
        a)   babbling
        b)   cooing
        c)   telegraphic speech
        d)   holophrases

Rationale:

_____

_____

21. By about 12 months, most infants _____.
    a) begin to use intonation in their language
    b) build a vocabulary of one-word phrases, or holophrases
    c) begin to distinguish, in their language, between themselves and others
    d) begin to form two and three word sentences

    Rationale:

    _____

    _____

22. Infants in different cultures and of different languages, experience a different series of stages in language development.
    a) True
    b) False

    Rationale:

    _____

    _____

Objective 7.11

23. If an infant in Mary Ainsworth's Strange Situation was unwilling to explore, became very upset by the stranger, and demanded to be picked up by his mother but then kicked to get away, he would most likely be classified as
    a) secure
    b) avoidant
    c) ambivalent
    d) disorganized-disoriented

    Rationale:

    _____

    _____

24. Chester is irritable, loud, and negative most of the time. He really doesn't like when new people pick him up and hold him and has irregular sleeping, eating, and waking schedules. What temperament does he exhibit?
    a) active
    b) slow-to-warm-up
    c) difficult
    d) easy

    Rationale:

    _____

    _____

25.   Erikson's theory of social development viewed the ages of 3 to 6, his third stage, as being
        characterized by the major challenge of _____.
        a) identity versus role diffusion
        b) industry versus inferiority
        c) initiative versus guilt
        d) autonomy versus shame and doubt

        Rationale:

        _____

        _____

26.   According to Erikson, when children between the ages of 5 and 12 succeed at learning new skills,
        they develop a sense of _____, and if they fail to develop new abilities, they feel

        _____.
        a) shame, doubt
        b) trust, guilty
        c) industry, inferior
        d) identity, despair

        Rationale:

        _____

        _____

Objective 7.13

27.   _____theorists believe that gender identity is learned through direct reinforcement and
        observational learning.
        a) Social learning
        b) Cognitive
        c) Psychoanalytic
        d) Humanistic

        Rationale:

        _____

        _____

28.   The growth spurt for boys typically begins at age_____.
        a) 9
        b) 12
        c) 10
        d) 15

        Rationale:

        _____

        _____

29.   Fifteen-year-old Todd is writing an impassioned novel about growing up in America. In his novel he describes his experiences in a way that portrays himself as unique and special, such that no one has ever thought such deep thoughts or experienced such ecstasy before. Todd's writings most clearly reflect _____.
   a)   his sense of autonomy
   b)   the personal fable
   c)   the period of rebellion common to all adolescents
   d)   his developing sense of conscience

Rationale:

_____

_____

30.   Which of the following questions would an adolescent who has NOT reached Piaget's stage of formal operations have trouble thinking about?
   a)   What date did Columbus arrive in America?
   b)   How many 2-inch pieces can a 10-inch rope be cut into?
   c)   What if you had been born to different parents?
   d)   What is the definition of democracy?

Rationale:

_____

_____

Objective 7.15

31.   Jeremy is 17 years old. According to Erikson, his chief task will be acquiring a sense of _____.
   a)   identity
   b)   intimacy
   c)   generativity
   d)   autonomy

Rationale:

_____

_____

Objective 7.16

32.   The cessation of menstruation and ovulation is called _____.
   a)   climacteric
   b)   perimenopause
   c)   menopause
   d)   andropause
Rationale:

_____

_____

33.   A young adult who is having difficulty trusting others is most likely still trying to resolve Erikson's stage of
        a)   autonomy vs. shame and doubt
        b)   ego integrity vs. despair
        c)   industry vs. inferiority
        d)   intimacy vs. isolation

Rationale:

_____

_____

34.   Which of the following is an example of generativity?
        a)   completing a cross-word puzzle
        b)   becoming a mentor
        c)   getting married
        d)   finding your own identity

Rationale:

_____

_____

35.   The _____theory of aging suggests that unstable oxygen molecules cause damage to the structure of cells, increasing with age.
        a)   wear and tear
        b)   cellular clock
        c)   disengagement
        d)   free radical

Rationale:

_____

_____

36.   Which theory correctly explains why the aging process occurs?
        a)   cellular clock theory
        b)   free radical theory
        c)   wear and tear theory
        d)   no theory to date has thoroughly explained the aging process

Rationale:

_____

_____

37.   Several weeks of diagnostic tests have revealed that cancer has spread throughout Barry's body. His physician suggests that he "take care of important matters." Barry realizes his family's home needs repairs, so he arranges to have that done right away. To relieve his family of the agony of planning his funeral, he makes all the arrangements. Barry tells his minister he has had a good life and just wants to make sure he provides for his family after his death. This description fits the stage Kubler-Ross called_____.

      a)   denial
      b)   acceptance
      c)   bargaining
      d)   depression

Rationale:

_____

_____

38.   Attention deficit hyperactivity disorder has not been observed to occur in adults.

      a)   True
      b)   False

Rationale:

_____

_____

1.   d   D is correct; cross-sectional design studies several different age groups at the same time.

2.   b   B is correct because a longitudinal study involves the study of a group of individuals at two or more points in their lives. It may be helpful to remember that a <u>long</u>itudinal study takes a <u>long</u> time to complete.

3.   c   Genetics is a field that investigates the effects of genes and environmental influences on behavior, whereas psychobiology is the study of the biological bases of behavior.

4.   b   Nature refers to everything you inherit biologically. Nurture refers to the effects of your surroundings, or environment.

5.   a   DNA, genes, and chromosomes all contain the genetic material of an organism, but DNA is the only molecule listed.

6.   c   A gene is a section of DNA that contains instructions for making proteins. Chromosomes are large strands of DNA that contain many genes.

7.   d   In the twenty third pair of chromosomes, females have an XX pair and males have an XY pair. The Y chromosome is smaller than the X chromosome, so some genes on the X chromosome don't have a "match" on the Y chromosome. Because there is no competition, a recessive gene on the X chromosome is more likely to be expressed in males than in females.

8.   b   "Di" means two and zygotic refers to the zygote, which is formed when the egg and sperm unite. Dizygotic (or fraternal) twins are formed from two eggs and two sperm.

9.   a   Monozygotic twins are formed from one egg and one sperm ("mono" means one). After the egg and sperm unite, they split to form two zygotes. Because all the DNA comes from the same egg and sperm, monozygotic twins are genetically identical.

10.   d   Conjoined twins (commonly referred to as Siamese twins) are physically joined due to the fact that the zygotes do not completely separate from each other.

11.   b   Multiple studies have found that babies of mothers who smoked are smaller in weight and height than babies from mothers who didn't smoke.

12.   c   The fetal period is the longest and last stage of prenatal development and is when the most growth occurs in the fetus.

13.   c   The rooting reflex is thought to help the baby with breast-feeding.

14.   b   Touch and taste are fairly well developed at birth, with touch being the most highly developed. The sense of sight takes the longest to fully develop after birth.

15.   c   Even if the disease has been eliminated in a specific area or country, there are possibilities of infection from other countries.

16.   b   The sensorimotor stage involves exploring the world through the use of the sensory and motor systems. During the sensorimotor stage, infants interact deliberately with objects by chewing, grasping, and tasting them. It is the first of Piaget's four stages of cognitive development.

17.   a   Information processing theory looks at the way in which people deal with the information that comes in through the senses. Metamemory is one's knowledge about the workings of memory and memory strategies.

18.   c   In the preoperational stage of development, children are still very egocentric and have a very hard time seeing the world from someone else's viewpoint.

19.   a   Scaffolding is the process of helping a child develop by providing the framework for learning.

20.   b   Cooing is the first visible sign of language development in infants, following by

babbling, holophrases and then telegraphic speech.

21.　b　By about one year of age, children are communicating one-word "phrases." Telegraphic speech, which consists of two or three word sentences, usually develops around one and a half to two years of age.

22.　b　It appears that all infants experience the same stages of language development.

23.　c　The ambivalent child exhibits ambivalent behaviors towards his or her mother. For example, they beg to be picked up by their mother and then struggle to get away from their mother once they are picked up.

24.　c　Difficult babies tend to be irritable, are not comfortable with change, and have irregular schedules.

25.　c　Initiative vs. guilt is Erikson's third stage of development. Autonomy vs. shame and doubt is the second stage and industry vs. inferiority is the fourth stage.

26.　c　Industry vs. inferiority is Erikson's fourth stage of development and corresponds closely with the primary school years.

27.　a　Social learning theorists focus on how personality is learned.

28.　b　Boys show a growth spurt around age 12, whereas girls typically show a growth spurt earlier around age 10.

29.　b　The personal fable describes a phenomenon commonly seen in adolescents in which they feel that no one else has experienced the emotions or thoughts that they are currently experiencing.

30.　c　The key to Piaget's fourth and final stage of cognitive development is the ability to consider hypothetical and abstract situations. The question in "C" is the only question requiring abstract thought.

31.　a　Erikson believed most of the adolescent years involved the crisis of identity vs. role confusion.

32.　c　Menopause is the correct answer. Perimenopause is the term used to describe the period of five to ten years during which a woman's reproductive system begins to decline.

33.　d　In Erikson's intimacy vs. isolation stage, young adults try to form intimate relations with others and learn to trust in someone other than themselves.

34.　b　Generativity involves helping a younger generation and engaging in activities that will leave a legacy.

35.　d　Radicals are oxygen molecules in the cells that are thought to cause damage.

36.　d　None of the theories to date have thoroughly explained the aging process.

37.　b　Kubler-Ross described the stage of acceptance as an emotional state of acknowledging one's impending death and being at peace with the idea.

38.　b　ADHD has been observed in adults with increasing frequency in recent years.

APPLY IT

One of the best ways to learn something is to have to teach it to someone else. In this chapter, you saw the importance Vygotsky placed on teachers in helping individuals move to the next stage of cognitive development. For this challenge, you will play the role of teacher in helping someone else understand the important concepts of this chapter.

Step 1: Pick someone who you will teach this material to. This can be another student in the class or an interested family member or friend.

Write the person's name here: _____

Step 2: Pick three of the most important concepts from this chapter that you will teach to your "student." Some possible choices are:

      Piaget's stages of cognitive development
      Erikson's stages of personality development
      Kohlberg's theory of the development of moral reasoning
      Stages of prenatal development
      The basic stages of language development
      Attachment theory, including the research by Ainsworth and Harlow
      The issue of nature versus nurture and the surrounding controversies

List the three topics you select here:

      Topic 1: _____

      Topic 2: _____

      Topic 3: _____

Step 3: Now your task is to teach these topics to your student. You might want to break it up into several sessions. Think about how you will present the information and what type of visual aids might be useful. Also, think about how you will know when the person has learned the material. Think about one question you would ask your student for each topic to test their understanding on the material. Write your question in the space below.

➤ Topic 1 question: _____

➤ Topic 2 question: _____

➤ Topic 3 question: _____

Step 4: Now go teach your student! When you are done, have them write their answers to your questions in the space above. Have fun!

CHAPTER 8 LEARNING OBJECTIVES

8.1	How do people use mental images to think?
8.2	What is the nature of a concept?
8.3	What methods do people use to solve problems and make decisions?
8.4	What are the barriers to solving problems?
8.5	What is creative thinking?
8.6	What is the definition of intelligence?
8.7	How do intelligence tests measure intelligence?
8.8	How are intelligence tests constructed?
8.9	What is artificial intelligence?
8.10	What is mental retardation and what causes it?
8.11	What is giftedness?

8.12   Does being intellectually gifted guarantee success in life?

8.13   What are the theories of intelligence and how do they differ?

8.14   What is the influence of heredity and environment on the development of intelligence?

8.15   What is the definition of language?

8.16   What are the different elements of a language and its structure?

8.17   Does language influence the way people think?

8.18   Are animals capable of learning language?

8.19   What are some ways to improve thinking?

SUMMARY

Thinking, or **cognitions,** can be defined as mental activity that goes on in the brain when a person is processing information. Cognition includes both verbal and non-verbal processes. Two examples of cognitions are **mental images**, which are picture-like representations that stand in for objects or events, and **concepts**, or ideas that represent a class of objects. Concepts can be ranked from general to specific by applying the terms **superordinate**, **basic level** type, and **subordinate**. **Formal concepts** are defined by specific rules, while **natural concepts** are formed as a result of experience. A **prototype** is a specific example of a concept that closely resembles the defining features of a concept. Concepts are formed through experience and culture and have an impact on our thinking.

Problem-solving involves using our thoughts or cognitions to reach a goal and consists of at least four different techniques. **Trial-and-error** problem solving makes use of mechanical solutions. When someone uses **algorithms** to problem-solve, they are following step by step procedures to solve the problem. **Heuristics** are general "rules of thumb" that can be applied to many situations, and **insight** consists of solving the problem by having a sudden moment of inspiration or "aha moment." Some factors that interfere with problem-solving include **functional fixedness,** when a person thinks about objects only in terms of their typical uses, **mental sets** which are tendencies to use the same problem-solving strategies that worked in the past, and **confirmation bias,** which consists of the search for evidence that fits your beliefs while ignoring any contradictory information. **Creativity** occurs when a person solves problems by combining ideas and behaviors in a new way. Many methods of problem solving utilize **convergent thinking,** which assumes that one single answer exists for the problem. **Divergent thinking** is the opposite process of convergent thinking. When an individual uses divergent thinking, they start from one point and come up with many possibilities or ideas based on that point.

Intelligence can be defined as the ability to learn from one's experiences, acquire knowledge, and use resources effectively in adapting to new situations or solving problems. In France in 1916, **Alfred Binet** and Theodore Simon developed the first formal test for intelligence in order to determine a child's mental age. The Stanford-Binet test used a ratio of mental age to chronological age to determine an individual's **intelligence quotient** or I.Q. In the U.S., the Wechsler intelligence tests are now used more frequently than the Stanford-Binet, and IQ scores are now based on individual **deviation IQ scores** rather than a ratio. The Wechsler tests are designed for specific age groups and can be administered individually.

To determine the quality of a psychological test, you need to look at the test's **validity**, **reliability**, and procedure used to obtain the **norms**. Validity refers to how well the test measures what it claims to measure, while reliability indicates the test's ability to produce the same result when given to the same person under similar conditions. Norms are determined by the **standardization group** selected by the researchers and should be a representative sample of the population who will be taking the test. All psychological tests should also be examined for cultural biases. Adrian Dove created an intelligence test call the Dove Counterbalance General Intelligence Test (also known as the Chitling Test) to demonstrate the cultural biases present in many of the intelligence tests currently in use. **Artificial intelligence** is the creation of a machine that can think like a human and is represented today through computer program such as Deep Blue.

Mental retardation, now more commonly referred to as **developmental delay**, occurs in about 3% of the U.S. population and is defined by an I.Q. score of 70 (two standard deviations below the mean) or lower along with adaptive behaviors significantly below the expected level for the person's age group. Diagnosis of developmental delay is determined by the person's intellectual and adaptive behavior skills, psychological and emotional levels, physical health considerations and environmental factors. Developmental delay is classified from mild to moderate, severe and profound. The three most common biological causes of developmental delay are Down syndrome, fetal alcohol syndrome, and fragile X syndrome. Individuals who receive scores of 130 or above on intelligence tests are referred to as **gifted**. **Lewis Terman** conducted a longitudinal study of the traits and behaviors of over 1,500 gifted children. The children were known as Terman's Termites and his findings showed that many of the common myths about the "nutty genius" were unfounded.

Currently, there is still much disagreement on exactly what is meant by the term "intelligence." In 1904, **Charles Spearman** proposed that intelligence was split between two abilities. The first ability was a general intelligence, labeled the **g factor**, and the other was a specific intelligence referred to as the **s factor**. Spearman believed that both the g and s factors could be measured using standardized intelligence tests. **Howard Gardner**, on the other hand, proposed that at least nine different kinds of intelligence exist. **Robert Sternberg** proposed the **triarchic theory of intelligence,** which states that intelligence can be divided into three types: analytical, creative, and practical. More recently, the concept of **emotional intelligence** has been suggested as an important factor for success in life. Further research in this area is still needed. The role of a person's environment (**nurture**) and heredity (**nature**) on the development of intelligence continues to be debated. Studies of identical and fraternal twins raised together and apart have provided one method for investigating the role of nature and nurture.

Language is defined as a system for combining symbols (such as words) so that an unlimited number of meaningful statements can be made for the purpose of communicating with others and can be analyzed at many levels. **Phonemes** are the most basic units of sounds used in a specific language, **morphemes** combine the units of sound into the smallest units that have meaning, **grammar** includes all the rules for combining morphemes into words and **syntax** are the rules for combining words into sentences. **Pragmatics** deal with the practical aspects of communicating with others. The relationship between language and thought has been studied extensively. The **Sapir-Whorf Hypothesis**, also known as the **linguistic relativity hypothesis**, proposes that the words people use determine how they think about themselves and the world. An opposing theory, known as **cognitive universalism**, proposes that certain ways of thinking are shared among all groups of people and influence the development of language in similar ways. Animals other than humans demonstrate a diverse ability to communicate, but it is unclear whether or not they have the capability for language as demonstrated by the ability to use abstract symbols to communicate. Kanzi, a bonobo chimpanzee has demonstrated an ability to understand about 150 spoken English words. However, none of the animals studied to date appear to have been able to use and comprehend syntax.

Research has shown that people who regularly "exercise" their brain are less likely to develop senile dementia. Examples of several brain exercises are listed at the end of the chapter in your textbook.

KEY POINTS

- Introduce the concept of cognition as it relates to mental images, concepts and problem-solving.
- Describe artificial intelligence.
- Discuss the measurement of intelligence, including the Stanford-Binet and Wechsler intelligence tests, test construction issues, and the determination of developmental delay.
- Describe several prominent theories of intelligence.
- Explain the basis of language and the relationship between language and thought processes.

KEY CONCEPTS

cognition	Mental activity that goes on in the brain when a person is organizing and attempting to understand information and communicating information to others.
mental images	Mental representations that stand in for objects or events and have a picture-like quality.
concepts	Ideas that represent a class or category of objects, events, or activities.
superordinate	The most general form of a type concept, such as "animal" or "fruit."
basic level type	An example of a type concept around which other, similar concepts are organized, such as "dog," "cat," or "pear."
subordinate	The most specific category of a concept, such as one's pet dog or a pear in one's hand.
formal concepts	Concepts that are defined by specific rules or features.
natural concepts	Concepts people form as a result of their experiences in the real world.
prototype	An example of a concept that closely matches the defining characteristics of a concept.
problem-solving	Process of cognition that occurs when a goal must be reached by thinking and behaving in certain ways.
trial-and-error	Problem-solving method in which one possible solution after another is tried until a successful one is found.
algorithms	Very specific, step-by-step procedures for solving certain types of problems.
heuristics	A general strategy that may help narrow down the possible solutions for a problem. Also known as a "rule-of-thumb."

insight	When the solution to a problem comes suddenly; also referred to as an "aha moment."
functional fixedness	A block to problem-solving that comes from thinking about objects in terms of only their typical functions.
mental set	The tendency for people to persist in using problem-solving patterns that have worked for them in the past.
confirmation bias	The tendency to search for evidence that fits one's beliefs while ignoring any evidence that does not fit those beliefs.
creativity	The process of solving problems by combining ideas or behavior in new ways.
convergent thinking	Type of thinking in which a problem is seen as having only one answer, and all lines of thinking will eventually lead to that single answer using previous knowledge and logic.
divergent thinking	Type of thinking in which a person starts from one point and comes up with many different ideas or possibilities based on that point.
intelligence	The ability to learn from one's experiences, acquire knowledge, and use resources effectively in adapting to new situations or solving problems.
Alfred Binet	1857-1911. French psychologist who developed the first formal test for intelligence.
intelligence quotient (I.Q)	A number representing a measure of intelligence, resulting from the division of one's mental age by one's chronological age and then multiplying that quotient by 100.
deviation IQ score	A type of intelligence measure which assumes that IQ is normally distributed around a mean of 100 with a standard deviation of about 15.
validity	The degree to which a test actually measures what it's supposed to measure.
reliability	The tendency of a test to produce the same scores again and again each time it is given to the same people.
norms	The standards used to assess the score of any individual who completes a standardized test.
standardization group	A randomly selected group chosen to represent the population for whom a psychological test is intended. Norms are calculated based off of the scores of the standardization group.

developmental delay	Condition in which a person's behavioral and cognitive skills exist at an earlier developmental stage than the skills of others who are the same chronological age. A more acceptable term for mental retardation.
gifted	The two percent of the population falling on the upper end of the normal curve and typically possessing an IQ of 130 or above.
Lewis Terman	1877-1956. Cognitive psychologist well known for his longitudinal study of gifted children, affectionately referred to as Terman's Termites.
Charles Spearman	1863-1945. English psychologist who proposed the two-factor theory of intelligence consisting of the g factor and the s factor.
g factor	The ability to reason and solve problems, or general intelligence.
s factor	The ability to excel in certain areas, or specific intelligence.
Howard Gardner	1943–present. Cognitive psychologist who has acted as a major proponent on the concept of multiple intelligences. Current theory suggests that nine types of intelligence exist.
Robert Sternberg	1949–present. Proposed the triarchic theory of intelligence, which states that intelligence is composed of three different abilities.
triarchic theory of intelligence	Sternberg's theory that there are three kinds of intelligences: analytical, creative, and practical.
emotional intelligence	The awareness of and ability to manage one's own emotions as well as the ability to be self-motivated, able to feel what others feel, and socially skilled.
nurture	The role a person's environment plays in their development.
nature	The role a person's heredity plays in their development.
language	A system for combining symbols (such as words) so that an unlimited number of meaningful statements can be made for the purpose of communicating with others.
phonemes	The basic units of sound in language.
morphemes	The smallest units of meaning within a language.
grammar	The system of rules by which the symbols of language are arranged.

syntax	The system of rules for combining words and phrases to form grammatically correct sentences.
pragmatics	Aspects of language involving the practical aspects of communicating with others, or the social "niceties" of language.
linguistic relativity hypothesis (Sapir-Whorf Hypothesis)	The theory that thought processes and concepts are controlled by language.
cognitive universalism	Theory that concepts are universal and influence the development of language.

HINTS

1. In this chapter, you were presented with four different approaches to problem-solving. In order to better understand how these approaches differ from each other, take the following problem and come up with an example of how you could solve the problem using each of the four different approaches.

    Problem: You are packing up to move to college and you have one more box to fit in the trunk of your car, but it looks like there is simply no room left. You don't want to leave the box behind. How will you solve this problem?

Approach	Solution
trial and error	
algorithm	
heuristics	
insight	

2. The two most commonly used methods to assess any psychological test is to determine the validity and reliability of the test. Examine the following test descriptions and determine whether the test has a potential problem with its reliability or validity.

Example	Validity or Reliability Issue?
A personality test gives a very different score for the same person when they retake it six months later.	
An individual takes an online IQ test that measures how long she can hold her breath.	
A five-year-old child is diagnosed as developmentally delayed based on his IQ scores, but when he is brought back and given the same test, his scores fall in the above average range.	

3. One issue that can get confusing is the various components of language analysis. Use the chart below to write a brief explanation of each component and come up with a specific example.

Component	Explanation	Example
phonemes		
morphemes		
grammar		
syntax		
pragmatics		

Suggested answers to Question 1:

Approach	Solution
trial and error	*Keep placing the box in various places and positions in your car until you find one that works.*
algorithm	*Go online and find a website that deals with physics. Enter in the dimensions of your car and the exact dimensions of every box and item that you are trying to fit in your car. Get a printout of the optimal placement for each box and follow it step by step to fit everything in.*
heuristics	*Think back to how your mom always told you to pack the big things first and then squeeze the little ones in. Take your boxes out and pack them again using this general rule of thumb to guide you.*
insight	*Sit back with your friends for a few minutes and relax, as you are talking with your friends, all of a sudden you remember that your family has a "Big Mac" container that will attach to the top of the car. Strap the container on, place your box in the container, and take off for school.*

Suggested answers to Question 2:

Example	Validity or Reliability Issue?
A personality test gives a very different score for the same person when they retake six months later.	*reliability – the scores are not consistent over time for the same person.*
An individual takes an online IQ test that measures how long she can hold her breath.	*validity – does holding your breath give a very accurate assessment of your IQ?*
A five-year-old child is diagnosed as developmentally delayed based on his IQ scores, but when he is brought back and given the same test, his scores fall in the above average range.	*This question illustrates that without reliability a test will also lack validity. The test scores are inconsistent over time, which indicates that the test is not really measuring what it claims to measure since we assume that intelligence is a fairly constant factor.*

Suggested answers to Question 3:

Component	Explanation	Example
phonemes	*most basic units of sound*	*"ay," "eee," "oh," "ahh"*
morphemes	*smallest unit of sound that has a meaning*	*"run," "ing"*
grammar	*system of rules to form words*	*To make girl plural, add an s.*
syntax	*system of rules to form sentences*	*Syntax tells you to say, "Where are you going?" instead of "Where go you?"*
pragmatics	*"social rules" of language*	*speak to a baby in a higher tone, emphasize "how" and not "you" in the question "how are you?"*

SAMPLE EXAM

For the following multiple choice questions, select the answer you feel best answers the question and explain the rationale or reason for your selection in the space provided.

Objective 8.1

1.   Mental images _____
        a)   represent abstract ideas
        b)   have a picture-like quality
        c)   consist entirely of unconscious information
        d)   are always prototypes

Rationale:
B is the correct answer. Mental images are mental representations of objects that have a picture-like quality.

2.   If three people used mental images to tell you how many windows they each had in their individual houses, which person would take the longest to answer?
        a)   the person with two windows in their house
        b)   the person with eight windows in their house
        c)   the person with twelve windows in their house
        d)   they would all take the same amount of time to answer

Rationale:
C is the correct answer. Research has found that if the individuals used mental images to answer the question they would actually visualize the house and have to count the windows, so the person with the most windows would take the longest time to answer.

Objective 8.2

3.   Concepts are ideas that represent _____
        a)   a class or category of objects, events, or activities
        b)   thoughts, images, muscle patterns of behavior
        c)   higher order conditioning and secondary reinforcers
        d)   none of these

Rationale:

_____

_____

4.   A very general form of a concept, such as "vegetable," represents which concept level?
        a)   subordinate
        b)   superordinate
        c)   basic level
        d)   hyperordinate

Rationale:

_____

_____

5.　　The trial and error method of solving problems is also known as
　　　　a)　the use of a heuristic device
　　　　b)　the use of algorithms
　　　　c)　the mechanical solution
　　　　d)　the A.I. solution

　　　Rationale:

　　　_____

　　　_____

6.　　Zach could not remember the four-digit combination needed to open the lock on his bicycle. After struggling to figure out what to do, he turned to start the long walk home and all of a sudden he remembered the combination to the lock. The problem-solving strategy Zach used would be best described as
　　　　a)　trial-and-error
　　　　b)　algorithm
　　　　c)　heuristic
　　　　d)　insight

　　　Rationale:

　　　_____

　　　_____

Objective 8.4

7.　　Which of the following examples would qualify as artificial intelligence according to the definition given in the textbook?
　　　　a)　A "smart" toaster that pops up when the toast starts to burn.
　　　　b)　A global positioning system installed in a car that can tell the driver exactly where they are located and how to get to their desired destination.
　　　　c)　A door that automatically opens when someone steps in front of it.
　　　　d)　A computerized black jack program that uses heuristics to attempt to beat its opponents.

　　　Rationale:

　　　_____

　　　_____

8.　　The term *artificial intelligence* was coined first by _____.
　　　　a)　Mary Shelly in *Frankenstein*
　　　　b)　Karel Capek in *RUR*
　　　　c)　Isaac Asimov in *I, Robot*
　　　　d)　John McCarthy

　　　Rationale:

　　　_____

　　　_____

9.   The tendency for people to persist in using problem-solving patterns that have worked for them in the past is known as
      a)   mental set
      b)   confirmation bias
      c)   creativity
      d)   divergent thinking

Rationale:

_____

_____

10.   Luann needs to hammer a nail into the wall, but the only tool she can find in the house is a screwdriver. Luann's inability to see how the handle of the screwdriver could be used as a hammer best represents the concept of
      a)   functional fixedness
      b)   confirmation bias
      c)   creativity
      d)   artificial bias

Rationale:

_____

_____

Objective 8.6

11.   The ability to produce solutions to problems that are unusual, inventive, novel and appropriate is called _____
      a)   creativity
      b)   insight
      c)   heuristics
      d)   latent learning

Rationale:

_____

_____

12.   Which of the following activities would NOT increase your creativity?
      a)   keeping a journal
      b)   brainstorming
      c)   subject mapping
      d)   convergent thinking

Rationale:

_____

_____

13. The ability to understand the world, think rationally or logically, and use resources effectively when faced with challenges or problems, or the characteristics needed to succeed in one's culture is the psychologist's working definition of _____
      a) divergent problem solving
      b) creative thinking
      c) heuristic usage
      d) intelligence

      Rationale:

      _____

      _____

Objective 8.8

14. An 8-year-old child who scored like an average 10-year-old on an intelligence test would have a mental age of _____ and an IQ of _____.
      a) Eight; 80
      b) Eight; 125
      c) Ten; 100
      d) Ten; 125

      Rationale:

      _____

      _____

Objective 8.9

15. Because of the need to measure the IQ of people of varying ages, newer IQ tests base their evaluation of IQ on_____
      a) mental age alone
      b) Deviation scores from the mean of the normal distribution
      c) Giving extra points for older folks to compensate for their slower processing times
      d) none of these

      Rationale:

      _____

      _____

16. If a test consistently produces the same score when administered to the same person under identical conditions, that test can be said to be high in
    a) reliability
    b) validity
    c) accuracy
    d) norms

Rationale:

_____

_____

Objective 8.10

17. Denny has a flat upper lip, wide-set eyes, and problems with his heart in addition to being mildly retarded. Denny most likely suffers from
    a) Down syndrome
    b) fetal alcohol syndrome
    c) fragile X syndrome
    d) cretinism

Rationale:

_____

_____

18. Which two of the following aspects are included in the definition of developmental delay?
    a) IQ scores and adaptive behavior
    b) age and socioeconomic status
    c) race and country of origin
    d) only IQ scores are considered

Rationale:

_____

_____

Objective 8.11

19. The two percent of the population who fall on the upper end of the normal curve and typically posses an IQ of 130 or above are referred to as
    a) special
    b) gifted
    c) extraordinary
    d) nutty

Rationale:

_____

_____

20.   Which was **NOT** a finding of the Terman and Oden (1974) study of gifted kids?
        a)   they were socially well adjusted
        b)   they were more resistant to mental illness
        c)   they were clearly much more likely to be females
        d)   they were average in weight, height and physical attractiveness

Rationale:

_____

_____

Objective 8.13

21.   Sternberg has found that _____ intelligence is a good predictor of success in life, but has a low relationship to _____ intelligence.
        a)   practical; analytical
        b)   practical; creative
        c)   analytical; practical
        d)   academic; creative

Rationale:

_____

_____

22.   What three types of intelligence constitute Sternberg's Triarchic theory of intelligence?
        a)   global, intuitive, and special
        b)   general, global, and specific
        c)   analytical, creative, and practical
        d)   mathematical, reasoning, and verbal

Rationale:

_____

_____

23.   The "g" in Spearman's g-factor of intelligence stands for
        a)   gifted intelligence
        b)   general intelligence
        c)   graded intelligence
        d)   the g does not stand for anything

Rationale:

_____

_____

24.   If intelligence is determined primarily by heredity, which pair should show the highest correlation between IQ scores?
        a)   fraternal twins
        b)   identical twins
        c)   brothers and sisters
        d)   parents and children

Rationale:

_____

_____

25.   If a researcher believed that <u>nature</u> was the most important factor in determining an individual's intelligence level, she would most closely agree with which of the following statements?
        a)   Intelligence is largely inherited from your parents.
        b)   Intelligence has no relationship to your biological family.
               The environment is the most important factor in determining a child's intelligence
        c)   level.
               A child's intelligence can be greatly increased by providing stimulating toys while
        d)   they are young.

Rationale:

_____

_____

26.   Which of the following statements are true about language?
        a)   is symbolic
        b)   can be written, spoken or signed
        c)   is capable of an infinite set of meaningful utterances
        d)   all of these

Rationale:

_____

_____

27.   The basic units of sound are called
        a)   morphemes
        b)   phonemes
        c)   semantics
        d)   syntax

Rationale:

_____

_____

28. Syntax is
    a) a system of rules for combining words and phrases to form sentences.
    b) the smallest units of meaning within a language.
    c) the basic units of sound.
    d) the rules to determine the meaning of words.

Rationale:

_____

_____

Objective 8.17

29. The linguistic relativity hypothesis suggests that _____.
    a) one's language determines the pattern of one's thinking and view of the world
    b) one's thinking and view of the world determines the structure of one's language
    c) we decide which objects belong to a concept according to what is most probable or sensible, given the facts at hand
    d) perception of surface structure precedes deep structure in understanding a sentence

Rationale:

_____

_____

30. Which theory would support the idea that certain concepts are shared by all people regardless of the language spoken?
    a) Sapir-Whorf hypothesis
    b) linguistic relativity hypothesis
    c) cognitive universalism
    d) heuristic theory

Rationale:

_____

_____

Objective 8.18

31. Dolphins, according to TV and movies, are very intelligent and have strong language abilities. They might even be able to talk! However, which statement is true from the research?
    a) Dolphins have been shown to master syntax.
    b) Dolphins have the language abilities of a three-year-old.
    c) Dolphin communication with parrots has been firmly established.
    d) None of these are true.

Rationale:

_____

_____

32. You are worried about your aging parent. Perhaps they might develop senile dementia. Thus you suggest:
    a) They stop reading as it will tire their brain out faster
    b) They start a program of extreme physical exercise to push more blood through their brain
    c) They need to start reading, doing puzzles, getting involved in a hobby, etc. to exercise their brain
    d) Nothing will help – don't bother to suggest anything

Rationale:

_____

_____

SAMPLE EXAM ANSWERS & RATIONALES

1. b   Mental images are mental representations of objects that have a picture-like quality.
2. c   Research has found that if the individuals used mental images to answer the question, they would actually visualize the house and have to count the windows, so the person with the most windows would take the longest time to answer.
3. a   The definition for concepts is ideas that represent a class or category of objects or events.
4. b   Superordinate is the highest or most general level of a concept. Basic level is the level most commonly used (such as potato or lettuce), subordinate is the most specific, such as a russet potato or romaine lettuce.
5. c   Again, this is asking for the straight definition of trial-and-error problem solving.
6. d   Insight problem solving occurs when you get a sudden inspiration that leads you to the solution to your problem.
7. d   Artificial intelligence is defined as a machine that thinks like a human, in particular the problem-solving skills of the machine. The first three examples are all simple procedures the machines are programmed to perform, but the last example represents an active problem solving ability.
8. d   The term artificial intelligence was coined by John McCarthy.
9. a   A mental set exists when someone continues to use the same approaches that worked in the past. Confirmation bias occurs when someone pays attention to information that confirms their ideas and ignores any contradictory input.
10. a   Functional fixedness occurs when an individual is *fixed* on only one *function* of a particular object.
11. a   This is the definition of creativity.
12. d   Convergent thinking occurs when you assume there is only one single answer or solution to a problem. Typically, convergent thinking decreases creative ability.
13. d   As can be seen, intelligence is a broad idea that can be difficult to define.
14. d   The IQ is based on a mental age of 10 divided by a chronological age of 8 and multiplied by 100. This gives an IQ = 125.
15. b   Deviation IQ scores are based on the norms of a representative sample of the population (also known as the standardization group).
16. a   Reliability indicates a test consistency, while validity indicates accuracy, or how well the test measures what it says it measures.
17. b   Denny most likely suffers from fetal alcohol syndrome.
18. a   The diagnosis of developmental delay is based on IQ scores as well as how well the individual is able to function in day-to-day life.
19. b   Gifted is the term used by psychologists to describe this group of people.
20. c   There were actually slightly more males than females in the sample of subjects selected for the Terman study.
21. a   Sternberg has found that practical intelligence is a good predictor of success in life, but has a low relationship to analytical intelligence.
22. c   Sternberg proposed that intelligence should actually be broken down into three components that can be thought of as book smarts, street smarts, and creativity.
23. b   Spearman proposed a two-factor theory of intelligence. The g-factor was for general intelligence and the s-factor was for specific intelligence.
24. b   Identical twins should show the strongest correlation since they share 100% of the same genes.
25. a   Nature refers to the influence of heredity on behaviors and traits, so "a" is the only selection that focuses on inheritance of genes.
26. d   The definition of language includes all three of these attributes.

27. b   Phonemes are the basic units of sound.
28. a   Syntax refers to the rules we use to form meaningful sentences.
29. a   *Linguistic relativity* hypothesis (also referred to as the Sapir-Whorf hypothesis) states that our thought processes are *relative* to the *language* (or linguistic setting) in which we grew up.
30. c   Cognitive universalism proposes that our basic thought processes, or cognitions, are universally shared by all people.
31. d   Chimpanzees have demonstrated a vocabulary equal to a two-year-old child, but no animal to date has demonstrated the ability to use and comprehend syntax.
32. c   In some ways the brain can be thought of as a muscle, in which increased activity can actually strengthen the brain.

APPLY IT

This chapter dealt with our thought processes and suggested methods for keeping our brains sharp. As you learned in Chapter 7, most forgetting occurs within the first hour after learning the material. For this study challenge, you should combine your knowledge of learning and memory with your new concept of exercising the brain.

1. After class, spend two minutes thinking about the information you just learned. Pick the three facts or concepts that you feel were the most important discussed in class.
2. In the space below, write down the concepts.
3. Next to the concepts, write down your own thoughts about them. Do you agree or disagree with the concept? Does the concept remind you of something from the past? The more associations you can form with the concepts, the more likely you are to remember them.

Class Period:_____

Concept	What you think about them
1.	
2.	
3.	

Class Period:_____

Concept	What you think about them
1.	
2.	
3.	

CHAPTER 9 LEARNING OBJECTIVES

9.1	What is motivation?	9.9	What happens in the body to cause hunger?
9.2	What are instinct approaches to motivation?	9.10	How do social factors influence hunger?
9.3	What are drive-reduction approaches to motivation?	9.11	What are some problems in eating behavior?
9.4	What are three types of needs?	9.12	What biological factors play a part in obesity?
9.5	What are arousal approaches to motivation?	9.13	What are the three elements of emotion?
9.6	What are incentive approaches to motivation?	9.14	What is the James-Lange theory of emotion?
9.7	What is Maslow's hierarchy of needs?	9.15	What is the Cannon-Bard theory of emotion?
9.8	What is the self-determination theory of motivation?	9.16	What is the cognitive arousal theory of emotion?
		9.17	What happened in Schachter and Singer's classic study of emotion?
		9.18	What is the facial feedback hypothesis?
		9.19	What is cognitive-mediational theory?
		9.20	What is the positive psychology movement?

SUMMARY

Motivation is the process by which activities are started, directed, and continued so that physical or psychological needs or wants are met. When motivation comes from outside the self it is called **extrinsic motivation**; on the other hand, if a person does something because it is satisfying in some internal manner, the motivation is called **intrinsic motivation**. Several theories have been proposed to explain the process of motivation including the theories of instinct, drive-reduction, needs, arousal, incentive, humanistic, and self-determination. **Instinct theory** suggests that people are motivated by biologically determined internal forces. Unfortunately, instinct theory only describes behavior and is unable to explain why people did what they did. The **drive-reduction approach** proposes that a **need**, or requirement, produces a **drive** and that people act in order to reduce these drives. The drives can be **primary drives,** such as hunger and thirst, or **secondary drives** such as the need for money. The rationale for drive-reduction includes the idea that the body has tendency to try to maintain a steady state referred to as **homeostasis**. When the body is out of balance, a need develops and the tension provides the drive to reduce the need and return the body to a state of balance. Drive-reduction theory, however, cannot explain why people would increase their internal tension by doing things like parachuting out of an airplane. **Need theory** attempts to explain motivation by understanding three specific needs, the **need for achievement (nAch), need for affiliation (nAff)**, and **need for power (nPow)**. **Arousal theory** suggest that people are motivated to maintain an optimal level of arousal or tension. The level of arousal is achieved by increasing or decreasing stimulation. The **Yerkes-Dodson law** demonstrates that for an easy task, performance is best when arousal is a little higher than average, whereas for a difficult task, performance is best when arousal is a little below average. Individuals who consistently seek out high levels of arousal have been labeled as **sensation seekers**. According to **incentive approaches** of motivation, people's acts are determined by the rewards or **incentives** for their behaviors. **Abraham Maslow** was a major proponent of the **humanistic approach** to motivation and proposed a **hierarchy of needs** that individuals must fulfill before they can reach the highest need of **self-actualization,** where a person reaches their fullest potential. According to Maslow, basic needs such as hunger and thirst must be satisfied before the higher level needs can be achieved. Also, Maslow referred to the times in which self-actualization is attained as **peak experiences**. The **self-determination theory** proposes that there are three inborn and universal needs that humans work to satisfy. These needs are the need for autonomy, competence, and relatedness.

One specific area of motivation that has been studied extensively is the motivation to eat, also known as hunger. The hunger drive can be divided into physiological and social components. Physiologically,

insulin and **glucagons** are hormones that regulate the level of glucose in the bloodstream. Insulin increases blood sugar levels, which leads to feelings of hunger. Several areas in the **hypothalamus** also play an important role in regulating eating behavior, perhaps by influencing the specific weight that our bodies try to maintain, or the **weight set point**. Another factor that influences the weight set point is the **basal metabolic rate**, which decreases as we age, causing a corresponding increase in the weight set point. The social factors that influence hunger include the times of day when a person typically eats, using food to reduce stress or provide comfort, and the appeal of a tempting dessert item. Some problems associated with eating behaviors are **obesity**, in which a person weighs 20 percent over their ideal weight; **anorexia nervosa**, in which a person weighs 15 percent less than their ideal weight; and **bulimia**, in which a person develops a cycle of overeating, followed by deliberate vomiting.

Emotions can be defined as the "feeling" aspect of consciousness, characterized by a certain physical arousal, a certain behavior, and an inner awareness of feelings. As can be seen in the definition, emotions can be divided into three components: physiology, behaviors, and subjective experience. Different emotions have been found to be associated with different physiological reactions. The **amygdala** has been found to play a role in the regulation of emotions in humans as well as other animals. The behaviors of emotions include facial expressions, body movements and other actions. Research has supported the idea that at least seven basic facial expressions are recognized and mimicked in cultures around the world. However, the **display rules**, or exactly when, where and how these emotions can be expressed, appears to differ across cultures. The subjective experience of emotions involves the cognitive process of assigning a label, such as happy, to your feelings. Several theories have been developed in an attempt to explain the process humans use to label our emotions. **Common sense theory** suggests that a stimulus causes a particular emotion to occur, which then leads to the behavioral and physiological response. The **James-Lange theory** of emotion proposes that a stimulus leads to a particular physiological response, which then leads to the subjective experience of an emotion. The **Cannon-Bard theory** suggests that the physical and subjective experience of emotions occur at the same time. A stimulus leads to activation of the thalamus, which then simultaneously activates the sympathetic nervous system and higher cortical areas which interpret the signal as a particular emotion. **Schachter and Singer** proposed the **cognitive arousal theory,** which proposes that after a stimulus occurs, your body has a physical reaction and we make a cognitive appraisal of the situation. Based on feedback from both these sources, we then come up with a subjective label for the emotion we are experiencing. The **facial feedback hypothesis** assumes that facial expressions provide feedback to the brain regarding the emotion being expressed and can then intensify or even cause the emotion. Lazarus's **cognitive-mediational theory** of emotion suggests that following a stimulus, we engage in a cognitive appraisal of the situation, which then triggers a subjective experience of an emotion followed by a physiological response.

In his book, *The Pursuit of Happiness*, David G. Myers suggests a number of ways to try to increase your emotional response of happiness. Some of the suggestions include acting happy, getting enough sleep, and exercising.

KEY POINTS

- Introduces the concept of motivation and discusses the major theories proposed to explain motivated behavior.
- Discusses the specific motivation of hunger and examines the physiological and social components in addition to three common eating disorders.
- Describes the three elements of emotion and presents six theories on how emotions are processed.

KEY CONCEPTS

motivation	The process by which activities are started, directed, and continued so that physical or psychological needs or wants are met.

extrinsic motivation	Type of motivation in which a person performs an action because it leads to an outcome that is separate from or external to the person.
intrinsic motivation	Type of motivation in which a person performs an action because the act itself is rewarding or satisfying in some internal manner.
instinct theory of motivation	Approach to motivation that assumes people are governed by instincts similar to those of other animals.
instincts	The biologically determined and innate patterns of behavior that exist in both people and animals.
drive-reduction theory	Approach to motivation that assumes behavior arises from physiological needs that cause internal drives to push the organism to satisfy the need and reduce tension and arousal.
need	A lack of some material (such as food or water) that is required for survival of the organism.
drive	A psychological tension and physical arousal arising when there is a need that motivates the organism to act in order to fulfill the need and reduce the tension.
primary drives	Those drives that involve needs of the body, such as hunger and thirst.
secondary drives	Those drives that are learned through experience or conditioning, such as the need for money or social approval.
homeostasis	The tendency of the body to maintain a steady state.
needs theory of motivation	Theory of motivation that examines the three specific needs for achievement, affiliation, and power.
need for achievement (nAch)	A need which involves a strong desire to succeed in attaining goals, not only realistic ones but also challenging ones.
need for affiliation (nAff)	The need for friendly social interactions and relationships with others.
need for power (nPow)	The need to have control or influence over others.
arousal theory of motivation	Theory of motivation in which people are said to have an optimal (best or ideal) level of tension that they seek to maintain by increasing or decreasing stimulation.
Yerkes-Dodson law	Predicts that a certain level of arousal will be motivating, but too much arousal or too little arousal will decrease motivation. The

optimal level of arousal appears to depend on the individual and the difficulty of the task.

sensation seeker	Someone who needs more arousal than the average person.
incentive theory of motivation	Theories of motivation in which behavior is explained as a response to the external stimulus and its rewarding properties.
incentives	Things that attract or lure people into action.
humanistic theory of motivation	Theories of motivation that focus on human potential and the drive to be the best a person can be.
self-determination theory (SDT)	Theory of human motivation in which the social context of an action has an effect on the type of motivation existing for the action.
Abraham Maslow	1908-1970. American psychologist who was a major proponent of the humanistic movement in psychology.
hierarchy of needs	A theory of motivation proposed by Maslow which suggests that as people meet their basic needs they seek to satisfy successively higher needs as laid out in the hierarchy.
self-actualization	According to Maslow, the seldom-reached point at which people have sufficiently satisfied the lower needs and achieved their full human potential.
peak experiences	According to Maslow, times in a person's life during which self-actualization is temporarily achieved.
insulin	A hormone secreted by the pancreas to control the levels of fats, proteins, and carbohydrates in the body by reducing the level of glucose in the bloodstream.
glucagons	Hormones that are secreted by the pancreas to control the levels of fats, proteins, and carbohydrates in the body by increasing the level of glucose in the bloodstream.
hypothalamus	Small structure in the brain located below the thalamus and directly above the pituitary gland, responsible for motivational behavior such as sleep, hunger, thirst, and sex.
weight set point	The particular level of weight that the body tries to maintain.
basal metabolic rate	The rate at which the body burns energy when the organism is resting.
obesity	Condition in which a person weighs 20 percent or more over their ideal weight.

anorexia nervosa	A condition in which a person reduces eating to the point that a weight loss of 15 percent below the ideal body weight or more occurs.
bulimia	A condition in which a person develops a cycle of "binging" or overeating enormous amounts of food at one sitting, and "purging" or deliberately vomiting after eating.
emotion	The "feeling" aspect of consciousness, characterized by a certain physical arousal, a certain behavior that reveals the emotion to the outside world, and an inner awareness of feelings.
amygdala	Brain structure located near the hippocampus, responsible for fear responses and memory of fear.
display rules	Learned ways of controlling displays of emotion in social settings.
Common sense theory	Idea held by most people that a stimulus leads to the subjective experience of an emotion, which then triggers a physiological response.
James-Lange theory of emotion	Theory in which a physiological reaction leads to the labeling of an emotion.
Cannon-Bard theory of emotion	Theory in which the physiological reaction and the emotion are assumed to occur at the same time.
Schachter and Singer	Two psychologists responsible for proposing the Cognitive Arousal theory of emotions.
cognitive arousal theory	Theory of emotion in which both the physical arousal and the labeling of that arousal based on cues from the environment must occur before the emotion is experienced.
facial feedback hypothesis	Theory of emotion which assumes that facial expressions provide feedback to the brain concerning the emotion being expressed, which in turn causes and intensifies the emotion.
cognitive-mediational theory	Theory of emotion in which a stimulus must be interpreted (appraised) by a person in order to result in a physical response and an emotional reaction.

HINTS

1. By far, the most confusing concept of this chapter is keeping track of the theories of emotion. The following hints are designed to help you work through this process. To start with, try filling in the following table correctly. Remember; when we are discussing emotions, there are several components we are interested in. The theories vary according to which component comes first. The components are:
    - physiological experience of emotion (increased heart rate, sweating, etc.)

- subjective experience of emotion (the "feeling" of happiness, sadness or anger)
- cognitive appraisal (using your thought process to assess the situation)
- subcortical brain activity (not considered cognitive types of action)

Using these key components, fill in the following table. The first row has already been filled in for you.

Theory	Event	1st response	2nd response	3rd response
Common Sense	*stimulus (dog barking)*	*subjective experience (fear)*	*physiological experience (increased heart rate)*	
James-Lange Theory				
Cannon-Bard Theory				
Schachter-Singer Theory				
Facial Feedback Hypothesis				
Cognitive-mediational Theory				

2. Now look over the chart you just completed. Which of the theories are similar and which are different? Can you come up with a way to group the theories together based on similarity?

As you learned in the chapter on memory, processing the information in this manner will help you better retain the material and make retrieval for the exam an easier process. Try grouping the theories into the following three categories:

Category 1: Physiological experience occurs after you "feel" the emotion.

_____

_____

Category 2: "Feeling" the emotion occurs after the physiological changes.

_____

_____

_____

Category 3: "Feeling" the emotion and the physiological changes occur at the same time.

_____

3.   And now just look at the theories for Category 2. These theories propose that we first experience a physical change in our body and then somehow that signals our subjective experience of a particular emotion. Can you break these theories down any further? What is it specifically that is triggering our subjective experience of an emotion? Write out your answers to each of the theories in the space below:

James-Lange: _____

Schachter-Singer: _____

Facial Feedback: _____

Suggested answers for Question 1

Theory	Event	1st response	2nd response	3rd response
Common Sense	*stimulus (dog barking)*	*subjective experience (fear)*	*physiological experience (increased heart rate)*	
James-Lange Theory	*stimulus (dog barking)*	*physiological (increased heart rate)*	*subjective (fear)*	
Cannon-Bard Theory	*stimulus (dog barking)*	*subcortical brain activity*	*physiological and subjective at the same time*	
Schachter-Singer Theory	*stimulus (dog barking)*	*physiological response (increased heart rate)*	*cognitive appraisal (there is a scary looking dog barking at me)*	*subjective experience (fear)*
Facial Feedback Hypothesis	*stimulus (dog barking)*	*facial expression of fear*	*subcortical brain activity*	*subjective experience (fear)*
Cognitive-mediational Theory	*stimulus (dog barking)*	*cognitive appraisal (there is a scary looking dog barking at me)*	*subjective experience (fear)*	*physiological experience (increased heart rate)*

Suggested answers for Question 2:

Category 1: Physiological experience occurs after you "feel" the emotion.

   common sense theory

   cognitive-mediational theory

197

Category 2: "Feeling" the emotion occurs after the physiological changes.

_____ *James-Lange theory* _____

_____ *Schachter-Singer theory of cognitive arousal* _____

_____ *Facial Feedback Hypothesis* _____

Category 3: "Feeling" the emotion and the physiological changes occur at the same time.

_____ *Cannon-Bard theory* _____

Suggested answers for Question 3:

James-Lange: *physiological changes themselves (for example, increased blood pressure)*

Schachter-Singer: *Our cognitive assessment of the immediate environment (for example, if your blood pressure rises and you are standing next to an attractive person, you might interpret the rise in blood pressure to feelings of attraction and excitement. If you were standing next to a spider, you might interpret the rise in blood pressure to feelings of fear.)*

Facial Feedback: *Subcortical feedback* _____

SAMPLE EXAM

For the following multiple choice questions, select the answer you feel best answers the question and explain the rationale or reason for your selection in the space provided.

Objective 9.1

1. Which statement about motivation is **true?**
    a) A motive energizes and directs behavior.
    b) We are always aware of motivational processes.
    c) Different motives always lead to different behaviors.
    Two people motivated by the same factor will satisfy that motive through similar
    d) means.

    Rationale:
    A is the correct answer; this is simply the definition of motive.

Objective 9.2

2. In the early twentieth century, psychologists were inclined to explain motivated behavior by attributing it to _____.
    a) emotions
    b) incentives
    c) learned responses
    d) instincts

    Rationale:

    _____

    _____

3. William McDougal proposed ___ instincts for humans early in the twentieth century.
    a) 5
    b) 9
    c) 18
    d) 24

    Rationale:

    _____

    _____

4. Each of the following is a valid criticism of instinct theories of motivation **EXCEPT** _____.
    a) human behavior is rarely rigid, inflexible, and found throughout the species
    b) instinct theories name behaviors without pinpointing their origins
    c) they were the dominant explanation for human behavior early in the twentieth century
    d) description is more important than explanation
    Rationale:

    _____

    _____

5.   One positive outcome of instinct approaches was:
      a)   that it gave birth to psychoanalytic theory.
      b)   that psychologists began focusing on learning theories.
      c)   that psychologists were now forced to consider the effects of heredity on behavior.
      d)   a better explanation of behavior.

Rationale:

_____

_____

Objective 9.3

6.   Homeostasis is like a:
      a)   scale
      b)   thermostat
      c)   carburetor
      d)   bicycle

Rationale:

_____

_____

Objective 9.4

7.   Which of the following is correct for people high in need achievement?
      a)   They look for careers that make a lot of money.
      b)   They look for careers and hobbies that allow others to evaluate them.
      c)   They look for careers that require little education.
      d)   They look for careers that will make them famous.

Rationale:

_____

_____

Objective 9.5

8.   Indiana Jones goes off to foreign lands in search of artifacts hidden in dangerous places and
      guarded by fierce protectors. Dr. Jones would be described as a _____ in arousal
      theory.
      a)   sensation seeker
      b)   nAff
      c)   fool-hardy
      d)   high nPow

Rationale:

_____

_____

9.   As a class assignment you are required to collect advertising slogans and describe how they may be relevant to concepts in psychology. You select the <u>Jell-O</u> slogan, "There's always room for Jell-O," and describe in class that it is relevant to one of the theories of motivation. Which theory is it?

      a)   instinctive
      b)   incentive
      c)   drive-reduction
      d)   optimum-level

Rationale:

_____

_____

10.   Which of the following shows a focus on the *lowest* of Maslow's hierarchy of needs?

      a)   Joan wants to live in a house with all the modern conveniences so she may have more time to seek fulfillment from her career and family.
      b)   Frank feels he is a good salesman because he likes what he does and knows how to do it well.
      c)   Barbara knows that as a teacher, she is a good person because she realizes the importance of imparting knowledge to society.
      d)   Mark works hard as an attorney only so that he can attract more clients, more money, and be secure in the knowledge that his family can survive.

Rationale:

_____

_____

11.   Self-determination theory (SDT) best fits which type of motivation?

      a)   the need for affiliation
      b)   intrinsic motivation
      c)   extrinsic motivation
      d)   a mastery goal

Rationale:

_____

_____

12.   The lateral hypothalamus (LH) may be involved in:
        a)   stoppage of eating
        b)   the onset of eating
        c)   processing low fats
        d)   food allergies

        Rationale:

        _____

        _____

13.   Anna Nicole weighed about 125 lbs most of her adult life. However, it seemed like whenever Anna Nicole gained weight it was easy to lose and get back to 125. But when she wanted to go below 125, it took forever and even the slightest deviation from her diet got her back to 125. What explanation would you give Anna Nicole?
        a)   Use better diet products.
        b)   Start a reality TV show.
        c)   Her weight, 125, is her set point. Leave it alone.
        d)   Her BMR is causing all the problems.

        Rationale:

        _____

        _____

Objective 9.10

14.   The concept of "comfort food" suggests that food:
        a)   may be influenced by social factors.
        b)   has genetic ways to comfort.
        c)   may release hormones and neurotransmitters that are comforting.
        d)   is reflexive.

        Rationale:

        _____

        _____

15.   Which component of hunger is most likely contributing to the fact that sometimes a person who has just had a late breakfast will still feel hungry at noon?
        a)   social
        b)   behavioral
        c)   physiological
        d)   intrinsic

        Rationale:

        _____

        _____

16.   Which individual has the highest risk for developing anorexia nervosa?
        a)   lower-class 26-year-old European man
        b)   an upper-class 16-year-old American boy
        c)   a lower-class 26-year-old European woman
        d)   an upper-class 16-year-old American girl

        Rationale:

        _____

        _____

Objective 9.12

17.   You are a hormone. You are secreted into the bloodstream by fatty tissue and your job is to signal
        the hypothalamus that the body has enough food, reducing appetite and increasing the feeling of
        being full. Who are you?
        a)   adrenalin
        b)   peptic acid
        c)   leptin
        d)   lippotor

        Rationale:

        _____

        _____

18.   Which individual has the highest risk for developing anorexia nervosa?
        a)   lower-class 26-year-old European man
        b)   an upper-class 16-year-old American boy
        c)   a lower-class 26-year-old European woman
        d)   an upper-class 16-year-old American girl

        Rationale:

        _____

        _____

Objective 9.13

19.   According to Ekman, which of the following is **NOT** one of the universal facial expressions?
        a)   disgust
        b)   fear
        c)   contempt
        d)   shame

        Rationale:

        _____

        _____

20. Which one of the following is **NOT** one of the three elements of emotion discussed in the text?
    a) physiology
    b) labeling
    c) behavior
    d) environment

Rationale:

_____

_____

Objective 9.14

21. Which statement is most consistent with the James-Lange theory of emotion?
    a) "I run because I'm afraid."
    b) "I'm laughing because I am happy."
    c) "I'm crying because I'm sad."
    d) "I'm anxious because I perspire."

Rationale:

_____

_____

Objective 9.15

22. What is the correct sequence of events in emotional response, according to the Cannon-Bard theory?
    a) stimulus --> emotion --> physiological changes
    b) stimulus --> physiological changes --> emotion
    c) physiological changes --> stimulus --> emotion
    d) stimulus --> emotion <u>AND</u> physiological changes (simultaneous)

Rationale:

_____

_____

Objective 9.16

23. "I think I'm afraid, therefore I am afraid."
    a) the James-Lange theory
    b) activation theory
    c) cognitive arousal theory
    d) the Cannon-Bard theory

Rationale:

_____

_____

24.	You just finished a cup of very strong coffee, which causes your body to have a general feeling of arousal. That afternoon you attend the funeral of a friend. According to Schachter and Singer, which of the following would most likely occur?
   a)	Your emotion would be happy in spite of the funeral because of the arousal.
   b)	You would work very hard to control your emotion.
   c)	Your emotion would be sad since the context would affect your labeling.
   d)	Your emotional state would be impossible to predict.

Rationale:

_____

_____

Objective 9.17

25.	According to the theory of emotion proposed by Schachter and Singer, what is the most important determinant of your subjective experience of emotion?
   a)	physiological reactions
   b)	cognitive appraisal of the situation
   c)	facial expressions
   d)	intensity of the stimulus

Rationale:

_____

_____

26.	In the classic study of emotion conducted by Schachter and Singer, after receiving the epinephrine, the subjects placed in the room with the angry man reported feeling
   a)	angry
   b)	happy
   c)	both angry and happy
   d)	no emotions were reported

Rationale:

_____

_____

27.   Which recent study below casts doubt on the facial feedback hypothesis?
   a)   a woman with a paralyzed face still responded emotionally to slides meant to stimulate emotions
   b)   a blind woman still responded emotionally to slides meant to stimulate emotions
   c)   a woman paralyzed from the waist down still responded emotionally to slides meant to stimulate emotions
   d)   a woman with Down syndrome still responded emotionally to slides meant to stimulate emotions

   Rationale:

   _____

   _____

28.   According to the facial feedback hypothesis, if you would like to make yourself feel more happy you should
   a)   spend time with friends
   b)   talk to a counselor
   c)   think about all the positive aspects of your life
   d)   smile

   Rationale:

   _____

   _____

Objective 9.19

29.   "I see a dog, but it is behind a fence, and I don't have anything to worry about, so I feel calm" is a statement that is most consistent with which of the following theories?
   a)   James-Lange theory
   b)   Cannon-Bard theory
   c)   Schachter-Singer theory
   d)   Cognitive-mediational theory

   Rationale:

   _____

   _____

30. According to the cognitive-mediational theory, which factor would be most important in determining whether you feel nervous when asked to speak in front of the class?
    a) your physiological reaction to the request
    b) activation of subcortical brain activity
    c) your cognitive appraisal of the situation
    d) your change in blood pressure

Rationale:

_____

_____

Objective 9.20

31. Positive psychology is best defined as
    a) An area in psychology that only focuses on positive test results (that is, those tests that actually show a difference between two groups).
    b) A movement in psychology that emphasizes the positive aspects of the human experience as opposed to the negative.
    c) A movement in psychology that attempts to incorporate simple mathematical functions as a means of understanding human behavior.
    d) An area in psychology that promotes a theory for treating depressed patients in which the patient is encouraged to think positively.

Rationale:

_____

_____

32. Which of the following is not a suggestion given by David Myers in his book *The Pursuit of Happiness*?
    a) Spend time alone
    b) Take control of your time
    c) Nurture your spiritual self
    d) Keep a gratitude journal

Rationale:

_____

_____

SAMPLE EXAM ANSWERS & RATIONALES

1.   a   This is simply the definition of motive.
2.   d   Instinct theory was one of the first proposed theories of motivation in psychology. Be careful not to confuse incentive with instincts!
3.   c   McDougal proposed a total of 18 basic instincts.
4.   c   This is not a criticism but simply a statement. For D, the criticism was that description is LESS important than explanation.
5.   c   Instinct approaches were based on heredity and psychologists started looking at inherited influences on behavior.
6.   b   A is not correct because a scale only has one direction.
7.   b   High achievers need feedback from others.
8.   a   His actions indicate that he needs a higher level of arousal than most people.
9.   b   Incentive theory suggests that we often eat food items because of their reward value and not simply because we are hungry.
10.   d   This is the only situation in which the person is focusing on basic needs for him and his family. In all the other examples, the individuals were focused on growth needs.
11.   b   Self determination theory is characterized by intrinsic motivations.
12.   b   When the lateral hypothalamus was removed in experimental animals, the animals stopped eating and had to be force-fed food.
13.   c   The set point is the level of weight the body tends to maintain.
14.   a   Social factors in hunger include the social cues associated with food.
15.   a   Social factors can have a strong impact on feelings of hunger.
16.   d   According to government statistics, white upper-class females in the U.S. show the highest prevalence rates for anorexia.
17.   c   Leptin appears to be the hormone that causes you to feel full.
18.   d   Anorexics are typically young and female.
19.   d   Shame was not found in all cultures. The seven facial expressions he did find were anger, fear, disgust, happiness, surprise, sadness and contempt.
20.   d   Emotion was broken down into its physical, behavioral, and subjective (or labeling) components.
21.   d   The physiological change comes before the experience of the emotion.
22.   c   Cannon-Bard believed the subjective and physiological experience occurred simultaneously.
23.   c   The cognitive aspect (or thinking component) is the factor that determines your emotions, according to the cognitive arousal theory.
24.   c   According to Schachter and Singer, the coffee causes an arousal and then you seek environmental cues to come up with a label for your arousal.
25.   b   See the answer to number 24.
26.   a   In accord with their theory, the participants use the environmental cues of an angry co-subject to determine that their own arousal was due to anger as well.
27.   a   If her face is paralyzed, she would not be able to send feedback to her brain regarding her facial expression, and thus her emotions would be significantly reduced according to the facial feedback hypothesis.
28.   d   The facial feedback hypothesis proposes that our brain receives feedback on our facial expressions, which then serves to enhance whatever emotion we are expressing.
29.   d   The cognitive-mediational theory believes that we first assess the situation before we have a subjective experience of emotion or a physiological reaction.
30.   c   See the answer to number 29.
31.   b   This is the definition given in your textbook.
32.   a   Myers suggests spending time with others and those you care about.

APPLY IT

This section will help you use the concepts you are learning in this class to improve your study skills.

This chapter focused on understanding motivation and emotion. One specific type of motivation that was discussed and one that is particularly helpful for success in college is the need for achievement (nAch). The following activity is designed to help you learn how to increase your need for achievement.

Think about the following four steps and try to answer the questions as accurately as possible. Following these suggestions should help you improve your motivation levels for achievement.

1. Be aware of the barriers you create.
The first step is to take a personal inventory of the barriers you create yourself to block your feelings of success and achievement. Some examples would be if you...

> *avoid taking hard classes*
> *skip classes before the test or the day a paper is due*
> *wait until the last minute to start working on a project or studying for an exam*

In the space below, come up with at least three barriers that you create yourself. Be specific!

_____

_____

_____

2. Examine your own idea of intelligence.
A number of research studies have found that your personal concept of intelligence is directly related to your drive for success. Individuals who feel that intelligence is fixed and cannot be shaped by experience tend to have lower motivation levels for achievement. On the other hand, individuals who view intelligence as something that can be increased by experiences tend to score higher on achievement motivation.

How do you view your own intelligence? Do you see your intelligence as fixed or changeable?

_____

To help you start thinking about your intelligence as a factor you can influence, list three things you could do that you feel would increase your level of intelligence.

_____

_____

_____

3. Shift your goals from externally motivated to internally motivated.
Research studies have supported the idea that people who are motivated by intrinsic goals tend to have higher and more consistent motivation levels, whereas people with externally motivated goals tend to get discouraged more easily. Intrinsic goals are goals you set for yourself because of your own personal desires and do not rely on comparisons or validation from others. On the other hand, extrinsic goals are goals those that are set by others for you or goals that depend on comparing yourself with other people's performances. Some examples include

Externally-motivated goal	Internally-motivated goal
• Working for an A because of pressure from your parents. • Wanting to get the highest score in the class.	• Working for an A to show yourself that you can do it. • Wanting to get a higher score on this exam than you got on the last exam.

Think about your own goals. How many of your goals are externally motivated and how many are internally motivated? Come up with at least three externally motivated goals and shift them to internally motivated goals.

Externally motivated ⟹ Internally motivated

_____   _____

_____   _____

_____   _____

4. When you succeed, praise your efforts, not just your success.
To reinforce the idea that intelligence is something that depends on how hard you work, when you achieve one of your goals, be sure to praise yourself for the effort you made as well as for the success itself. This will help you stay encouraged and motivated during those times when you don't attain your goal or don't have the results you were hoping for. Use the following examples to practice coming up with praise for effort as well as success. The first example has already been filled in.

Accomplishment	Praising your success	Praising your effort
You got an A on a test.	This A proves how smart I am.	This A how hard I really worked.
You get called to interview for a job you really want.		
You receive an award at school for your academic achievements.		
You complete a 10 K race in your fastest time ever.		

210

CHAPTER 10 LEARNING OBJECTIVES

10.1   What are the physical differences between females and males?

10.2   What is gender?

10.3   How much influence do biology and learning have on gender role development?

10.4   What are the theories about how children learn their gender roles?

10.5   What is gender stereotyping?

10.6   What is androgyny?

10.7   What are the differences in thinking, social behavior, and personality between women and men?

10.8   What is the controversy concerning the treatment of intersexed infants?

10.9   What happens in the bodies of women and men during sexual intercourse?

10.10 How did Masters and Johnson investigate the human sexual response?

10.11 How did Kinsey study human sexual behavior?

10.12 What were the findings of the Janus Report?

10.13 What are the different sexual orientations and how do they develop?

10.14 What are the sexual dysfunctions caused by physical problems or stress?

10.15 What are the sexual dysfunctions known as paraphilias?

10.16 What are sexually transmitted diseases?

10.17 How can people protect themselves and prevent the spread of STDs?

SUMMARY

Sex is defined as the physical differences between males and females. **Primary sex characteristics** are those physical characteristics that are present at birth and are directly involved in human reproduction. In the female, the primary sex characteristics include the **vagina**, **uterus**, and **ovaries**. In the male, the primary sex characteristics include the **penis**, the **testes** (also called the testicles), the **scrotum**, and the **prostate gland**. In the female embryo, the development of the gonads into ovaries causes the release of **estrogen,** which leads to the development of the remaining sex organs, while in the male, the development of the gonads into testes leads to the release of **androgens** and further development of the male sex organs. **Secondary sex characteristics** develop during **puberty** and are indirectly involved in human reproduction. Female secondary sex characteristics include a growth spurt after the first menstrual cycle, enlarged breasts, wider hips, pubic hair, and fat deposits on the buttocks and thighs. Male secondary sex characteristics include a deepening voice, facial, chest, and pubic hair, development of coarser skin texture, and a growth spurt.

Gender is defined as the psychological aspects of being feminine or masculine. **Gender roles** are a culture's expectation for behavior of a person who is perceived as male or female, and **gender typing** is the process by which individuals learn their expected gender role. A person's sense of being female or male is called their **gender identity** and is influenced by both biology and environment. For example, some researchers believe that exposure to certain hormones during fetal development influences gender identity in addition to the strong environmental pressures or family and friends to behave in the "expected" manner. **Social learning theory** proposes that individuals learn their gender identities by observing the behaviors of the people around them and being rewarded for imitating the appropriate gender behavior. **Gender schema theory** suggests that children acquire their gender role by organizing their own behavior around their internalized schema of "boy" or "girl." A **gender stereotype** is a generalization about males or females that ignores individual differences. Female gender stereotypes often include characteristics such as illogical, emotional, sensitive, and nurturing, while male gender stereotypes can include characteristics such as aggressive, logical, decisive and unemotional. Sexism refers to prejudice about males and females. Psychologist Sandra Bem coined the term **androgyny** to describe people who display both male and female characteristics. With regard to cognitive differences between gender, men tend to perform better than women on certain spatial tasks, while women tend to perform better than men on tests of perceptual speed. Researchers are still investigating the relative contributions of the environment and heredity on these gender differences. With regard to communication, women tend to use a "relate" style of communication, while men often use a "report" style.

Approximately 1 out of 1,500 children in the U.S. are born with ambiguous sexual organs, a condition referred to as **intersexed**. Many physicians view the condition as an abnormality that should be repaired by sexual reassignment surgery. However, many intersexed individuals feel that the decision regarding surgery should be made by the individual themselves when they are old enough to make their own choice.

Three landmark studies have provided much of the information available today in the U.S. about human sexuality. In 1957, **William Masters and Virginia Johnson** conducted the first direct observational study on the physical aspects of the human sexual response by recording the physiological reactions of 700 female and male volunteers while they were engaged in sexual intercourse or masturbation. Their research led them to propose four stages of the sexual response cycle: **excitement**, **plateau**, **orgasm**, and **resolution**, respectively. Men show a **refractory period** after the fourth phase during which time they cannot achieve erection. The valuable research of Masters and Johnson has helped a tremendous number of individuals but was extremely controversial when it was originally published. In 1948, **Alfred Kinsey** published his findings from a large survey of adult sexual behavior in the United States. His findings were based on face-to-face interviews with participants and included details about the frequency of behaviors such as masturbation, anal sex, premarital sex, and sexual orientation. Some have criticized the Kinsey Study on the basis of methodological issues. The next large-scale study of human sexual behavior was published in 1993 by **Samuel Janus** and **Cynthia Janus**. The Janus Report described sexual behaviors in the U.S. based on the survey responses of 3,000 individuals from across the U.S.

Sexual orientation refers to a person's sexual attraction for members of a particular sex. The term **heterosexual** refers to people who are sexually attracted to members of the opposite physical sex and the term **homosexual** refers to individuals who are attracted to members of their own physical sex. A person who is **bisexual** may be either male or female and is attracted to both sexes. A great deal of time and energy has been invested into answering the question of whether sexual orientation is learned or inherited from your parents. A well-known study by Simon LeVay found differences in posthumous hypothalamus size between heterosexual and homosexual men. Although this study was corroborated by a similar study in sheep, both studies are correlational in nature and do not tell us the actual cause of sexual orientation.

A **sexual dysfunction** is a problem with sexual functioning or the actual physical workings of the sex act and can be caused by a number of factors. **Organic or stress-induced dysfunctions** are the sexual problems that are caused by physical disorders or by psychological distress. The sexual problems can be in three areas of sexual activity: sexual interest, arousal, and response. **Paraphilia** is a sexual dysfunction in which the person achieves sexual arousal and fulfillment through sexual behavior that is unusual or socially unacceptable. **Pedophilia** is a sexual deviancy that involves recurring sexual thoughts or behaviors toward children who have not yet entered puberty. Pedophilia is illegal and considered immoral in almost every culture. **Transvestism** is a dysfunction in which the individual receives sexual pleasure from dressing in the clothing of the opposite sex.

Sexually transmitted diseases or STDs are any disease that is spread through sexual contact. Some common STDs in the United States include **chlamydia**, **syphilis**, **gonorrhea**, **genital herpes**, **genital warts**, and AIDS (or **acquired immune deficiency syndrome**). AIDS is cause by the **human immunodeficiency virus** (HIV), which wears down the body's immune system, making the individual highly susceptible to infections. The virus can be transmitted from person to person through exposure to blood, vaginal fluid, semen, and breast milk. There are no documented cases of the spread of AIDS through tears or saliva. In the United States, approximately 900,000 people have the virus and about 300,000 of those individuals have developed AIDS. The medications used to treat the virus are called antiretrovirals and work by slowing down the action of the virus. Researchers are working on a vaccine that would prevent HIV infection.

Individuals can protect themselves from STDs by using condoms, having a sexual relationship with one uninfected partner, not sharing needles or other drug equipment, having regular exams for STDs, learning the common symptoms of STDs, talking openly with your partner about diseases and condom use, and realizing that abstinence is the only 100 percent effective prevention.

KEY POINTS

- Discuss physical sex differences between males and females.
- Describe the psychological gender differences between males and females, including gender development and gender stereotypes.
- Introduce three of the most influential studies on sexual behavior in the United States.
- Explain the concept of sexual orientation.
- Describe the physical and psychological problems that can lead to sexual dysfunction.
- Discuss the most common sexually transmitted diseases in the United States.

KEY CONCEPTS

sex	Physical properties that distinguish males from females
primary sex characteristics	Sexual organs present at birth and directly involved in human reproduction.
vagina	The tube that leads from the outside of a female's body to the opening of the womb.
uterus	The womb in which the baby grows during pregnancy.
ovaries	The female sexual glands.
penis	Male external sex organ.
testes	The male sex glands.
scrotum	External sack that hold the testes.
prostate gland	Gland that secretes most of the fluid holding the male sex cells or sperm.
estrogen	Female sex hormones.
androgens	Male sex hormones.
secondary sex characteristics	Sexual organs and traits that develop at puberty and are indirectly involved in human reproduction.
puberty	Period during which the secondary sex characteristics begin to develop and the capability of sexual reproduction is attained.
gender	The psychological aspects of being male or female.

gender roles	The culture's expectations for masculine or feminine behavior, including attitudes, actions, and personality traits associated with being male or female in that culture.
gender typing	The process of acquiring gender role characteristics.
gender identity	The individual's sense of being male or female.
social learning theory	Theory of gender identity acquisition that emphasizes learning through observation and imitation of models.
gender schema theory	Theory of gender identity acquisition in which a child develops a mental pattern, or schema, for being male or female and then organizes observed and learned behavior around that schema.
gender stereotype	A concept held about a person or group of people that is based on being male or female.
androgyny	Characteristic of possessing the most positive personality characteristics of males and females regardless of actual sex.
intersexed	A person who possesses ambiguous sexual organs, making it difficult to determine actual sex from a visual inspection at birth.
William Masters	1915-2001. Gynecologist famous for his pioneering research into the nature of human sexual response and the diagnosis and treatment of sexual disorders and dysfunctions from 1957 until the 1990s.
Virginia Johnson	b. 1925. Psychologist famous for her pioneering research into the nature of human sexual response and the diagnosis and treatment of sexual disorders and dysfunctions from 1957 until the 1990s
excitement	First phase of sexual arousal during which the pulse rate increases, blood pressure rises, breathing quickens and the skin may show a rosy flush.
plateau	Second phase of sexual arousal during which the physical changes in the first phase continue.
orgasm	A series of rhythmic contractions of the muscles of the vaginal walls or the penis, also the third and shortest phase of sexual response.
resolution	The final phase of the sexual response in which the body is returned to a normal state.
refractory period	Time period in males just after orgasm in which the male cannot become aroused or achieve erection.
Alfred Kinsey	1894-1956. Regarded by some as the father of the scientific study

of human sexuality. Published a series of reports called the Kinsey Reports which described common sexual behaviors in the U.S.

Samuel and Cynthia Janus	In 1993, published the most recent nationwide survey of common sexual behaviors. The publication is called The Janus Report.
sexual orientation	A person's sexual attraction preference for members of a particular sex.
heterosexual	Person sexually attracted to the opposite sex.
homosexual	Person sexually attracted to the same sex.
bisexual	Person sexually attracted to both men and women.
sexual dysfunction	A problem in sexual functioning.
Organic or stress-induced dysfunctions	Sexual problem caused by physical disorder or psychological stress.
paraphilia	A sexual disorder in which the person's preferred method of sexual arousal and fulfillment is through sexual behavior that is unusual or socially unacceptable.
pedophilia	Deriving sexual arousal and pleasure from touching or having sexual relations with prepubescent (non-sexually mature) children, or fantasizing about such contact.
transvestism	Deriving sexual arousal and pleasure from dressing in the clothing of the opposite sex.
sexually transmitted diseases (STDs)	Any disease that is spread through sexual contact.
Chlamydia	Sexually transmitted disease which can cause damage to the female and male reproductive systems resulting in infertility. Chlamydia may remain undetected for long periods of time
syphilis	Sexually transmitted disease with the initial symptom of a painless open sore that usually appears on the penis or around or in the vagina. If untreated, syphilis may go on to more advanced stages, including a transient rash and, eventually, serious involvement of the heart and central nervous system
gonorrhea	Sexually-transmitted disease that affects the genitals of both sexes, gonorrhea causes burning or difficulty with urination, itching, and a yellow or green discharge. It is easily treated with antibiotics
genital herpes	Sexually transmitted infection caused by the herpes simplex virus, which causes a painful rash of fluid-filled blisters on the genitals.

genital warts	Lesions produced by the human papillomavirus (HPV) and transmitted through sexual contact. The lesions may be raised and bumpy, or flat and almost impossible to see.	
acquired immune deficiency syndrome (AIDS)	Sexually transmitted viral disorder that causes deterioration of the immune system and eventually results in death due to complicating infections that the body can no longer fight.	
human immunodeficiency virus (HIV)	A virus that steadily weakens the body's defense (immune) system until it can no longer fight off infections such as pneumonia, diarrhea, tumors and other illnesses.	

HINTS

1. It is important to be able to distinguish the primary from the secondary sex characteristics. The primary characteristics are those that we are born with and the secondary characteristics develop during puberty. Use your own knowledge and your memory of the information from the text to fill in the following table.

	Primary Sex Characteristics	Secondary Sex Characteristics
Female		
Male		

2. This chapter introduced three of the most important studies on human sexuality conducted to date. Use the following table to help you summarize the details of these studies.

Researcher(s)	Date of Study	Method used	Major Findings

3. Try matching each of the STDs listed on the left with the correct set of symptoms on the right.

Chlamydia

Initial symptoms of a painless open sore that usually appears on the penis or in or around the vagina. If untreated, may go on to more advanced stages, including a transient rash and, eventually, serious involvement of the heart and central nervous system.

syphilis

Infection caused by the herpes simplex virus, which causes a painful rash of fluid-filled blisters on the genitals.

gonorrhea

Affects the genitals of both sexes, causes burning or difficulty with urination, itching, and a yellow or green discharge. It is easily treated with antibiotics.

genital herpes

Lesions produced by the human papillomavirus (HPV) and transmitted through sexual contact. The lesions may be raised and bumpy, or flat and almost impossible to see.

genital warts

Causes damage to the female and male reproductive systems resulting in infertility; it may remain undetected for long periods of time

acquired immune deficiency syndrome (AIDS)

Viral disorder that causes deterioration of the immune system and eventually results in death due to complicating infections that the body can no longer fight.

Suggested Answers for Question 2

Researcher(s)	Date of Study	Method used	Major Findings
Masters and Johnson	late 1950's; published in 1957	direct observation in a laboratory	Four phases of human sexual response. Men and women both go through the four phases, but men have a refractory period that is not typically seen in women.
Alfred Kinsey	1948	one-on-one personal interviews	Sexual orientation was seen more along a continuum. Frequency of masturbation, pre-marital and extra-marital sex was much higher than many people previously thought.
Samuel Janus and Cynthia Janus	1993	one-on-one interviews as well as mass questionnaires	Findings on typical sexual behavior as well as sexual deviance, single people's sexual behavior, marriage, divorce and decisions to have children.

Answers for Question 3

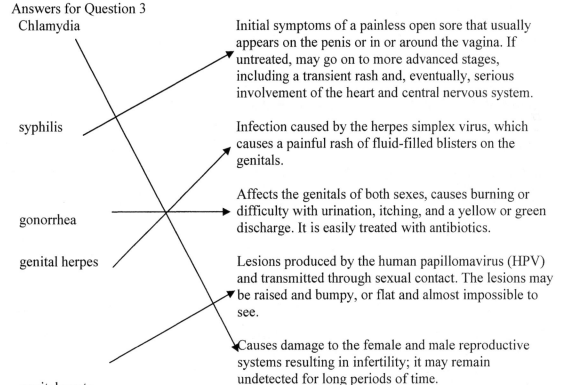

Chlamydia

syphilis

gonorrhea

genital herpes

genital warts

Initial symptoms of a painless open sore that usually appears on the penis or in or around the vagina. If untreated, may go on to more advanced stages, including a transient rash and, eventually, serious involvement of the heart and central nervous system.

Infection caused by the herpes simplex virus, which causes a painful rash of fluid-filled blisters on the genitals.

Affects the genitals of both sexes, causes burning or difficulty with urination, itching, and a yellow or green discharge. It is easily treated with antibiotics.

Lesions produced by the human papillomavirus (HPV) and transmitted through sexual contact. The lesions may be raised and bumpy, or flat and almost impossible to see.

Causes damage to the female and male reproductive systems resulting in infertility; it may remain undetected for long periods of time.

219

acquired immune deficiency
syndrome (AIDS) ⟶ Viral disorder that causes deterioration of the immune
system and eventually results in death due to
complicating infections that the body can no longer
fight.

SAMPLE EXAM

For the following multiple choice questions, select the answer you feel best answers the question and
explain the rationale or reason for your selection in the space provided.

Objective 10.1

1.   The growth spurt in <u>female</u> puberty usually starts at around _____ years of age
     a)   8-10
     b)   10-12
     c)   12-14
     d)   14-16

Rationale:

*B is the correct choice. The female growth spurt starts at around age 10-12, while the male
growth spurt starts at around age 12-14.*

2.   Which of the following is NOT a secondary sex characteristic in males?
     a)   facial and chest hair
     b)   deepening voice
     c)   development of coarser skin texture
     d)   the prostate gland

Rationale:

D is the correct answer; the prostate gland represents a primary sex characteristic in males.

Objective 10.2

3.   _____ is the process by which people learn their culture's preferences and expectations for
     proper "masculine" and "feminine" behavior.
     a)   gender role
     b)   gender identity
     c)   gender typing
     d)   gender stereotyping

Rationale:

_____

_____

4. Whereas _____ can be defined as the physical characteristics of being female or male, _____ is defined as the psychological aspects of being feminine or masculine.
   a) sex, gender
   b) gender roles, gender identity
   c) gender typing, gender
   d) gender, sex

Rationale:

_____

_____

Objective 10.3

5. Traditional views of gender roles are more likely found in
   a) collectivist cultures
   b) individualistic cultures
   c) countries like the Netherlands, Germany, Italy, and England
   d) none of these answers are correct

Rationale:

_____

_____

6. If an individual's gender identity was completely determined by the DNA he or she inherited, we would say that gender identity is determined by:
   a) nature
   b) nurture
   c) both nature and nurture
   d) we would not be able to say

Rationale:

_____

_____

7. When children observe their same-sex parents behaving in certain ways and imitate that behavior, a psychologist uses which theory to explain the situation?
   a) Freudian psychoanalysis
   b) Piaget's theory of development
   c) gender schema theory
   d) social learning theory

   Rationale:

   _____

   _____

8. A child who develops her identity and organizes her behavior around a mental concept of "girl" is relying on
   a) simple imitation
   b) positive reinforcement
   c) social pressures
   d) a gender schema

   Rationale:

   _____

   _____

Objective 10.5

9. Desperate for help with her computer, Dana calls her fiancé, thinking that he will know what to do because he is a man, and men are natural fixers. Dana's thinking in this instance is an example of
   a) androgyny
   b) schema error
   c) benevolent sexism
   d) negative stereotyping

   Rationale:

   _____

   _____

10. Stereotypes about males and females consist of only negative characteristics.
    a) True
    b) False

    Rationale:

    _____

    _____

Objective 10.6

11. Psychologist Sandra Bem (1975, 1981) developed the concept of _____.
      a) androgyny
      b) benevolent sexism
      c) social learning theory
      d) ambiguity

     Rationale:

     _____

     _____

Objective 10.7

12. MRI technology has demonstrated that men listen with _____
      a) the right hemisphere of the brain
      b) the left hemisphere of the brain
      c) both hemispheres of the brain
      d) there is no consistent pattern of listening

     Rationale:

     _____

     _____

13. One difference that has been reported in the communication styles of men and women is that
      a) no differences have been found in communication styles
      b) men talk more than women
      c) men are more likely to switch topics frequently
      d) women are more likely to interrupt

     Rationale:

     _____

     _____

Objective 10.8

14. Approximately how many children in the U.S. are born with both male and female sex organs?
      a) 1 out of 100
      b) 1 out of 1,500
      c) 1 out of 100,000
      d) there are currently no estimates of the number

     Rationale:

     _____

     _____

15.   The final phase of the sexual response is _____

      a)   excitement
      b)   plateau
      c)   orgasm
      d)   resolution

Rationale:

_____

_____

16.   The research of Masters and Johnson represents the first major contribution to our understanding of

      a)   common sexual behaviors
      b)   prevalence of sexually transmitted diseases
      c)   common sexual disorders
      d)   the physical response during sexual activity

Rationale:

_____

_____

Objective 10.10

17.   One seemingly amazing aspect of Masters and Johnson's research program concerning human sexual response was _____

      a)   their ability to get senior citizens to volunteer as subjects in the first studies
      b)   that the study was funded by churches open to discovering ways to prevent masturbation
      c)   that they were able to convince the newspapers to keep the research secret for a long period of time
      d)   none of these are correct

Rationale:

_____

_____

Objective 10.11

18.   The Kinsey Report, which was published in 1948 by Alfred Kinsey, reported on common sexual behaviors of adults in U.S., and was based on what type of research method?

      a)   direct observation
      b)   anonymous surveys
      c)   experimental laboratory studies
      d)   one-on-one personal interviews

Rationale:

_____

_____

19. According to Kinsey, what percentage of husbands reported anal sex with their wives?

   a) 11%
   b) 14%
   c) 92%
   d) 26%

Rationale:

_____

_____

Objective 10.12

20. The first large-scale study of human behavior to be done after the Kinsey and Masters and Johnson reports was conducted by _____.

   a) Janus and Janus
   b) Hite and Rose
   c) Hilton and Paris
   d) Erickson and Schlomo

Rationale:

_____

_____

Objective 10.13

21. If homosexuality were definitively found to be due to genetic or hormonal influences, then

   _____.

   a) discrimination against homosexuals would be equivalent to racism or sexism
   b) it would no longer be seen as a matter of simple choice
   c) society could no longer demand that homosexuals change their behavior
   d) all of these are true

Rationale:

_____

_____

22. When a person refers to themselves as "heterosexual" or "homosexual," the person is referring to their

   a) sexual identity
   b) sex
   c) gender identity
   d) sexual orientation

Rationale:

_____

_____

23. A controversial study by Simon LeVay found that the _____ was significantly larger in heterosexual men than in homosexual men or women.
    a) hypothalamus
    b) hippocampus
    c) cerebral cortex
    d) corpus callosum

    Rationale:

    _____

    _____

Objective 10.14

24. Jaime enjoys sexual activity with his partner. However, he cannot reach an orgasm during sexual intercourse even though fully aroused. Jaime is suffering from _____
    a) male erectile disorder
    b) male orgasmic disorder
    c) dyspareunia
    d) premature ejaculation

    Rationale:

    _____

    _____

Objective 10.15

25. Aaliyah became sexually aroused or gratified through rubbing up against an unwilling person, usually in a crowded public place. He has a condition known as _____
    a) foyeurism
    b) frotteurism
    c) necrophilia
    d) transvestism

    Rationale:

    _____

    _____

26. A _____ is a disorder in which an individual achieves sexual arousal and fulfillment through sexual behavior that is unusual or not socially acceptable.
    a) schizophrenia
    b) borderline personality disorder
    c) gender identity disorder
    d) paraphilia

    Rationale:

    _____

    _____

27.   Which cause of a sexually transmitted disease is hardest to treat?
        a)   bacterial
        b)   fungal
        c)   viral
        d)   all are equally difficult to treat

Rationale:

_____

_____

28.   AIDS can be passed from one individual to the next through each of the following ways EXCEPT
        a)   vaginal fluid
        b)   semen
        c)   tears
        d)   blood

Rationale:

_____

_____

29.   AIDS is caused by
        a)   a bacterial infection
        b)   an airborne fungus
        c)   a viral infection
        d)   the cause is not yet known

Rationale:

_____

_____

30.   Shallice has had several sexual partners in the past year. What is the **BEST** advice you could give her about how she can lower the odds of contracting a sexually transmitted disease in the future?
        a)   use condoms
        b)   learn the symptoms of the common sexually transmitted diseases
        c)   practice abstinence
        d)   all of these are good advice

Rationale:

_____

_____

SAMPLE EXAM ANSWERS & RATIONALES

1. b The female growth spurt starts at around age 10-12, while the male growth spurt starts at around age 12-14.
2. d The prostate gland is a primary sex characteristic in males.
3. c Gender typing is the process of learning proper masculine and feminine behaviors. Gender roles are the actual expectations each culture has for males and females and gender identity is the individual's sense of being male or female.
4. a Sex refers to physical differences and gender refers to psychological and social differences.
5. a Several research studies have supported the idea that collectivist cultures, such as those found in many Asian and South American countries, display more traditional views on gender roles.
6. a Nature refers to inherited, biological differences, while nurture refers to the effects of the environment.
7. d Social learning theory emphasizes observational learning, which is reinforced through attention and positive remarks.
8. d A gender schema is a mental concept of what it means to be a "boy" or a "girl."
9. c Benevolent sexism is the result of thinking that all men or all women have some particular desirable trait, simply because of their sex.
10. b Stereotypes can be both negative and positive.
11. a Androgyny describes people who exhibit both male and female typical behaviors.
12. b Several studies have shown that males listen primarily with the left hemisphere of the brain, while females tend to show activity in both hemispheres while they are engaged in listening activities.
13. c Men are more likely to use a "report" style of communication, which involves switching topics frequently, while women are more likely to use a "relate" style of communication.
14. b The best estimate to date is that about 1 in every 1,500 children in the U.S. are born with ambiguous sexual genitalia.
15. d Masters and Johnson labeled the fourth and final phase of the human sexual response as the "resolution" phase.
16. d Masters and Johnson used direct observations in the laboratory to investigate the physical human sexual response.
17. c Masters and Johnson were able to convince the newspapers to keep the research secret for almost 12 years.
18. d Alfred Kinsey traveled across the country with a team of researchers and conducted one on one personal interviews to gather data on sexual behavior.
19. a According to Kinsey, 11% of husbands reported anal sex with their wives.
20. a The Januses did the first major study on common sexual behaviors after Kinsey.
21. a If homosexuality were definitively found to be due to genetic or hormonal influences, then it would no longer be seen as a matter of simple choice, society could no longer demand that homosexuals change their behavior, and discrimination against homosexuals would be equivalent to racism.
22. d Sexual orientation refers to a person's attraction for members of a particular sex.
23. a LeVay's study reported differences in the size of the hypothalamus. The hypothalamus controls the pituitary gland, which regulates many important hormonal levels in the body.
24. b Jaime does get fully aroused, which means he does have erections and is therefore not suffering from an erectile disorder. Instead, he has a condition known as male

orgasmic disorder.

25. b   Frotteurism is the practice of obtaining sexual arousal or gratification by rubbing against an unwilling person.

26. d   Paraphilias are a group of disorders in which sexual arousal is achieved through unusual or socially unacceptable methods.

27. c   Bacterial infections can normally be treated with antibiotics but viral diseases are very hard to treat.

28. c   Currently, there are no documented cases of a person becoming infected with AIDS through exposure to tears.

29. c   AIDS is caused by the human immunodeficiency virus, more commonly referred to as HIV.

30. c   Although all of the options are good advice, the best way to prevent STDs is through abstinence.

APPLY IT

This section will help you use the concepts you are learning in this class to improve your study skills.

This chapter discussed several research studies that used the survey technique to find out about trends and attitudes among the general population. Having that information is useful for individuals to see where they fall in comparison to others and to gain knowledge about overall behaviors. One behavior that might be helpful to you as a student would be to get some general knowledge of the study strategies and behaviors your fellow students engage in. This challenge will help you understand the usefulness of the survey approach in quickly gathering information about overall trends and attitudes.

Come up with at least three pieces of information you would like to know about your fellow students' study habits, and write three questions that you will use to gather the answers. The questions can be open-ended or restricted. An open-ended question might be something like, "How do you study for an exam?" A restricted question would be something like "Do you study with the TV on or off?" or "How many hours do you study per week?"

Write your three questions here.

1. _____

2. _____

3. _____

Now, go and collect your data. Get to class a little early one day or stay behind afterwards and ask the other students to answer your questions. You can record the answers to the questions here.

Question 1	Question 2	Question 3

Now look over your data and try to summarize it. For example, if you asked how many hours students studied per week, what is the average for all the students? Or, what is the most commonly used method for studying? Or, what percentage of the students study with the TV on versus off? Write your summaries here:

Question 1: _____

_____

Question 2: _____

_____

Question 3: _____

_____

Now look over your summaries. What can you say about the students' study habits in your class in general? How do your own study habits compare to those of the other students? Did you get any ideas or suggestions to improve your own study habits from learning about others? If so, be sure to list those.

Overall Conclusions:

_____

_____

_____

CHAPTER 11 LEARNING OBJECTIVES

11.1 What is stress?

11.2 What are the cognitive factors in stress?

11.3 What kinds of experiences can cause stress?

11.4 What are some sources of stress in everyday life?

11.5 Why do people commit suicide?

11.6 What are the different types of conflicts people must face?

11.7 What is happening in the body when a person experiences stress?

11.8 What is the relationship between stress and the immune system?

11.9 What is the relationship between stress and personality?

11.10 What is the relationship between stress and social factors?

11.11 What are two ways that people can deal with stress?

11.12 What are the psychological defense mechanisms?

11.13 How can meditation help relieve stress?

11.14 What are the cultural influences on stress?

11.15 Can being religious help people cope with stress?

11.16 What are some ways to promote wellness in one's life?

SUMMARY

Stress is the physical, emotional, cognitive, and behavioral responses to events that are perceived as threatening or challenging. When a person's stress response is unpleasant or undesirable, it is called **distress,** and when it is an optimal amount that helps a person function it is called **eustress**. The events that cause stress are called **stressors** and can be either internal or external events. The **cognitive-mediational theory** of emotions proposed by Richard Lazarus states that the way people think about and appraise a stressor is a major factor in their stress response. The first step in appraising a stressor is called **primary appraisal** and involves estimating the severity of the stressor and classifying it as a threat, challenge, or loss. In **secondary appraisal**, an individual determines what resources they have available for dealing with the threat or loss.

Stressors can include external events such as catastrophes, major life changes, and hassles, along with internal experiences such as pressure, uncontrollability, and frustration. A **catastrophe** is an unpredictable event that happens on a large scale such as a tornado or flood. Catastrophes are one cause of an anxiety disorder known as **post-traumatic stress disorder** (PTSD), in which an individual has recurring nightmares, sleep disturbances and flashbacks of the event that persist for more than one months time. A number of researchers have suggested that any **major life change**, such as moving, getting married, or getting a new job, would result in stress. Holmes and Rahe developed the **Social Readjustment Rating Scale** (SRRS) to measure the amount of change and thus stress in a person's life. Researchers have found a moderate correlation between scores on the SRRS and physical health. Alternate forms of the SRRS have been designed for specific populations, such as the College Undergraduate Stress Scale for college students. A majority of the stressors that people have to deal with are the little daily annoyances, or **hassles**. Surveys that measure the number of hassles an individual has to deal with are actually a better predictor of short term illnesses than the SRRS. The internal experience of **pressure** is also considered a stressor. Pressure is the psychological experience produced by demands and expectations from outside sources. Two additional internal causes of stress are **uncontrollability**, or a lack of control in a situation, and **frustration**, or being blocked from achieving a desired goal. Typical reactions to frustration include persistence and **aggression**, or actions meant to harm or destroy. **Displaced aggression** occurs when a person takes out their frustrations on less threatening, more available targets.

An extreme reaction to stress is **suicide**, or intentionally taking one's own life. Statistics from the Office of the Surgeon General indicate that rates of suicide increase with age, men are more likely to complete a suicide than women, and the most common method of committing suicide is the use of a gun. Symptoms of suicide include feelings of hopelessness, lack of energy, irritability, and sleep disturbances, among others. Some of the ways to help someone who is contemplating suicide is to listen with true concern, stay with them, and call the police for emergency intervention.

Conflict is another source of stress and occurs when a person feels pulled toward two or more goals but can only achieve one of them. In 1935 a researcher by the name of Lewin defined three types of conflict. **Approach-approach conflict** occurs when an individual is attempting to choose between two desirable goals. **Avoidance-avoidance conflict** occurs when someone must choose between two undesirable goals. **Approach-avoidance conflict** describes a single goal that has both desirable and undesirable outcomes. An individual faced with two or more options in which each option has positive and negative aspects is dealing with a **multiple approach-avoidance conflict**.

Psychologist **Hans Selye** was a pioneer in the study of the physical consequences of exposure to stressors. He proposed that the body goes through a sequence of three stages he called the **general adaptation syndrome**. The initial stage is called **alarm** and represents the immediate reaction to stress mediated by our **sympathetic nervous system**. Typical alarm reactions include increased heart rate and blood pressure and release of sugar into the blood stream. As the stress continues, the body enters the **resistance** stage, in which the sympathetic nervous system works overtime to give the body more energy. When the body's resources have been exhausted, the **parasympathetic nervous system** is activated and the body enters the **exhaustion** stage. Selye believed that it was the prolonged release of stress hormones during the resistance stage that led to the breakdown on the body's **immune system** and the onset of the stress-related physical conditions. Researchers in the field of **psychoneuroimmunology** who study the effects of psychological factors on the immune system have found that stress actually causes an increase in the activity of the immune system. High levels of stress have been linked to increased risk of heart disease. Also, stress has been shown to decrease the amount of **natural killer cells** which are the cells responsible for fighting cancerous growths.

Personality has also been linked to stress related health risks. In 1974, Meyer Freidman and Ray Rosenman published a book describing the **Type A** and **Type B** personalities and their link to heart disease. Based on studies of their own patients, Freidman and Rosenman proposed that individuals with Type A personality (a person who is competitive, ambitious, workaholic, with a constant sense of pressure) were more likely to develop heart disease than someone with a Type B personality. Several studies found that the specific trait of hostility in Type A individuals was the best predictor of future heart problems. A third personality type called **Type C** (in which a person holds in their emotions and tends to be pleasant) was later identified and is currently being investigated as to its possible link with cancer rates. Finally, research has suggested a fourth personality type, the **hardy personality**, which is associated with decreased illness due to stress. An individual with a hardy personality shows commitment, displays a sense of control, and sees stresses as challenges to be met and answered. In addition to personality, links have been found between an individual's attitude and their physical reactions to stress. Specifically, **pessimists** have been found to have significantly more stress related health problems than **optimists**. One way to become an optimist is to recognize any negative thoughts you are having and to work to get rid of them.

Social factors also play a key role in the amount of stress an individual experiences. Living in **poverty** and **job stress** are two major sources of stress. A serious consequence of job stress is **burnout**, or negative changes in thoughts, emotions and behaviors as a result of prolonged stress or frustration. **Acculturative stress** describes the stress an individual experiences when having to adapt to a new culture. The method of adaptation can affect the stress level. Some of the methods of adapting to a new culture include integration, assimilation, separation, and marginalization. The effects of negative social factors on health can be minimized by a strong **social support system**, or network of family and friends who can offer help when a person is in need.

Coping strategies are actions that people take to master, tolerate, reduce, or minimize the effects of stressors and include both behavioral and psychological strategies. **Problem-focused coping** occurs when a person tries to eliminate the source of a stress or reduce its impact by taking some action, while **emotion-focused coping** involves changing the way you feel or react to a stressor. One example of emotion-focused coping involves the use of **psychological defense mechanisms**, such as denial, repression, rationalization and projection, among others. Both **concentrative and receptive meditation** have also been found to be effective coping strategies. Culture and religion have also been found to affect an individual's level of stress as well as the strategies used to cope with that stress.

A few ways that individuals can promote wellness in their own lives include exercising, getting involved with others, getting enough sleep, eating healthy foods, reserving time for fun, managing your time, and even breathing deeply.

KEY POINTS

- Define stress and identify the role cognitive factors play in an individual's experience of stress.
- Discuss the causes of stress.
- Describe the physical reaction to stress and the relation of this reaction to personality and social factors.
- Explain the methods used to cope with stress.

KEY CONCEPTS

stress	The term used to describe the physical, emotional, cognitive, and behavioral responses to events that are appraised threatening or challenging.
distress	The effect of unpleasant and undesirable stressors.
eustress	The effect of positive events, or the optimal amount of stress that people need to promote health and well-being.
stressors	Events that cause a stress reaction.
cognitive-mediational theory	Theory of emotions proposed by Richard Lazarus that states the way people think about and appraise a stressor is a major factor in their stress response.
primary appraisal	The first step in assessing stress involves estimating the severity of a stressor and classifying it as either a threat or a challenge.
secondary appraisal	The second step in assessing a threat involves estimating the resources available to the person for coping with the stressor.
catastrophe	An unpredictable, large-scale event that creates a tremendous need to adapt and adjust as well as overwhelming feelings of threat.
post-traumatic stress disorder (PTSD)	A disorder resulting from exposure to a major stressor, with symptoms of anxiety, nightmares, poor sleep, reliving the event, and concentration problems, lasting for more than one month.
major life change	Any event that requires an individual to adapt to a new set of circumstances, such as moving, getting a job, or getting married.
Social Readjustment Rating	Assessment that measures the amount of stress in a person's life

Scale (SRRS)	Over a one-year period resulting from major life events.
hassles	The daily annoyances of everyday life.
pressure	The psychological experience produced by urgent demands or expectations for a person's behavior that come from an outside source.
uncontrollability	The psychological experience caused by having no ability to change your particular set of circumstances.
frustration	The psychological experience produced by the blocking of a desired goal or fulfillment of a perceived need.
aggression	Actions meant to harm or destroy.
displaced aggression	Taking out one's frustrations on some less threatening or more available target; a form of displacement.
suicide	Intentionally taking one's own life.
conflict	Psychological experience of being pulled toward or drawn to two or more desires or goals, only one of which may be attained.
approach-approach conflict	Conflict occurring when a person must choose between two desirable goals.
avoidance-avoidance conflict	Conflict occurring when a person must choose between two undesirable goals.
approach-avoidance conflict	Conflict occurring when a person must choose or not choose a goal that has both positive and negative aspects.
multiple approach-avoidance conflict	Conflict in which the person must decide between more than two goals, with each goal possessing both positive and negative aspects.
Hans Selye	1907-1982. Canadian endocrinologist who studied the physical response to stress and developed the concept of the general adaptation syndrome.
general adaptation syndrome (GAS)	The three stages of the body's physiological reaction to stress, including alarm, resistance, and exhaustion.
sympathetic nervous system	The division of the autonomic nervous system responsible for mobilizing the body's energy and resources during times of stress and arousal.
alarm	The first stage of Hans Selye's General Adaptation Syndrome during which the sympathetic nervous system prepares the body for action.

resistance	The second stage of Hans Selye's General Adaptation Syndrome during which the sympathetic nervous system recruits resources to maintain an elevated level of activity and energy.
parasympathetic nervous system	The division of the autonomic nervous system responsible for regulating the routine functions of the body, such as heartbeat, digestion, and sleeping.
exhaustion	The third stage of Hans Selye's General Adaptation Syndrome during which the parasympathetic nervous system takes over and the body experiences any number of physical illnesses.
immune system	The system of cells, organs, and chemicals of the body that respond to attacks from diseases, infections, and injuries.
psychoneuroimmunology	The study of the effects of psychological factors such as stress, emotions, thoughts, and behavior on the immune system.
natural killer cells	Immune system cell responsible for the suppression of viruses and destroying tumor cells.
Type A	Person who is ambitious, time-conscious, extremely hard-working, and tends to have high levels of hostility and anger as well as being easily annoyed.
Type B	Person who is relaxed and laid-back, less driven and competitive than Type A and slow to anger.
Type C	Pleasant but repressed person who tends to internalize their anger and anxiety and who find expressing emotions difficult.
hardy personality	A person who seems to thrive on stress but lacks the anger and hostility of the Type A personality.
pessimists	People who expect negative outcomes.
optimists	People who expect positive outcomes.
poverty	The state of having little or no money and few or no material possessions.
job stress	Damaging physical and emotional responses that can occur when the requirements of a job do not match the capabilities, resources, or needs of the worker.
burnout	Negative changes in thoughts, emotions, and behavior as a result of prolonged stress or frustration.
acculturative stress	Stress resulting from the need to change and adapt one's ways to the majority culture.

social support system	The network of family, friends, neighbors, coworkers, and others who can offer support, comfort, or aid to a person in need.
coping strategies	Actions that people can take to master, tolerate, reduce, or minimize the effects of stressors.
problem-focused coping	Coping strategies that try to eliminate the source of a stress or reduce its impact through direct actions.
emotion-focused coping	Coping strategies that change the impact of a stressor by changing the emotional reaction to the stressor.
psychological defense mechanisms	Unconscious distortions of a person's perception of reality that reduce stress and anxiety.
concentrative meditation	Form of meditation in which a person focuses the mind on some repetitive or unchanging stimulus so that the mind can be cleared of disturbing thoughts and the body can experience relaxation.
receptive meditation	Form of meditation in which a person attempts to become aware of everything in immediate conscious experience, or an expansion of consciousness.

HINTS

1. One important component to understanding this chapter is to understand the difference between a stressor and stress. The stressor is the event that causes us to experience stress. The event can be external, such as getting stuck in traffic, or internal, such as worrying about an upcoming exam. Our reaction to the event is called stress and can be physical, emotional, mental, and behavioral. Try coming up with some examples of events that could be considered stressors along with possible stress reactions. The first example has already been completed for you.

Stressor   Stress Reaction

Having to take an exam   *increased heart rate*

_____   _____

_____   _____

_____   _____

2. Many students find the different types of conflicts confusing. Look over the Key Concepts area to refresh yourself on the meaning of each type of conflict and then try to come up with an example from your own life that illustrates each type of conflict. List your examples in the space below.

Approach-Approach Conflict: _____

_____

Approach-Avoidance Conflict: _____

_____

Avoidance-Avoidance Conflict: _____

_____

Multiple Approach-Avoidance Conflict: _____

_____

3. The textbook discusses a number of different types of coping strategies. Many of the coping strategies can be divided into those that deal with taking action (problem-focused) and those that deal with changing your own emotions or thoughts (emotion-focused). Think about the types of coping strategies you use. Do you focus on emotions or actions? For each of the situations listed below, come up with one example of a problem-focused strategy and one example of an emotion-focused strategy and list them in the space below. The first one has already been completed for you.

Stressor	Problem-Focused Strategy	Emotion-Focused Strategy
You get in an accident and wreck your car.	*You take photographs of the accident and call the insurance company daily to check on the status of your claim.*	*Whenever you start to feel discouraged about not having a car, you think to yourself how lucky you are that you did not get injured in the*

You get in a fight with your boyfriend or girlfriend.		
You are late for work.		
You get a low score on an important exam.		
You have a "bad hair day."		

SAMPLE EXAM

For the following multiple choice questions, select the answer you feel best answers the question and explain the rationale or reason for your selection in the space provided.

Objective 11.1

1. The term used to describe the physical, emotional, cognitive and behavioral <u>responses</u> to events that are viewed as threatening or challenging is _____.
    a)   stress
    b)   stressors
    c)   uncontrollability
    d)   pressures

    Rationale:
    A is the correct choice. The response itself is called stress and the event that causes the response is called a stressor.

2. The response an individual might have to an unpleasant stressor, such as losing their job, would be called
    a)   eustress
    b)   distress
    c)   stress appraisal
    d)   negative stressors

    Rationale:
    B is the correct answer. The response to negative stressors is called distress and the response to positive stressors or the optimal level of stressors is referred to as eustress.

Objective 11.2

3. After we have decided that a certain event is a stressor, we must decide how we will deal with it and what resources are available for coping with the stressor. This process is called_____.
    a)   primary appraisal
    b)   secondary appraisal
    c)   stress-related decision
    d)   hassle-related decision

    Rationale:

    _____

    _____

4. According to the cognitive-mediational theory of emotions proposed by Richard Lazarus, which of the following would be the best way to reduce the stress of losing a job?
   a) try to ignore the problem
   b) try to understand all the negative implications of the loss
   c) list all the resources that you do not have available and will need to acquire
   d) view the loss as a challenge and opportunity to explore a new career

Rationale:

_____

_____

Objective 13

5. Which of the following is an example of a stressor that would be classified as a hassle, according to Richard Lazarus?
   a) getting married
   b) locking your keys in the car
   c) losing your house due to a flood
   d) the death of a family member

Rationale:

_____

_____

6. The Social Readjustment Rating Scale (SRRS) measures stress related to _____.
   a) positive and negative life events
   b) only negative life events
   c) only positive life events
   d) internal stressors

Rationale:

_____

_____

Objective 11.4

7. Gloria is a tax account who is very busy from January to April 15, which is the tax return filing deadline. She feels that she must work very long hours during this time to meet the April 15 deadline for all of her clients. Gloria is experiencing_____.
   a) anxiety
   b) pressure
   c) overload
   d) cognitive dissonance

Rationale:

_____

_____

8. A parent who has an unpleasant confrontation with his boss and then comes home and yells at the dog would be displaying
    a) uncontrollability
    b) pressure
    c) displaced aggression
    d) catastrophe

Rationale:

_____

_____

Objective 11.5

9. Which of the following is a fact about suicide, according to the Office of the Surgeon General of the United States?
    a) Men attempt suicide more than women.
    b) More people die from suicide than from homicide.
    c) The most common method of committing suicide is with pills.
    d) Suicide is a spontaneous act.

Rationale:

_____

_____

10. People who talk about suicide just want attention and won't really follow through with it.

    a) True
    b) False

Rationale:

_____

_____

Objective 11.6

11. Which of the following is an example of an avoidance-avoidance conflict?
    a) A person who enjoys the ocean has to choose between retiring in the Bahamas or in Tahiti.
    b) A student has to decide whether to turn in an unfinished paper and receive a failing grade or hand it in late and lose many points.
    c) Someone wanting to eat some cake but not wanting the calories.
    d) A person who loves chocolate must choose between a chocolate cake or chocolate ice cream.

Rationale:

_____

_____

12. Trying to decide on taking a trip to the Bahamas, which would be very enjoyable but would severely limit the amount of money you would have to spend on other items, is an example of a
   a) approach-approach conflict
   b) approach-avoidance conflict
   c) avoidance-avoidance conflict
   d) multiple approach-avoidance conflict

Rationale:

_____

_____

Objective 11.7

13. The general adaptation syndrome proposed by Hans Selye describes how we respond to stress with regard to our
   a) psychological reactions
   b) emotional reactions
   c) social reactions
   d) physical reactions

Rationale:

_____

_____

14. According to Selye, some people may develop illnesses such as high blood pressure or weakened immune system during the _____ stage of the GAS.
   a) alarm
   b) collapse
   c) exhaustion
   d) resistance

Rationale:

_____

_____

Objective 11.8

15. Stress has been shown to be related to _____.
   a) increased resistance to environmental threats
   b) decreased efficiency of the reticular formation
   c) increased galvanic skin response
   d) decreased efficiency of the body's immune system

Rationale:

_____

_____

16.   When stress levels are elevated, the amount of natural killer cells in the body tends to
        a) increase
        b) decrease
        c) stay the same
        d) there is not enough data to say at this point

        Rationale:

        _____

        _____

Objective 11.9

17.   The Type A behavior pattern is a significant predictor of _____.
        a) mental illness
        b) coronary heart disease
        c) cancer
        d) respiratory illnesses

        Rationale:

        _____

        _____

18.   Someone who would be classified as having a Type C personality would be likely to
        a) openly express their anger at someone
        b) try to always look on the bright side of a situation
        c) display a great deal of hostility when things don't go their way
        d) internalize their anger so that no one can see their true emotion

        Rationale:

        _____

        _____

Objective 11.10

19.   _____is the term used to describe the excessive anger exhibited by drivers in response to ordinary traffic frustration.
        a) Road rage
        b) Conflict
        c) Driving stress
        d) Frustration

        Rationale:

        _____

        _____

20. Pepe moved from Argentina to France. He chose not to learn to speak and write French, continues to maintain his old culture's styles of dress and customs, and lives in a neighborhood where only people from Argentina live. Pepe has used which method of entering the majority culture?
   a) integration
   b) assimilation
   c) separation
   d) marginalization

   Rationale:

   _____

   _____

21. Which method of acculturation would tend to lead to the greatest degree of stress?
   a) integration
   b) assimilation
   c) separation
   d) marginalization

   Rationale:

   _____

   _____

Objective 11.11

22. Vanna's mother is ill, and she is feeling overwhelmed and sad. To cope with this stress of her mother's illness, Vanna has been writing her feelings down in a journal. Vanna is using

   _____.
   a) problem-focused coping
   b) emotion-focused coping
   c) distraction
   d) reappraisal

   Rationale:

   _____

   _____

Objective 11.12

23. A student who is failing but does not study because she refuses to believe that the instructor will really assign her an "F" at the end of the term is using the psychological defense mechanism of

   _____.
   a) repression
   b) denial
   c) projection
   d) rationalization

   Rationale:

   _____

   _____

24. Which of the following examples best illustrates the psychological defense mechanism of projection?
   a) Suzan has a serious gambling addiction but refuses to admit it.
   b) John thinks to himself that he should watch one more hour of TV. before starting to study for his big exam so he will feel nice and relaxed while he is studying.
   c) Saul plans an elaborate "Congratulations party" for the co-worker who received the promotion that Saul was desperately hoping to receive.
   d) Alex feels guilty about not doing his part to keep the house clean, but when his wife comes home, he accuses her of being a slob and not helping out enough around the house.

Rationale:

_____

_____

Objective 11.13

25. Research shows that _____ lowers blood pressure in adolescents and adults.
   a) sensory deprivation
   b) concentrative meditation
   c) sublimation
   d) implosive meditation

Rationale:

_____

_____

Objective 11.14

26. You are a psychologist working with a new client, an immigrant from China, who is experiencing adjustment problems due to stress. Which of the following are you first going to consider when assessing your client's ability to cope?
   a) use of meditative strategies
   b) use of psychological defense mechanisms
   c) ability to use biofeedback equipment
   d) cultural background

Rationale:

_____

_____

27.   Several studies have found a positive correlation between level of religious commitment and life expectancies.
        a)   true
        b)   false

        Rationale:

        _____

        _____

28.   Eating a healthy breakfast _____.
        a)   has been shown to increase the risk of obesity.
        b)   has been shown to decrease the ability to concentrate.
        c)   has been shown to decrease the risk of obesity.
        d)   has been shown to increase the need for a morning nap.

        Rationale:

        _____

        _____

SAMPLE EXAM ANSWERS & RATIONALES

1. a   The response itself is called stress and the event that causes the response is called a stressor.

2. b   The response to negative stressors is called distress and the response to positive stressors or the optimal level of stressors is referred to as eustress.

3. b   Secondary appraisal involves deciding how to deal with a stressor and estimating the resources available for coping with it, while primary appraisal is the first step we take when facing a potential threat; it involves estimating its severity and determining whether it is a challenge or a threat.

4. d   The cognitive-mediational theory of emotions suggests that the way we think about or interpret a stressor is the biggest factor in determining our response.

5. b   Lazarus focused on the minor daily annoyances, such as losing your car keys, as a significant source of stress in our lives.

6. a   The SRRS assumes that any change (either positive or negative) will serve as a stressor in an individual's life.

7. b   Although anxiety may be a result of pressure, Gloria is experiencing pressure as a result of her need to work longer hours to meet a deadline.

8. c   Displaced aggression often occurs when the person or object that a person is really angry at is not an accessible target.

9. b   Although women attempt suicide more frequently than men, men actually complete suicide at a higher rate than women.

10. b   This is a common myth about suicide.

11. b   Avoidance-avoidance conflicts involve having to choose between two undesirable outcomes.

12. b   Approach-avoidance conflicts focus on one decision that has both positive and negative aspects to it.

13. d   The general adaptation syndrome describes our body's physical reactions to stress.

14. d   During the resistance stage, the body uses its resources to fight off the stressor. It is not until the next stage, exhaustion, that bodily resources are so depleted that stress-related diseases can develop.

15. d   Stress is related to decreased efficiency of the immune system.

16. b   Natural Killer cells are important cells in the body that server to limit the growth of cancerous cells. During times of stress, the level of natural killer cells tends to decrease, thus increasing the chances of tumor growth.

17. b   The original development of the idea of Type A personality was to describe and predict the individuals who were at high risk for heart disease.

18. d   Type C personalities tend to internalize their emotions.

19. a   Driving stress may be what a person with road rage feels, but road rage is the term for excessive anger exhibited by some drivers over ordinary traffic frustration.

20. c   Separation occurs when a person tries to maintain his or her original cultural identity. Assimilation occurs when a person completely gives up his or her old cultural identity and completely adopts the majority culture's ways.

21. d   Marginalization occurs when an individual is not a part of his original culture, nor is he a part of the new culture. This method of acculturation has been found to create the greatest amount of acculturative stress.

22. b   Vanna is coping with her stress by focusing on and thinking about her emotions.

23. b   Denial is the refusal to recognize or acknowledge a threatening situation. Rationalization is the defense mechanism that involves finding excuses for a behavior that is unacceptable.

24. d Alex is projecting his feelings of guilt onto his wife.
25. b Concentrative mediation places one in a state of relaxation and lowers blood pressure. There is no such term as implosive mediation.
26. d Psychological defense mechanisms are significant but would not be as important in your initial assessment as would cultural background, especially since the client is from a country with a very different culture.
27. a Although these studies do not prove a cause and effect relationship, they have shown a correlation between religious affiliation and longevity.
28. c Eating a healthy breakfast has been shown to decrease the risk of obesity.

APPLY IT

This section will help you use the concepts you are learning in this class to improve your study skills.

This study focused on stress and health. Several suggestions were mentioned in the chapter on how to reduce your own stress levels. High stress levels not only deteriorate your health but also can make it hard to achieve the goals you want in school. One of the most effective ways to reduce stress is through exercise. This application will give you a chance to test that out and see if exercise can work for you!

Some benefits of exercising include:
- Exercising strengthens your heart and lungs.
- People who exercise report having more energy.
- People who exercise are better able to concentrate.
- People who exercise get better sleep.

What do we mean when we say "exercise"?
- The National Heart, Lung, and Blood Institute recommends increased and sustained cardiovascular elevation for fifteen to thirty minutes three to four times a week.

Okay, so let's get an exercise plan.

Step 1: Begin slowly. If you are not used to exercising, start out with ten to fifteen minutes twice a week and build up from there.

Here's a weekly schedule. Fill in the next two weeks with the amount and type of exercise that you will be doing.

Monday	Tuesday	Wednesday	Thursday	Friday	Saturday	Sunday

Step 2: Keep track of your progress. Over the next two weeks, place a check mark or star or heart next to the day after you have accomplished your work out goal for that day.

Step 3: Assessment. After the two week period is over, think about how you feel. Did you have more energy? Sleep better? Feel less "stressed out" during the day? Write your comments here.

_____

_____

Step 4: Establish a regular routine for working out.
Now that you have completed your first two weeks of exercising, come up with an exercise plan that will work for you over the next several months. You can fill in your goals and keep track of your progress in the space below. There is enough space for a four-month plan. Have fun!

Monday	Tuesday	Wednesday	Thursday	Friday	Saturday	Sunday

12.1	What is personality?
12.2	How did Freud view the divisions of the conscious mind?
12.3	According to Freud, what are the three parts of the personality and how do they interact?
12.4	What are the stages of personality development in Freudian theory?
12.5	How did Jung, Adler, Horney, and Erikson modify Freud's theory?
12.6	How does modern psychoanalytic theory differ from that of Freud?
12.7	How do behaviorists explain personality?
12.8	How do humanists explain personality?
12.9	What was Roger's view of the self?
12.10	What is the trait perspective?
12.11	How do trait theorists today view personality?
12.12	What part do biology and heredity play in personality?
12.13	What were Hofstede's dimensions of cultural personality?
12.14	What are the advantages and disadvantages of using interviews to measure personality?
12.15	How are projective tests used to explore personality, and what are the problems with projective tests?
12.16	How can behavioral assessments be used in assessing personality?
12.17	What are the different kinds of personality inventories used to measure personality?
12.18	How good are the personality tests people can take on the Internet?

SUMMARY

Personality is the unique way in which each individual thinks, acts, and feels throughout life. Two components of personality are **character**, which refers to value judgments made about a person's morals or ethical behavior, and **temperament**, or the enduring characteristics a person is born with. There are at least four different perspectives regarding personality, including the psychoanalytic, behaviorist, humanistic and trait perspectives.

The **psychoanalytic perspective** originated with the theories of **Sigmund Freud** and focuses on the role of unconscious thoughts and desires in the development of personality. It is important to take into account the sexually repressed **Victorian era** in which Freud grew up when evaluating his theory or personality. Freud believed the mind was divided into three parts: the **conscious** mind contains all of the things a person is aware of at any given moment, the **preconscious** mind contains all the memories and facts that can be recalled with only minimal effort, and the **unconscious** mind is the part of our mind that remains hidden at all times. Freud believed the unconscious mind was the most important factor in directing behavior and personality. In addition to the divisions of the mind, Freud also believed that personality could be divided into three components: the id, ego, and superego. The **id** resides completely in the unconscious mind and represents the most primitive part of the personality containing all of the basic biological drives, such as huger, thirst, and sex. According to Freud, the id operates on **the pleasure principle,** which attempts to seek immediate gratification of needs with no regard for consequences. Freud referred to the psychological tension created by a person's unconscious desires as the **libido**. The **ego** represents the mostly conscious and rational aspect of personality, which operates on the **reality principle**, attempting to satisfy the desires of the id in a way that will minimize negative consequences. The **superego** is the last part of the personality to develop, according to Freud's theory, and represents the moral center of personality. The superego is divided into the **ego ideal**, or the set of standards an individual learns as a child, and the **conscience**, or the part of personality that makes a person feel good or bad depending on whether they do the right or wrong thing. According to Freud, the id demands immediate satisfaction, while the superego places restrictions on which behaviors are morally acceptable and the ego is left in the middle to come up with a compromise.

For Freud, the three components of personality develop in a series of **psychosexual stages** with each stage focused on a different **erogenous zone**, or area of the body that produces pleasurable feelings. Unresolved conflicts at any of the stages of development can lead to **fixation** and subsequent emotional or psychological problems as an adult. The first stage is called the **oral stage** because the erogenous zone is the mouth. Fixation can occur in this stage if the baby is weaned from the mother's breast too soon or too late. The second stage in Freud's theory is the **anal stage,** during which time the anus serves as the erogenous zone and the conflict centers around toilet training. Fixation resulting from openly rebelling against the toilet training results in adults who are characteristically messy and are referred to as **anal expulsive personalities**. Fixation resulting from overly strict toilet training results in adults who are stingy, stubborn and excessively neat and would be referred to as **anal retentive personalities**. The third stage is the **phallic stage** and focuses on the child's own genitals. During this stage, the child develops a sexual attraction to the opposite-sex parent, becomes jealous of the same-sex parent, develops anxiety due to the attraction and the jealousy, and resolves the anxiety through sexual repression and identification with the same sex parent. Freud referred to this process in boys as the **Oedipus complex,** and Jung suggested that it be termed the **Electra complex** in girls. The process of **identification** leads to the development of the superego, so that by the end of Freud's third stage of development, all three components of personality are in place. The fourth stage, known as the **latency stage,** consists of repressed sexual feelings during which children focus on intellectual, physical and social development but not sexual development. The final stage occurs around the start of puberty, when sexual feelings can no longer be repressed and is referred to as the **genital stage**.

A number of psychologists, referred to as **neo-Freudians**, agreed with parts of Freud's theories but not all aspects. **Carl Gustav Jung** believed that there were two parts of the unconscious: a **personal unconscious** similar to the unconscious described by Freud, and a **collective unconscious,** which contained universal human memories that Jung called **archetypes**. **Alfred Adler** felt that the motivating factor of behavior was not the pleasure-seeking drive of the libido suggested by Freud, but rather the seeking of superiority through defense mechanisms such as compensation. **Karen Horney** disagreed with Freud's emphasis on sexuality and thought personalities were shaped more by a child's sense of basic anxiety, which, if unattended to, could lead to the development of neurotic personalities. **Erik Erikson** developed eight psychosocial stages of development, which focused on role of social relationships in the development of personality.

Although Freud's theory has had a significant impact on the culture of modern western societies, his theory has been criticized on the scientific grounds due to the fact that it was not developed based on scientific experiments but rather on Freud's personal observations in his private practice as a psychiatrist, and that Freud's personal observations were limited to a specific group of wealthy Austrian women living in the sexually repressed Victorian era.

According to the behaviorists' perspective, personality consists of a set of learned responses or **habits**. A variation on the behaviorist perspective is that of the **social cognitive learning theorists**, who emphasize the role of conditioning along with an individual's thought processes in the development of personality. **Albert Bandura** suggested that the environment, behavior, and personal/cognitive factors all act together to determine an individual's actions in a process Bandura referred to as **reciprocal determinism**. An important component of the cognitive factors is the person's sense of **self-efficacy**, or perception of how effective a behavior will be in a particular context.

The **humanistic perspective** of personality focuses more on qualities that are considered uniquely human, such as free will and subjective emotions. **Carl Rogers** proposed that humans are always striving to fulfill their innate capacities in a process known as the **self-actualizing tendency**. In order for an individual to work towards self actualization, they need to be exposed to a certain level of **unconditional positive regard** from the significant others in their lives. Rogers felt that **conditional positive regard** would restrict a person's ability to become a fully functioning person. Rogers believed an individual's image of oneself, or **self-concept**, also played a role in becoming fully functional. According to Rogers, self-concept could be divided into a **real self** and an **ideal self**. If the real self and ideal self concept were too far apart, anxiety and neurotic behavior would result.

Trait theories of personality have focused on describing personality and predicting behavior based on that description. A **trait** is a consistent, enduring way of thinking, feeling or behaving. Gordon Allport identified approximately 200 traits in the English language that he felt were "wired" into each person's nervous system. Raymond Cattell narrowed the number of traits down further by dividing traits into **surface traits**, such as the 200 traits described by Allport, and **source traits**, or the more basic traits that underlie the surface traits and form the core of personality. Cattell believed that there were 16 basic, or source, traits. Later researchers narrowed this list to five source traits and developed the personality model known as the **five-factor model**, or the big five. The five trait dimensions are **openness**, **conscientiousness**, **extraversion**, **agreeableness**, and **neuroticism**. Critics of the five factor model have argued that the situation plays a more significant role in determining an individual's behavior than is suggested by trait theory.

The field of **behavioral genetics** studies the role of inherited traits in personality. Twin studies have found that identical twins are more similar to fraternal twins or unrelated people in certain aspects of personality, such as intelligence, leadership, tendency to follow rules, assertiveness and aggressiveness. Adoption studies have supported some of these findings and have suggested a biological basis for shyness and aggressiveness.

In an attempt to describe "national personalities," Geert Hofstede conducted a cross-cultural study for IBM, which resulted in a description of each country along four basic dimensions. The dimensions Hofstede observed were individualism/collectivism, power distance, masculinity/femininity, and uncertainty avoidance.

Methods for assessing personality have been developed based on specific theories of personality as well as the various goals of classification, self insight, and the diagnosis of psychological disorders. An **interview** is a method of personality assessment in which the professional asks questions of the client and allows the client to answer in either a structure or unstructured manner. Interviews are limited by the fact that clients can lie, intentionally or unintentionally, and the interviewers can bring their own biases into their interpretations. Psychoanalysts have developed **projective tests** in an attempt to assess a person's unconscious conflicts or desires by having them *projected* onto an ambiguous visual stimulus. Two of the most commonly used projective tests are the **Rorschach inkblot test** and the **Thematic Apperception Test or TAT**. Projective tests have been found to have very low reliability and validity. A behaviorist would be more likely to measure personality by directly observing an individual's actions. In **direct observation**, the psychologist would observe an individual in a specific setting and record their behaviors through the use of a **rating scale** or a **frequency count**. Critics of this approach have pointed out the possibility for both the observer effect and observer bias. Trait theorists would be most likely to use a **personality inventory**, which consists of a questionnaire that has a standard list of questions that require specific answers such as "yes" or "no." Examples of commonly used personality inventories include Cattell's 16 PF, the Neuroticism/Extraversion/Openness Personality Inventory (NEO-PI), the Myers-Briggs Type Indicator (MPTI) and the Minnesota Multiphasic Personality Inventory, Version II (MMPI-2). The advantage of personality inventories is that they are scored objectively, which eliminates the possibility of observer bias, and they have been found to have very high reliability and validity scores. However, the inventories are still based on self-report.

A large number of personality tests are accessible over the Internet; however, the results of such tests should be interpreted with an appropriate level of skepticism.

KEY POINTS

- Define personality.
- Discuss Freud's psychoanalytical perspective on personality, including the division of the mind, components of personality, stages of development, and modifications of the Neo-Freudians.
- Describe the behaviorists' perspective on personality, with an emphasis on Albert Bandura's social cognitive model.
- Introduce the humanistic perspective of personality, including Carl Rogers' view of the self and concept of unconditional positive regard.
- Discuss trait theory with regard to the description of personality.

- Explain what is known about the role of biology and heredity in personality development.
- Describe major methods of personality assessment, including interviews, projective tests, behavioral assessment and personality inventories.

KEY CONCEPTS

personality	The unique and relatively stable ways in which people think, feel, and behave.
character	Value judgments of a person's moral and ethical behavior.
temperament	The enduring characteristics with which each person is born.
psychoanalytic perspective	Freud's term for both the theory of personality and the therapy based upon it.
Sigmund Freud	1856-1939. Founder of the psychoanalytic school of thought, which focuses on the role of the unconscious on behavior.
Victorian era	Years between 1837 and 1901 when Queen Victoria ruled England. Culturally, this was a very repressive time period.
conscious mind	Level of the mind that is aware of immediate surroundings and perceptions.
preconscious mind	Level of the mind in which information is available, but not currently conscious.
unconscious mind	Level of the mind in which thoughts, feelings, memories, and other information is kept that is not easily or voluntarily brought into consciousness.
id	Part of the personality present at birth and completely unconscious.
the pleasure principle	Principle by which the id functions; the immediate satisfaction of needs without regard for the consequences.
libido	The instinctual energy that may come into conflict with the demands of a society's standards for behavior.
ego	Part of the personality that develops out of a need to deal with reality; mostly conscious, rational and logical.
reality principle	Principle by which the ego functions; the satisfaction of the demands of the id only when negative consequences will not result.
superego	Part of the personality that acts as a moral center.

255

ego ideal	Part of the superego that contains the standards for moral behavior.
conscience	A person's sense of morality or sense of right and wrong.
psychosexual stages	Five stages of personality development proposed by Freud and tied to the sexual development of the child.
erogenous zone	An area of the body especially sensitive to sexual stimulation.
fixation	Disorder in which the person does not fully resolve the conflict in a particular psychosexual stage, resulting in personality traits and behavior associated with that earlier stage.
oral stage	First stage occurring in the first year of life, in which the mouth is the erogenous zone and weaning is the primary conflict.
anal stage	Second stage occurring from about one to three years of age, in which the anus is the erogenous zone and toilet training is the source of conflict.
anal expulsive personalities	A person fixated in the anal stage who is messy, destructive, and hostile.
anal retentive personalities	A person fixated in the anal stage who is neat, fussy, stingy, and stubborn.
phallic stage	Third stage occurring from about three to six years of age, in which the child discovers sexual feelings.
Oedipus complex	Situation occurring in the phallic stage in which a child develops a sexual attraction to the opposite sex parent and jealousy of the same sex parent.
Electra complex	The female equivalent of the Oedipus complex in which the female child experiences an erotic desire for her father and simultaneous fear of her mother.
identification	Defense mechanism in which a person tries to become like someone else to deal with anxiety.
latency stage	Fourth stage occurring during the school years, in which the sexual feelings of the child are repressed while the child develops in other ways.
genital stage	Fifth stage of Freud's theory, occurring from adolescence on; sexual energy is focuses on sexual activity with others.
Neo-Freudians	Followers of Freud who developed their own, competing theories of psychoanalysis.

Carl Jung	1875-1961. Swiss psychiatrist who was a pioneer in the psychoanalytic school of thought and was heavily influenced by Freud.
personal unconscious	Jung's name for the unconscious mind as described by Freud.
collective unconscious	Jung's name for the memories shared by all members of the human species.
archetypes	Jung's collective, universal human memories.
Alfred Adler	1870-1937. One of the Neo-Freudians who continued the pursuit of the unconscious. Adler focused on the need for power as a driving force in an individual's life.
Karen Horney	1885-1952. A Neo-Freudian who focused on more equal representation of men and women in psychoanalytic theory and also the role of basic anxiety as a motivating force.
Erik Erikson	1902-1994. Developmental psychologist who believed that personality developed through a series of psychosocial crises.
habits	In behaviorism, sets of well-learned responses that have become automatic.
social cognitive learning theorists	Theorists who emphasize the importance of both the influences of other people's behavior and of a person's own expectancies on learning.
Albert Bandura	Born 1925. Bandura developed the theory of reciprocal determinism to explain personality development.
reciprocal determinism	Bandura's explanation of how the factors of environment, personal characteristics, and behavior can interact to determine future behavior.
self-efficacy	Individual's perception of how effective a behavior will be in any particular circumstance.
humanistic perspective	The "third force" in psychology that focuses on those aspects of personality that make people uniquely human, such as subjective feelings and freedom of choice.
Carl Rogers	1902-1987. Humanist psychologist who focused on the role of the self-concept and positive regard on personality development.
self-actualizing tendency	The striving to fulfill one's innate capacities and capabilities.
unconditional positive regard	Positive regard that is given without conditions or strings attached.
conditional positive regard	Positive regard that is given only when the person is doing what

the providers of positive regard wish.

self-concept	The image of oneself that develops from interactions with important, significant people in one's life.
real self	One's perception of actual characteristics, traits, and abilities.
ideal self	One's perception of who one should be or would like to be.
trait theories	Theories that endeavor to describe the characteristics that make up human personality in an effort to predict future behavior.
trait	A consistent, enduring way of thinking, feeling, or behaving.
surface traits	Aspects of personality that can easily be seen by other people in the outward actions of a person.
source traits	The more basic traits that underlie the surface traits, forming the core of personality.
five-factor model	Also known as the Big Five; model of personality traits that describes five basic trait dimensions.
openness	One of the five factors; willingness to try new things and be open to new experiences.
conscientiousness	The care a person gives to organization and thoughtfulness of others; dependability.
extraversion	Dimension of personality referring to one's need to be with other people.
agreeableness	The emotional style of a person, which may range from easy-going, friendly and likeable, to grumpy, crabby, and unpleasant.
neuroticism	Degree of emotional instability or stability.
behavioral genetics	Field of study devoted to discovering the genetic bases for personality characteristics.
interview	Method of personality assessment in which the professional asks questions of the client and allows the client to answer, either in a structured or unstructured fashion.
projective tests	Personality assessments that present ambiguous visual stimuli to the client and ask the client to respond with whatever comes to mind.
Rorschach inkblot test	Projective test that uses 10 inkblots as the ambiguous stimuli.
Thematic Apperception Test	Projective test that uses twenty pictures of people in ambiguous

(TAT)	situations as the visual stimuli.
direct observation	Assessment in which the professional observes the client engaged in ordinary, day-to-day behavior in either a clinical or natural setting.
rating scale	Assessment in which a numerical value is assigned to specific behavior that is listed in the scale.
frequency count	Assessment in which the frequency of a particular behavior is counted.
personality inventory	Paper and pencil or computerized test that consists of statements that require a specific, standardized response from the person taking the test.

HINTS

1. Students often confuse the levels of awareness suggested by Freud with his three components of personality. The next two exercises should help you keep them straight. To start with, let's think about your levels of awareness. For each of the levels listed, list at least three examples of the information or memories that would be found there. Start with the conscious level.

My <u>conscious</u> level of awareness might contain the following:

_____

_____

My <u>preconscious</u> level of awareness might contain the following:

_____

_____

My <u>unconscious</u> level of awareness might contain the following:

_____

_____

259

2. Now think about the three components that Freud suggested make up an individual's personality; the id, the ego, and the superego. For each of the situations listed below, describe how a person's id, ego, and superego might respond. The first example has been completed for you. Notice how the ego always represents the compromise between the two extremes.

Situation	Id	Ego	Superego
Someone cuts you off in traffic as you are driving down the freeway.	*Speed up, cut in front of them and then slow way down.*	*I'll yell a few words at the driver from my own car but remain driving at the speed limit.*	*It's wrong to break the law and we don't know what is happening with that person; maybe they have an emergency.*
Your alarm goes off for school but you still feel completely exhausted.			
Your co-worker asks you to work her shift for you so that she can have the night off to go to a concert.			
Your roommate just made a batch of chocolate chip cookies and said he is going to take most of them to work with him tomorrow.			
You just finished watching two hours of TV and still have a lot of homework to do for tomorrow, but you don't feel like doing it.			

3. For each of the personality assessment techniques listed below, come up with an example of who would be most likely to use it and what goal they would be trying to achieve.

Assessment	Who would use it	Goal
Rorschach	*psychoanalytic psychologist*	*Observe a projection of the person's unconscious concerns.*
MMPI-II		
TAT		
MPTI		
Frequency count		

SAMPLE EXAM
For the following multiple choice questions, select the answer you feel best answers the question and explain the rationale or reason for your selection in the space provided.

Objective 11.1

1.   The unique way in which each individual thinks, acts, and feels throughout life is called _____ .
          a)   character
          b)   personality
          c)   temperament
          d)   the unconscious

     Rationale:
     B is the correct choice, temperament and character are both part of personality. Character refers to value judgments made about a person's morals, and temperament refers to the enduring characteristics that a person is born with.

2.   One limitation of the trait perspective compared to the other perspectives is there is not much:
          a)   description
          b)   research
          c)   material
          d)   explanation

     Rationale:
     A is the correct answer. Trait theories are descriptive and deal with the actual end result of personality.

Objective 12.2

3.   Many have compared Freud's idea of the mind to an iceberg. If that were the case and you were standing on the deck of a ship in Alaska, what part of the mind would you see above the water?
          a)   ego
          b)   superego
          c)   id
          d)   preconscious

     Rationale:

     _____

     _____

4.   Information that cannot be recalled even when a person makes a determined effort to retrieve it would be said by Freud to be residing in the
          a)   conscious
          b)   preconscious
          c)   unconscious
          d)   superego

     Rationale:

     _____

     _____

5. In Sigmund Freud's theory, the _____ operates according to the pleasure principle.
    a) id
    b) ego
    c) thanatos
    d) superego

    Rationale:

    _____

    _____

6. According to Freud, the last component of an individual's personality to develop is the
    a) ego
    b) superego
    c) id
    d) libido

    Rationale:

    _____

    _____

7. What is Freud's term for the executive of the personality that has a realistic plan for obtaining gratification of an individual's desires?
    a) id
    b) ego
    c) superego
    d) preconscious

    Rationale:

    _____

    _____

Objective 12.4

8. Freud called the developmental stage in which the Oedipus Complex occurs the
    a) oral stage
    b) anal stage
    c) phallic stage
    d) latency stage

    Rationale:

    _____

    _____

9. Freud believed that the personality characteristics of overeating, gum chewing, being too dependent or overly optimistic developed due to fixation during the
    a) oral stage
    b) anal stage
    c) phallic stage
    d) latency stage

Rationale:

_____

_____

Objective 12.5

10. Which neo-Freudian viewed personality disturbances as resulting from the feelings of inferiority all people share?
    a) Carl Jung
    b) Alfred Adler
    c) Carl Rogers
    d) Karen Horney

Rationale:

_____

_____

11. Karen Horney disagreed with Freud about the unconscious force that influences behavior. She believed the force was not sexual desire, but rather
    a) feelings of inferiority
    b) basic anxiety
    c) the collective unconscious
    d) self regard

Rationale:

_____

_____

Objective 12.6

12. Which of the following is NOT a current criticism of Freud's psychoanalytic theory?
    a) the significant impact it has had on culture
    b) the lack of empirical evidence
    c) observations based on Freud's personal clients
    d) role of women in Freud's theory

Rationale:

_____

_____

13. Albert Bandura's notion that people are affected by their environment but can also influence that environment is known as
    a) self-efficacy.
    b) locus of control.
    c) phenomenology.
    d) reciprocal determinism.

    Rationale:

    _____

    _____

14. A baseball player's son is quite talented; he has received lots of awards over the years. When he gets up to bat he expects to get a hit, and when he is in the field he expects to make every catch. According to Bandura, what characteristic does this young man seem to have?
    a) self-regard
    b) self-centeredness
    c) self-efficacy
    d) self-actualization

    Rationale:

    _____

    _____

Objective 12.8

15. _____ theory is called the third force in personality theory.
    a) Psychoanalytic
    b) Behaviorist
    c) Cognitive
    d) Humanistic

    Rationale:

    _____

    _____

16.   In Carl Rogers's theory, our perception of our abilities, behaviors, and characteristics is known as

_____.
- a) personality
- b) self-regard
- c) self-esteem
- d) self-concept

Rationale:

_____

_____

17.   Which of the following represents an example of unconditional positive regard?
- a) A mother telling her son that she hopes he becomes an engineer like his father.
- b) A father telling his daughter that he will really only be proud of her if she gets all A's like she did last semester.
- c) An owner pays attention to her dog only when he is well-behaved.
- d) A parent telling his son he loves him even though he just wrecked the family car.

Rationale:

_____

_____

Objective 12.10

18.   What did Gordon Allport think about traits?
- a) He thought they were like stages.
- b) He thought they were wired into the nervous system.
- c) He thought they were learned.
- d) He thought they were the result of cognitive modeling.

Rationale:

_____

_____

19.   How many source traits did Raymond Cattell discover through the process of factor analysis?
- a) 5
- b) 16
- c) 200
- d) 4,500

Rationale:

_____

_____

20. What psychoanalytic theorist most notably influenced the big five theory of personality?
   a) Freud
   b) Jung
   c) Erikson
   d) Horney

Rationale:

_____

_____

Objective 12.11

21. The fact that an outgoing extravert might be very talkative at a party but very quiet at a funeral is an example of:
   a) trait-situation interaction
   b) cross-cultural similarities
   c) source trait reliability
   d) neuroticism

Rationale:

_____

_____

Objective 12.12

22. What major conclusion about personality traits emerged from the Minnesota twin study?
   a) Identical twins are more similar than any other type of sibling.
   b) Siblings reared apart were much more similar than identical twins
   c) Fraternal twins reared together were much more similar than identical twins..
   d) Personality scores for twins were not related in either case

Rationale:

_____

_____

Objective 12.13

23. Which of the following countries would not be considered a collectivist country, according to the studies by Geert Hofstede?
   a) Japan
   b) United States
   c) Mexico
   d) Korea

Rationale:

_____

_____

24. Which of the following terms describes the cultural personality of the United States, according to Hofstede's dimensions of cultural personality?
   a) individualistic
   b) high in power distance
   c) low in individualism
   d) high in uncertainty avoidance

   Rationale:

   _____

   _____

Objective 12.14

25. Which of the following is NOT considered a disadvantage in the use of interviews for personality assessment?
   a) halo effect
   b) answers are based on self-report
   c) bias of the interviewer
   d) natural flow of the questions

   Rationale:

   _____

   _____

Objective 12.15

26. Which personality test relies on the interpretation of inkblots to understand personality?
   a) MMPI
   b) 16PF
   c) TAT
   d) Rorschach

   Rationale:

   _____

   _____

27. Which of the following is NOT a criticism of projective tests?
   a) they are a projection of the person's unconscious concern
   b) they are low in reliability
   c) their interpretation is more an art than a science
   d) they lack validity

   Rationale:

   _____

   _____

28.　Direct observation is most like:
        a)　case studies
        b)　naturalistic observation
        c)　experimental methods
        d)　correlation

Rationale:

_____

_____

Objective 12.17

29.　The most commonly used personality inventory is the:
        a)　MMPI-2
        b)　MBTI
        c)　TAT
        d)　CPI

Rationale:

_____

_____

30.　Which of the following is an advantage to using personality inventories?
        a)　observer bias
        b)　they are standardized
        c)　biases of interpretation
        d)　they rely on self-report

Rationale:

_____

_____

Objective 12.18

31.　A personality test that results in statements that are so general that they could apply to just about anyone is a good example of
        a)　high validity
        b)　the Barnum Effect
        c)　observer bias
        d)　inter-rater reliability

Rationale:

_____

_____

SAMPLE EXAM ANSWERS & RATIONALES

1.   b   Temperament and character are both part of personality. Character refers to value judgments made about a person's morals, and temperament refers to the enduring characteristics that a person is born with.

2.   a   Trait theories are descriptive and deal with the actual end result of personality.

3.   a   The ego is the part of the mind that is conscious and in view.

4.   c   Freud thought that information sometimes seeped out of the unconscious through our dreams or slips of the tongue, but for the most part, the information was not readily available to our conscious awareness.

5.   a   According to Freud, the id represents the most basic part of the personality and operates on the pleasure principle. The ego operates on the reality principle.

6.   b   Freud's theory states that the superego develops during the phallic stage or when an individual is around 5-6 years old.

7.   b   The ego is in charge of reality and decisions, and the superego is there for moral judgments, but the ego makes the decisions.

8.   c   The Oedipus Complex leads to the development of the superego and occurs during the phallic stage.

9.   a   Freud described those personality traits as resulting from fixation during the oral stage of development.

10.   b   Adler viewed personality disturbances as resulting from the feelings of inferiority all people share. Jung focused on archetypes in the collective unconscious.

11.   b   Horney believed that basic anxiety was the unconscious driving force behind many of the behaviors people exhibited.

12.   a   The impact of Freud's theory on culture is not considered a criticism.

13.   d   Self-efficacy refers to one's perception of how effective a behavior will be in any particular circumstance, whereas reciprocal determinism is Bandura's notion that people are affected by their environment but can also influence that environment.

14.   c   Self-efficacy refers to one's perception of how effective a behavior will be in any particular circumstance. Self-actualization has to do with self-fulfillment and reaching one's full potential.

15.   d   Humanistic theory is called the third force in personality theory; the first two are psychoanalytic theory and behaviorist theory.

16.   d   Self-esteem has more to do with one's sense of worth.

17.   d   Rogers defined unconditional positive regard as being love, affection and respect with no strings attached.

18.   b   Allport thought traits were not learned, but rather were wired into the nervous system.

19.   b   Cattell proposed that there were 16 source traits of personality.

20.   b   Freud's views are not involved in trait theory, but Jung's theory mentioned extroversion, which is one of the big five traits.

21.   a   The trait-situation interaction focuses on the interaction of source traits with the specific environment or situation that a person is in.

22.   a   Identical twins, who share the same genes, are more similar in personality than are any other type of siblings.

23.   b   The Hofstede study found that the United States could be described as more of an individualistic culture.

24.   a   Americans expect power to be well distributed rather than held by an elite few; democracies are typically low in power distance.

25.   d   The natural flow of the interview process is one of the advantages of this method.

26.   d   The Rorschach is a projective test that relies on the use of ink blot interpretation.

27.   a   The reason a psychologist would use a projective test is in order to get a "projection" of that individual's unconscious concerns.

28.   b   In naturalistic observation, one directly observes behavior in a relatively natural environment. Doing case studies involves gathering information through interviews rather than through actually observing the individual in a natural setting.

29.   a   The MMPI-2 is used more than any other inventory.

30.   b   The fact that personality inventories are standardized represents one of the greatest advantages to using this assessment technique.

31.   b   The Barnum Effect can also be seen in daily horoscope readings.

APPLY IT

This section will help you use the concepts you are learning in this class to improve your study skills.

In Chapter 11, you learned about a number of different assessment tools used to identify an individual's personality. In this application, you will use a self-assessment strategy to try to get a better idea of your own "learning personality." One key ingredient to improve your study habits is to understand yourself and how you learn. The following assessment will help you examine your own learning strategies.

Just like personality, learning styles can be described a lot of different ways. One description divides learning styles into three types: visual, auditory, and kinesthetic. Answer the following questions to try to determine which learning style you use most frequently. For a more in-depth series of question, visit the following website: http://www.ulc.arizona.edu/learn_styl_ass.html.

Visual

A visual learning style focuses on retaining and recalling information visually. This includes activities such as reading text, viewing a diagram or outline notes on a PowerPoint, or writing out notes to study. Some questions you might ask yourself include:

> *Do you learn better by reading something than by listening to someone talk about it?*
> *Do your notes contain a lot of pictures, diagrams, charts, etc?*
> *When you are remembering items, do you picture the words or images in your head?*

Auditory

An auditory learning style relies on receiving and recalling information verbally. Activities used with this style include listening to a lecture or discussion, limited note taking, and studying verbally rather than writing information down. Some questions to ask yourself include:

> *Would you prefer to listen to someone than learn the material by reading it in a book?*
> *Do you find that you take very few notes in class and would rather just listen to and absorb the material presented in lecture?*
> *Do you study by reciting the information out loud to yourself or a study partner?*

Kinesthetic

The kinesthetic learning style focuses on actually doing something during the learning process.

> *When you are studying, do you find that you get up and move around a lot?*
> *Do you use your hands and gesture when explaining information to someone?*
> *Do you find yourself tapping your pencil or foot in class often?*
> *Do you prefer classes that use a lot of hands-on activities to teach the material?*

Which learning style do you feel you use most often? _____

For another assessment, visit the following website: http://www.ulc.arizona.edu/learn_styl_ass.html

After you are done, write your scores here:

Visual: _____

Auditory: _____

Kinesthetic: _____

Do these scores agree with your self-assessment above?_____

One mistake students often make after assessing their learning style is to feel limited to that learning style alone. Instead, it would be a much better strategy to use this information to strengthen and experiment with the learning styles you use less often. The following are some study suggestions for each of the learning styles. Try to expand your approach to a new style and see how that affects your learning.

Tips to improve the learning styles you use less often.

Visual
- Try taking extensive notes in class.
- Use pictures, diagrams, tables and charts in your notes.
- Study by reading through the textbook and reviewing your lecture notes.
- Try to redraw a key image or figure from memory.
- Read your notes (silently) again and again.
- Rewrite the key concepts of a chapter into your own words.
- Practice taking a sample exam with multiple choice questions.
- Arrange your notes into an outline form.

Auditory
- Attend classes, discussions and tutorials.
- Discuss topics and explain new ideas to someone else.
- Use a tape recorder in class instead of taking notes.
- After class, write down any hands-on activities or concrete examples, stories or jokes.
- Describe the overheads, pictures and other visuals to somebody who was not there.
- Put your summarized notes onto tapes and listen to them.
- Read your summarized notes aloud.
- Imagine talking with the professor as you answer the questions on the exam.
- Practice writing answers to old exam questions.
- Speak your answers aloud or inside your head.

Kinesthetic
- Use case studies and applications to help with principles and abstract concepts.
- Talk about your notes with another person.
- Use pictures and photographs that illustrate an idea.
- Recall the experiments, field trip, and in-class activities.
- Write practice answers and paragraphs.
- Role play the exam situation in your own room.

CHAPTER 13 LEARNING OBJECTIVES

13.1   What makes people want to conform to the actions of others?

13.2   What is groupthink?

13.3   What are four common ways to gain the compliance of another?

13.4   What makes people obey the instructions or orders of others?

13.5   How does the presence of other people affect a person's performance on a task?

13.6   What are the three components of an attitude, and how are attitudes formed?

13.7   How can attitudes be changed?

13.8   What happens when a person's attitudes don't match the person's actions?

13.9   What are social categorization and implicit personality theories?

13.10 How do people try to explain the actions of others?

13.11 What is the difference between prejudice and discrimination?

13.12 Why are people prejudiced, and how can prejudice be stopped?

13.13 What factors cause people to be attracted to each other?

13.14 What is love, and what are the different forms that love can take?

13.15 How is aggressive behavior determined by biology and learning?

13.16 What is altruism?

13.17 What is the bystander effect?

13.18 What did Latané and Darley discover about the presence of others and helping behavior?

13.19 What decisions have to be made before a person will help someone else?

13.20 Why do people join cults?

SUMMARY

Social psychology is the scientific study of how a person's behavior, thoughts, and feelings are influenced by the real, imagined, or implied presence of others. Social psychology can be broadly divided into the areas of social influence, social cognition, and social interaction.

Social influence is the process in which the presence of other people influences the behavior, feelings, and thoughts of an individual. **Conformity** involves changing one's own behavior to more closely match the actions of others. In 1951 **Solomon Asch** conducted a classic experiment on conformity by having subjects judge the length of a line after hearing a group of confederates all report an obviously incorrect answer. Asch found that the subjects conformed to the group answer around one-third of the time, and conformity increased as the group size increased, up to a group of four confederates. In a later study, Asch found that conformity greatly decreased when at least one confederate gave the right answer. **Groupthink** is a type of conformity in which people feel it is more important to maintain the group's cohesiveness than to consider the facts more realistically. Social influence can also be used to describe the phenomenon of **compliance,** which occurs when people change their behavior as a result of another person or groups asking or directing them to change. There are a number of techniques people use to obtain the compliance of others, including **foot-in-the-door technique** in which compliance with a small request is followed by a larger request, **door-in-the-face technique,** which is the process of making a large request that is almost always refused and then a smaller request that is often agreed to. The door-in-the-face technique relies on the **norm of reciprocity,** which states that if someone does something for you, you should do something in return. Two additional compliance techniques include the **lowball technique,** in which the cost of the commitment is increased *after* the commitment is already made, and the **that's-not-all technique** in which an offer is made, and before the individual can make a decision, something "extra" is added to the offer. In compliance, an individual changes their behavior because someone asks them; in **obedience**, an individual changes their behavior because an authority figure gives them an order. **Stanley Milgram** conducted one of the most famous experiments on obedience in which he measured the number of volts a participant would administer to another participant simply because the experimenter instructed him or her to do so. In reality, no electrical shocks were being administered. Milgram found that about two-thirds of the subjects (65%) administered electrical shocks up to a lethal level of 450 volts when instructed to do so. The presence of others can also influence how well an individual performs a specific task in a process called **social facilitation**. If the task is easy, the presence of others seems to improve performance, but if the task is difficult, the presence of others actually has a negative impact on performance. **Social loafing** describes the tendency for people to put less effort into a simple task when working in a group as opposed to working alone.

Social cognition deals with the ways people think about other people and includes attitudes, impressions, and attributions. An **attitude** can be defined as a tendency to respond positively or negatively toward a certain idea, person, object, or situation. Attitudes are composed of the way people feel, act and think. The affective component describes the feelings associated with attitudes, the behavior component describes the actions, and the cognitive component describes the thoughts. Attitudes have been found to be only weak predictors of actual behavior. Attitude formation is a learning process that occurs through direct contact, direct instruction, interaction with others, and vicarious (or observational) learning. **Persuasion** is the process by which one person tries to change the belief, opinion, position, or course of action of another person through argument, pleading, or explanation. Factors that influence the effectiveness of persuasion include the source, the message and the target audience. The **elaboration likelihood model** examines how likely it is that an individual will elaborate on a persuasive message and what the outcome of the elaboration will most likely be. When people attend to the content of the message, the model describes it as **central-route processing,** and when people pay attention to information outside of the message content itself, it is referred to as **peripheral-route processing**. **Cognitive dissonance** is a sense of discomfort that occurs when a person's behavior does not match up with that person's attitudes. When a person experiences cognitive dissonance, they typically change the conflicting behavior to match the attitude, change the attitude to match their behavior, or form new cognitions to justify their behavior. **Impression formation** involves the process of forming the first knowledge that a person has concerning another person, in other words, the "first impression." One component of impression formation involves **social categorization,** which is the assignment of a person to a category based on characteristics the person has in common with other people with whom one has had experience in the past. Social categorization can often result in **stereotypes**, or a set of characteristics that people believe are shared by all members of a particular social category. People often form their own categories based on **implicit personality theories**, or sets of assumptions about how different types of people, personality traits, and actions are all related. Most implicit personality theories are formed in childhood. The final aspect of social cognition discussed in the textbook is **attribution**, or the process of explaining one's own behavior and the behavior of others. **Fritz Heider** originally described attribution theory and divided attributions into two categories; **situational attributes** were explanations that relied on external causes and **dispositional attributes** assume behavior is the result of some internal factor. The **fundamental attribution error** is the most well-known bias of attribution and is the tendency for some people to almost exclusively use dispositional attributes to explain other people's behavior.

Social interaction, or the relationship between people, is the third main area of study in the field of social psychology. When a person holds an unsupported and often negative attitude about the members of a particular group, it is called a **prejudice,** and when a person acts differently towards a person based on that attitude it is called **discrimination**. The **realistic conflict** theory states that prejudice and discrimination will be increased between groups that are in conflict. Jane Elliot used her second-grade classroom to demonstrate the power of prejudice and discrimination by dividing her class based on the color of the students' eyes and observing the effects. Conflicts between groups tend to increase as pressures and stresses increase. Often the prejudice exists because of the need for a **scapegoat**, a person or group who serve as the target for the frustrations and negative emotions of the group with the prejudiced attitude. Several theories have been proposed to explain the formation and persistence of prejudice. **Social identity theory** suggests that the three processes of **social categorization**, **social identification**, and **social comparison** are involved in the formation of prejudice attitudes. **Stereotype vulnerability** refers to the effect that a person's knowledge of someone else's stereotyped opinion can have on that person's behavior. The resulting feeling of anxiety is referred to as **stereotype threat**. The negative impact of stereotype threat on an individual's performance can actually cause a person to act in the way that the stereotype predicts, thus confirming an outside observer's prejudicial attitude. **Self-fulfilling prophecy** occurs when a person acts according to their existing beliefs and their actions make it more likely that their beliefs are confirmed. The best defense against prejudice is becoming informed about people who are different from you. **Equal status contact**, in which all individuals involved have the same amount of power in the situation, is crucial for reducing prejudice. Educators have attempted to create situations of equal status in the classroom by setting up **jigsaw classrooms**, in which students have to work together to reach a specific goal. Another area of social interaction discussed in your textbook is **interpersonal attraction**, or liking or having the desire for a relationship with someone else. Several factors are involved in the attraction of one person to another, including physical attractiveness, proximity (or how close a person is to you physically), similarity, and **reciprocity of liking** (or liking someone who likes you). Robert Sternberg proposed a theory of love that contains three components: intimacy, passion, and commitment. He felt that seven types of love could be described by various combinations of these three components. A very different type of social interaction is that of violence. **Aggression** is defined as any behavior intended to hurt or destroy another person. Social psychologists have examined the role of both biology and the environment on aggression. Twin studies have shown a higher correlation of aggression levels in identical twins than in fraternal twins. Certain areas of the brain have been found to control aggressive responses and testosterone levels are related to aggression. However, a large portion of human aggression is influenced by learning. Several studies have suggested that taking on a particular **social role** can lead to an increase in aggressive behavior. A number of studies have also supported the link between exposure to violent media and aggression. The final area of social interaction discussed in your textbook is **prosocial behavior**, or socially desirable behavior that benefits others rather than bringing them harm. **Altruism** is a specific type of prosocial behavior in which an individual helps someone else with no expectation of reward. Sometimes the presence of other people can decrease the likelihood of prosocial behavior, as can be seen in the **bystander effect** and **diffusion of responsibility**. Bibb Latane and John Darley conducted a series of experiments that found that participants were less likely to respond to an emergency situation where other people were present than when they were alone. Some of the decisions an individual must make when deciding whether to offer help or not include noticing the situation, defining the situation as an emergency, taking responsibility, planning a course of action, and taking action.

Technically, a **cult** refers to any group of people with a particular religious or philosophical set of beliefs and identities; however, most people associate the term cult with a group of people whose beliefs are so different from the mainstream that they are view with suspicion.

KEY POINTS

- Describe the role social influence plays on conformity, compliance, obedience and social facilitation.
- Discuss the issues of social cognition, including the formation and development of attitudes, impressions, and attributions.
- Introduce concepts of social interaction, including prejudice, discrimination, interpersonal attraction, aggression and altruisim.

KEY CONCEPTS

social psychology	The scientific study of how a person's thoughts, feelings, and behavior are influenced by the real, imagined, or implied presence of others.
social influence	The process through which the real or implied presence of others can directly or indirectly influence the thoughts, feelings, and

behavior of an individual.

conformity	Changing one's own behavior to match that of other people.
Solomon Asch	1907-1996. Pioneer in the field of social psychologist; well-known for his experiments on conformity.
groupthink	The kind of thinking that occurs when people place more importance on maintaining group cohesiveness than on assessing the facts of the problem with which the group is concerned.
compliance	Changing one's behavior as a result of other people directing or asking for the change.
foot-in-the-door technique	Asking for a small commitment and, after gaining compliance, asking for a bigger commitment.
door-in-the-face technique	Asking for a large commitment and being refused, and then asking for a smaller commitment.
norm of reciprocity	Assumption that if someone does something for a person, that person should do something for the other in return.
lowball technique	Getting a commitment from a person and then raising the cost of that commitment.
that's-not-all technique	The persuader makes an offer and then adds something extra to make the offer look better before the target person can make a decision.
obedience	Changing one's behavior at the command of an authority figure.
Stanley Milgram	1933-1984. Social psychologist at Yale University famous for his experiments on obedience to authority.
social facilitation	The tendency for the presence of other people to have a positive impact on the performance of an easy task.
social loafing	The tendency for people to put less effort into a simple task when working with others on that task.
social cognition	Deals with the ways people think about other people and includes attitudes, impressions, and attributions.
attitude	A tendency to respond positively or negatively toward a certain person, object, idea, or situation.
persuasion	The process by which one person tries to change the belief, opinion, position, or course of action of another person through argument, pleading, or explanation.

elaboration likelihood model	Model of persuasion stating that people will either elaborate on the persuasive message or fail to elaborate on it, and that the future actions of those who do elaborate are more predictable than those who do not.
central-route processing	Type of information processing that involves attending to the content of the message itself.
peripheral-route processing	Type of information processing that involves attending to factors not involved in the message, such as the appearance of the source of the message, the length of the message, and other non-content factors.
cognitive dissonance	Sense of discomfort or distress that occurs when a person's behavior does not correspond to that person's attitudes.
impression formation	The forming of the first knowledge that a person has concerning another person.
stereotypes	A set of characteristics that people believe are shared by all members of a particular social category.
implicit personality theories	Sets of assumptions about how different types of people, personality traits, and actions are related to each other.
attribution	The process of explaining one's own behavior and the behavior of others.
Fritz Heider	1896-1988. German social psychologist known for the development of attribution theory.
situational attributes	Cause of behavior attributed to external factors, such as delays, the action of others, or some other aspect of the situation.
dispositional attributes	Cause of behavior attributed to internal factors such as personality or character.
fundamental attribution error	The tendency to overestimate the influence of internal factors in determining behavior while underestimating situational factors.
social interaction	The relationship between people.
prejudice	Negative attitude held by a person about the members of a particular social group.
discrimination	Treating people differently because of prejudice toward the social group to which they belong.
realistic conflict theory	Theory stating that prejudice and discrimination will be increased between groups that are in conflict.

278

scapegoat	An individual who is punished for the mistakes of someone else.
social identity theory	Theory in which the formation of a person's identity within a particular social group is explained by social categorization, social identity, and social comparison.
social categorization	The assignment of a newly-met person to a category based on characteristics the new person has in common with other people with whom the person doing the assigning has had experience in the past.
social identification	The part of the self-concept including one's view of self as a member of a particular social category.
social comparison	The comparison of oneself to others in ways that raise one's self-esteem.
stereotype vulnerability	The effect that people's awareness of the stereotypes associated with their social group affects their behavior.
stereotype threat	The feeling of anxiety that a person's knowledge of someone else's stereotyped opinion can have on that person's behavior.
self-fulfilling prophecy	The tendency of one's expectations to affect one's behavior in such a way as to make the expectation more likely to occur.
equal status contact	Contact between groups in which the groups have equal status, with neither group having power over the other.
jigsaw classroom	Educational technique in which each individual is given only part of the information needed to solve a problem, causing the separate individuals to be forced to work together to find the solution.
interpersonal attraction	Liking or having the desire for a relationship with another person.
reciprocity of liking	Tendency of people to like other people who like them in return.
aggression	Behavior intended to hurt or destroy another person.
social role	The pattern of behavior that is expected of a person who is in a particular social position.
prosocial behavior	Socially desirable behavior that benefits others.
altruism	Prosocial behavior that is done with no expectation of reward and may involve the risk of harm to oneself.
bystander effect	Referring to the effect that the presence of other people has on the decision to help or not help, with help becoming less likely as the number of bystanders increases.

diffusion of responsibility

Occurs when a person fails to take responsibility for actions or for inaction because of the presence of other people who are seen to share the responsibility.

cult

Any group of people with a particular religious or philosophical set of beliefs and identity.

1. The text introduces four common methods that are used to gain the compliance of another person. In order to better understand the differences between these methods, assume that you are trying to get your friend to come pick you up and then go shopping at the mall with you. In the space below, come up with an example of how you might get your friend to comply with your request using each of the techniques listed.

Technique	Example
Foot-in-the-door	
Door-in-the-face	
Low ball	
That's-not-all	

2. The ABC's of attitudes. Attitudes can be broken down into three different components. For each of the following attitudes listed below, give an example of each of the components a person who holds this attitude might experience.

Attitude	Affective	Behavioral	Cognitive
a positive attitude towards traveling to foreign countries			
a negative attitude towards brussel sprouts			

3. Social psychology contains a large number of well-known researchers along with the famous studies they carried out. It is important to be able to remember which researcher goes with which study. Next to the researchers listed below, briefly describe the experiment they carried out along with the topic they studied. In the final column, come up with a mnemonic to help you remember the information.

Researcher	Experiment	Topic	Mnemonic
Solomon Asch			
Stanley Milgram			
Jane Elliot			
Latané and Darley			
Philip Zimbardo			

SAMPLE EXAM

For the following multiple choice questions, select the answer you feel best answers the question and explain the rationale or reason for your selection in the space provided.

Objective 13.1

1.   Vince has always believed children deserve the best prenatal care available. During a class discussion, he hears the first of several speakers express very negative attitudes toward spending tax money on prenatal care for the poor. When it is his turn to speak, he voices an opinion more in keeping with the previous speakers. Vince's behavior is an example of
     a)   compliance
     b)   persuasion
     c)   conformity
     d)   obedience

Rationale:
C is the correct choice; conformity involves going along with the group despite one's real opinion. Compliance would be the case if someone had asked him to voice an opinion in keeping with the previous speakers. In this case, Vince did it on his own as a result of internal pressure to conform.

2.   The following researcher conducted a series of studies on conformity that involved having a subject judge the length of three lines after a group of confederates all reported an obviously incorrect answer.
     a)   Jane Elliot
     b)   Stanley Milgram
     c)   Philip Zimbardo
     d)   Solomon Asch

Rationale:
D is the correct answer. Asch conducted the well-known studies on conformity. Milgram studied obedience in his famous studies with electrical shock.

Objective 13.2

3.   _____ occurs when people begin to think that it is more important to maintain a group's cohesiveness than to objectively consider the facts.
     a)   Groupthink
     b)   The lowball technique
     c)   Obedience
     d)   Social loafing

Rationale:

_____

_____

4. All of the following are causes for groupthink EXCEPT:
    a) The belief that the group can do no wrong.
    b) The belief that the group is invulnerable.
    c) The belief that opposition to the group is unsound.
    d) Openness to differing opinions.

    Rationale:

    _____

    _____

Objective 13.3

5. At the supermarket, a demonstrator gives away free samples of a new pizza. He also gives each taster a coupon worth $1 off his or her grocery bill. This manufacturer is depending on the social process of _____ to increase sales.
    a) norm of reciprocity
    b) deindividuation
    c) group polarization
    d) social facilitation

    Rationale:

    _____

    _____

6. Selena is trying to get her boyfriend to wash the dishes for her. To start with, she asks her boyfriend to cook dinner for her, when her boyfriend refuses, she asks "Well, will you at least wash the dishes then?" to which he readily agrees. Selena has just used the

    _____.
    a) foot-in-the-door technique
    b) door-in-the-face technique
    c) lowball technique
    d) that's-not-all technique

    Rationale:

    _____

    _____

Objective 13.4

7. Changing one's behavior due to a direct order of an authority figure is referred to as
    a) compliance
    b) obedience
    c) conformity
    d) persuasion

    Rationale:

    _____

    _____

8. Imagine 100 individuals are asked to take part in a replication of Milgram's famous study on obedience. How are these 100 people likely to respond?
    a) The majority would administer 450 volts as instructed.
    b) The majority would immediately realize the use of deception and leave.
    c) Most of the women would refuse to obey, whereas almost all of the men would obey.
    d) Most of the participants would work together to force the experimenter to end the experiment.

    Rationale:

    _____

    _____

Objective 13.5

9. A teacher decides against assigning group projects in which all group members get the same grade. What social psychological phenomenon might the teacher be concerned about?
    a) conformity
    b) social loafing
    c) social influence
    d) social facilitation

    Rationale:

    _____

    _____

10. Ashley has practiced her drum routine over and over. When she gets up to play it at the recital in front of 100 people, she performs it better than she ever has. Her improved performance is an example of
    a) social compliance
    b) persuasion
    c) social facilitation
    d) social impairment

    Rationale:

    _____

    _____

11. Which of the following is the best example of the behavioral component of an attitude?
    a) Bea feels recycling is a great concept.
    b) Bob is upset when he hears a corporation plans to build a polluting plant near his home.
    c) Bill struggles to understand the arguments both sides present in a debate over a new manufacturing plant.
    d) Betty writes a letter to her senator asking for support of a law making corporations responsible for the pollution they cause.

    Rationale:

    _____

    _____

12. Which of the following is NOT a factor that influences attitude formation?
    a) direct contact with an individual
    b) DNA inherited from your parents
    c) instructions from your parents
    d) observing someone else's actions

    Rationale:

    _____

    _____

13. Kerry's positive attitude toward China, even though she has never been there, seems to be related to the fact that her mother is Chinese and talks about China all the time with Kerry. Which method of attitude formation is involved in this example?
    a) direct contact
    b) direct instruction
    c) interaction with others
    d) classical conditioning

    Rationale:

    _____

    _____

Objective 13.7

14. Which communicator would likely be most persuasive?
    a) an attractive person who is an expert
    b) a moderately attractive person who is an expert
    c) an attractive person who has moderate expertise
    d) a moderately attractive person who has moderate expertise

    Rationale:

    _____

    _____

15. _____ describes the situation in which people attend to the content of a message.
    a) Central-route processing
    b) Cognitive dissonance
    c) Social facilitation
    d) Peripheral-route processing

Rationale:

_____

_____

Objective 13.8

16. Which of the following was a finding in the classic study by Festinger and Carlsmith (1959)?
    a) Those who got $1 to perform a boring task said the task was more interesting than did those who got $2.
    b) Those who got $20 to perform a boring task said the task was more interesting than did those who got $1.
    c) Paid groups said the task was less boring than did non-paid groups.
    d) Women performed the tasks for less money than men.

Rationale:

_____

_____

17. Which of the following represents an example of cognitive dissonance?
    a) A boy learns how to ride a bicycle without training wheels.
    b) A father tells his daughter that he will really only be proud of her if she gets all A's like she did last semester.
    c) A student stays up all night to study for an upcoming exam.
    d) A woman who is arguing that it is morally wrong to kill animals for food becomes upset when she is asked to explain why she is wearing a leather belt and leather shoes.

Rationale:

_____

_____

Objective 13.9

18. What is the term for the process of developing an opinion about another person?
    a) social interaction
    b) stereotyping
    c) impression formation
    d) interpersonal judgment

Rationale:

_____

_____

19. Toni sees a picture of the new international exchange student and notices that the student looks happy, so Toni automatically assumes that he is also friendly. This automatic assumption about the student's personality is an example of
   a) central-route processing
   b) implicit personality theory
   c) cognitive dissonance
   d) discrimination

Rationale:

_____

_____

Objective 13.10

20. The process of explaining one's own behavior and the behavior of other people is called

   _____.
   a) stereotyping
   b) attribution
   c) central-route processing
   d) cognitive dissonance

Rationale:

_____

_____

21. "Look, Officer, I didn't see the stop sign back there because the sun was in my eyes." The police officer responds, "You were not paying attention." How would a social psychologist describe this situation?
   a) Both individuals were making fundamental attribution errors.
   b) Both individuals were making situational attributions.
   c) The driver was making a dispositional attribution; the officer was making a situational attribution.
   d) The driver was making a situational attribution; the officer was making a dispositional attribution.

Rationale:

_____

_____

22. While watching the TV game show "Jeopardy," your roommate says, "The game show host, Alex Trebek, knows all the answers. He must be a genius." You tell your roommate she probably would not have said that if she had attended class the day the instructor discussed the topic of _____.
   a) social facilitation
   b) stereotyping illusions
   c) internal attribution biases
   d) fundamental attribution errors

Rationale:

_____

_____

Objective 13.11

23. A bank loan officer thinks people who speak with an accent are lazy; consequently, he refuses to grant them loans. The loan officer's belief is an example of _____. His refusal to grant them loans is an example of _____ .
   a) discrimination; prejudice
   b) stereotyping; attribution
   c) attribution; stereotyping
   d) prejudice; discrimination

Rationale:

_____

_____

Objective 13.12

24. The part of a person's self-concept that is based on his or her identification with a nation, culture, or ethnic group or with gender or other roles in society is called:
   a) fundamental attribution error
   b) self-serving bias
   c) ethnocentrism
   d) social identity

Rationale:

_____

_____

25. Which of the following does NOT represent an effective method for reducing prejudice?
   a) establishing a jigsaw classroom
   b) bringing diverse groups of people into contact with each other
   c) learning about people who are different from you
   d) establishing equal status contact between different groups of people

Rationale:

_____

_____

26. We tend to ___ attractive people more than we do less attractive people.
   a) like
   b) dislike
   c) ignore
   d) hate

Rationale:

_____

_____

27. When opposites attract it is said that they have _____ characteristics.
   a) proximal
   b) complimentary
   c) rewarding
   d) reciprocal

Rationale:

_____

_____

28. Which of the following was not a component of Robert Sternberg's theory of love?
   a) intimacy
   b) lust
   c) passion
   d) commitment

Rationale:

_____

_____

29. Behavior that is intended to hurt or destroy another person is referred to as _____ .
   a) empty love
   b) prejudice
   c) aggression
   d) dissonance

Rationale:

_____

_____

30. The fact that a social role can lead to an increase in aggressive behavior points to _____ as a major contributor to aggression.
    a) biology
    b) the environment
    c) DNA
    d) chemical influences

Rationale:

_____

_____

Objective 13.16

31. What term refers to helping behavior that is performed voluntarily for the benefit of another person, with no anticipation of reward?
    a) altruism
    b) collectivism
    c) interdependence
    d) humanitarianism

Rationale:

_____

_____

Objective 13.17

32. In a crowded mall parking lot, dozens of people hear a female voice yell, "He's killing me!" Yet, no one calls the police. What is the reason for the lack of action, according to Darley and Latane?
    a) people are too busy to respond
    b) most people "do not want to become involved"
    c) the fight-or-flight response is not activated when others are in danger
    d) diffusion of responsibility

Rationale:

_____

_____

Objective 13.18

33. In Latané and Darley's classic 1969 study, they found that _____ of the participants reported smoke in the room when the two confederates in the room noticed the smoke but then ignored it.
    a) all
    b) three-fourths
    c) one-half
    d) one-tenth

Rationale:

_____

_____

34.   All of the following are decision points in helping behavior EXCEPT:
       a)   noticing
       b)   defining an emergency
       c)   taking responsibility
       d)   diffusion of responsibility

Rationale:

_____

_____

35.   In 1995, there were approximately how many cults in the United States?
       a)   200
       b)   500
       c)   4,000
       d)   15,000

Rationale:

_____

_____

SAMPLE EXAM ANSWERS & RATIONALES

1. c   Conformity involves going along with the group despite one's real opinion. Compliance would be the case if someone had asked him to voice an opinion in keeping with the previous speakers. In this case, Vince did it on his own as a result of internal pressure to conform.

2. d   D is the correct answer. Asch conducted the well-known studies on conformity. Milgram studied obedience in his famous studies with electrical shock.

3. a   Groupthink describes the thought processes that can dominate a group of individuals.

4. d   Groupthink results in a lack of differing opinions. Believing that the group can do no wrong is actually a cause for groupthink.

5. a   The norm of reciprocity involves the tendency of people to feel obligated to give something in return after they have received something. Social facilitation is an increase in performance caused by greater arousal.

6. b   The door-in-the-face technique involves asking for a large request that you know will be refused, followed up by a smaller request, which many people then agree to.

7. b   Obedience involves changing your behavior due to an order from "above," while conformity involves changing your behavior to better "fit in" with others around you.

8. a   The Milgram experiment has been repeated at various times in the United States and in other countries, and the percentage of participants who went all the way consistently remained between 61 and 66 percent. In addition, few differences between males and females have been found.

9. b   The teacher knows that some students will slack off if they are not being evaluated for their individual performance due to a phenomenon known as social loafing.

10. c   Social facilitation is the term for the positive effect on one's performance caused by the perception that others are watching.

11. d   Writing is an action, or behavior. The fact that Bill struggled to understand indicates that what he is doing is cognitive.

12. b   Attitude formation is believed to occur solely through the learning process and is not considered to be something that is inherited biologically.

13. c   The fact that Kerry's mother talks about China all the time with Kerry and is Chinese indicates that her attitude is the result of interaction with her mother. Classical conditioning occurs when someone learns through repetition to respond in a certain way to a stimulus; it has nothing to do with classical music.

14. a   Attractiveness and expertise have been shown to increase persuasiveness.

15. a   In central-route processing, an individual pays attention to the content of the message, whereas in peripheral-route processing, an individual focuses on details other than the main content of the message.

16. a   The group that got paid less used cognitive dissonance to justify their poor pay for telling a lie.

17. d   Cognitive dissonance is an emotional disturbance that occurs when a person's actions don't match their statements.

18. c   While stereotyping may be a component of impression formation, it is not the term for the process of developing an opinion about another person.

19. b   Implicit personality theory represents the automatic associations a person makes about personality traits that are assumed to be related.

20. b   An attribute is an explanation for a person's behavior. Stereotypes are preconceived ideas about a group of people.

21.   d   The driver attributed his error to something in his situation, the sun, whereas the officer attributed his error to something internal to him, his lack of attention.

22.   d   Your roommate attributed something that is situational (Trebek gets the answers ahead of time) to an internal characteristic (genius). Although internal attribution bias sounds correct, it is not a term used in social psychology.

23.   d   Prejudice is an unsupported, often negative belief about all people in a particular group, whereas discrimination is an action taken that is based on this belief. In this case, the action is the refusal to grant loans.

24.   d   Social identity refers to a person's identity with their social group. Ethnocentrism is the process of viewing the world from your own viewpoint and failing to see alternative perspectives.

25.   b   Simply bringing groups together normally does not reduce prejudice unless all the members of the group have equal status and power in the group.

26.   a   Social psychologists have found that we tend to like attractive people more than unattractive people.

27.   b   Things that "complement" each other tend to be opposites. The term proximity refers to nearness.

28.   b   Sternberg's theory of love includes the three components of intimacy, passion and commitment.

29.   c   Aggression describes a type of behavior, whereas prejudice refers to a person's attitude.

30.   b   The impact of the social role points to learning and the influence of the surrounding environment on an individual's aggressive behavior.

31.   a   Altruism is defined as helping others for no personal benefit. Humanitarianism means almost the same thing as altruism but is not the term social psychologists use for the helping behavior that is performed voluntarily for the benefit of another person, with no anticipation of reward.

32.   d   According to Latane and Darley, most people say they do want to become involved; however, often diffusion of responsibility occurs. Diffusion of responsibility is what occurs as each person thinks someone else will call for help, i.e., take responsibility.

33.   d   About one tenth of the participants reported smoke when the confederates in the room noticed the smoke but did nothing about it. This number was much higher when the participants were in the room alone.

34.   d   Diffusion of responsibility <u>stops</u> a person from helping and is not considered a decision point.

35.   c   The estimate is between 3,000-5,000 cults in the U.S.

APPLY IT

This section will help you use the concepts you are learning in this class to improve your study skills.

In this chapter, you learned about the concept of the jigsaw classroom. This learning strategy uses the power of the group to enhance and strengthen learning. The basic idea of the jigsaw classroom is to divide up a task into smaller segments and have one person in each group be responsible for that segment. After the individual learns the smaller segment, they come back to the group and teach it to everyone else. In this application, you will utilize the jigsaw puzzle to study for your next upcoming test.

1. Identify a group of people to take part in this project with you. You need at least one other person. A group of four or five people would be ideal.

2. After you have identified your group, divide the material for the upcoming test into equal segments. This could be done by chapter or topic or by dividing up the sections of a study guide.

3. Now assign each individual a specific segment that they are responsible for. Write the details down here.

Group member	Segment to cover

4. Decide on a time when the group will meet to study for the test together. During this time, each group member will teach the group about the particular segment that they were assigned.

Write you meeting time, date and location here: _____

5. Have your group study session and give time for each member to discuss their assigned segment.

Write your conclusions here. Did you find this study method effective? What were the pros and the cons? Would you try this approach again in the future?

_____

_____

_____

14.1   How did people in earlier times explain mental illness?

14.2   What are the different ways in which abnormal behavior can be defined?

14.3   How are psychological disorders related to the brain and body chemistry?

14.4   How can psychological disorders be explained by the different viewpoints in psychology?

14.5   How is abnormality viewed in other kinds of cultures?

14.6   How do psychological professionals decide what kind of disorder a person has?

14.7   What are the different types of psychological disorders, and how common are they?

14.8   What are the different types of anxiety disorders and their symptoms?

14.9   How do psychologists explain the causes of anxiety disorders?

14.10 What are the different kinds of somatoform disorders?

14.11 What causes somatoform disorders?

14.12 What are the dissociative disorders?

14.13 How do dissociative disorders develop?

14.14 What is the controversy surrounding the famous case of Sybil?

14.15 What are the different types of mood disorders?

14.16 What are the causes of mood disorders?

14.17 What are the main symptoms of schizophrenia?

14.18 What are the different types of schizophrenia?

14.19 What are the possible causes of schizophrenia?

14.20 What are the different kinds of personality disorders?

14.21 What causes personality disorders?

14.22 What is seasonal affective disorder and how can it be treated?

SUMMARY

The study of abnormal behavior, or **psychopathology**, can be traced to at least as early as 3000 B.C. from evidence of trepanning, or drilling some holes in the skull. Today, abnormal behavior is considered to be any behavior that is rare, deviates from the social norm, causes subjective discomfort, or is maladaptive. **Psychological disorders** are defined as ay pattern of behavior that causes people significant distress, causes them to harm themselves or others, or interferes with their ability to function in daily life. The **biological model** of psychopathology proposes that psychological disorders arise from a physical or biological cause. The **psychoanalytical model** suggests that disorders are the result of repressed thoughts in the unconscious mind, while the **behaviorist model** explains disorders as a set of learned behaviors, and the **cognitive model** describe psychological disorders as resulting from faulty thinking patterns.

Currently in the United States, psychological disorders are assessed by referring to the Diagnostics and Statistical Manual of Mental Disorders, Version 4, Text Revision (**DSM-IV-TR**), which provides information about 250 different disorders, including common symptoms, prevalence rates, and criteria for diagnosis. The individual is assessed in five different categories, or axes. Axis 1 contains all the psychological disorders except personality disorders. Axis II includes personality disorders and mental retardation. Axis III includes an assessment of any physical disorders that affects a person psychologically. Axis IV consists of problems in a person's environment that may be affecting their psychological functioning, and Axis V is an assessment of a person's overall (or global) level of functioning ranging from 0 to 100. In a given year, about 22 percent of adults in the United States could be diagnosed with a mental disorder.

Anxiety disorders include all disorders characterized by excessive or unrealistic anxiety. **Phobias** are a specific form of anxiety, a disorder defined as an irrational and persistent fear of something and includes **social phobias**, **specific phobias** such as claustrophobia, and **agoraphobia,** or fear of being in a place that would be difficult to escape from if something happened to go wrong. **Obsessive compulsive disorder** involves a reoccurring thought (or obsession) that causes extreme anxiety and leads to some repetitive or ritualistic behavior (or compulsion). **Panic disorder** is characterized by frequent occurrences of panic attacks or sudden onsets of extreme panic. Individuals diagnosed with **generalized anxiety disorder** display excessive anxiety and worries with no real source that can be pinpointed as leading to the anxiety. The psychoanalytical model states that anxiety disorders are caused by repressed urges or conflicts that are threatening to surface, while the behaviorist model sees anxious behavior as learned or conditioned responses. Cognitive psychologists believe that anxiety disorders are caused by illogical thinking including maladaptive thinking process such as **magnification**, **all-or-nothing thinking**, **overgeneralization**, and **minimization**. Evidence also supports biological factors, such as an imbalance in neurotransmitter levels, as playing a role in anxiety disorders.

Disorders in which people believe they are sick when they are not are called **somatoform disorders**. Somatoform disorders include **hypochondrias**, a disorder in which a person worries excessively about becoming ill, **somatization disorder**, in which the person complains about a specific physical symptom for which there is no real physical cause, and **conversion disorder,** which includes the lost of motor and/or sensory function. Freud believed somatoform disorders were caused by the repression of unacceptable thoughts; behaviorists believe the disorders are learned through both positive and negative reinforcement, and cognitive psychologists point to faulty thinking such as magnification and false beliefs as the cause.

Dissociative disorders involve a break, or dissociation, in a person's sense of identity. In **dissociative amnesia**, an individual cannot remember information contained in long-term memory, such as their own name or where they live. A **dissociative fugue** occurs when a person suddenly travels away from their home and afterwards cannot remember the trip or even their own identity. In **dissociative identity disorder**, formerly referred to as multiple personality disorder, a person seems to experience at least two or more distinct personalities. According to the psychoanalytical model, dissociation is a defense mechanism and is associated with emotional or physical trauma. Behaviorists believe that "not thinking" about certain events can be negatively reinforced by reducing anxiety and unpleasant feelings, while cognitive psychologists focus on the feelings of guilt, shame or anxiety that may be avoided through "thought avoidance." Biological explanations for dissociative disorders also exist.

Mood disorders, also referred to as affective disorders, represent a disturbance in emotion. Two mild forms of mood disorders include **dysthymia**, a chronic depression that lasts for at least two years or more, and **cyclothymia**, a cycle of sadness and happiness that also persists for two or more years. The most common mood disorder is **major depression,** which is characterized by prolonged feelings of extreme sadness. **Bipolar disorder** involves all the symptoms of major depression in addition to brief periods of extreme mania, or excessive excitement, energy and feelings of happiness. Psychoanalyts explain depression as anger turned inward on the person, while many learning theorists attribute depression to learned helplessness. Biological explanations have focused on the role of brain chemicals such as serotonin, norepiniphrine and dopamine.

Schizophrenia is a severe psychotic disorder in which the person is not able to distinguish fantasy from reality and experiences disturbances in thinking, emotions, behavior and perception. Many people with schizophrenia experience **delusions** (false beliefs about the world), **hallucinations** (seeing or hearing things that are not really there) and **flat affect** (the display of little or no emotion). Schizoprenia can be divided into five basic categories; **disorganized**, characterized by confused speech along with frequent and vivid hallucinations; **catatonic**, in which the individual may sit without moving for hours or may move about wildly; **paranoid**, identified by hallucinations and delusions; **undifferentiated**, in which the individual does not fit in one of the three categories already mentioned; and **residual,** in which a person is in a state of recovery from the symptoms of schizophrenia. Schizophrenia can also be classified according to the kind of symptoms displayed. **Positive symptoms** reflect an excess or distortion of normal functions, such as hallucinations, whereas **negative symptoms** reflect a decrease of normal functions. Medication appears to be more effective in treating the positive symptoms of schizophrenia. The causes of schizophrenia have been most clearly explained with the biological model. Increased levels of dopamine and brain structural defects are currently the two explanations with the strongest support.

Disorders that affect a person's entire life adjustment are referred to as **personality disorders**. The DSM-IV-TR recognizes ten different personality disorders. An individual with **antisocial personality disorder** typically feels no remorse and often behave in an impulsive manner with no regard for the consequences. **Borderline personality disorder** is defined by moody, unstable behaviors in which the individual lacks a clear sense of identity. Psychoanalytic theorists point to an incomplete resolution of the Oedipus complex as explanation for personality disorders, while cognitive and learning theorists focus on how the specific behaviors are learned and reinforced over time.

    Seasonal affective disorder (SAD) is a mood disorder that is caused by the body's reaction to low levels of light, especially during the winter months. One of the most effective treatments for SAD is phototherapy, which involves daily exposure to bright light, typically from an artificial source such as a lamp.

KEY POINTS

- Define abnormality and briefly discuss the history of psychological disorders.
- Present the biological and psychological models of psychopathology.
- Discuss the diagnosis and prevalence rates of psychological disorders in the U.S.
- Describe specific categories of psychological disorders including anxiety, somatoform, dissociative, mood, schizophrenia, and personality disorders.

KEY CONCEPTS

psychopathology	The study of abnormal behavior.
psychological disorders	Any pattern of behavior that causes people significant distress, causes them to harm others, or harms their ability to function in daily life, or both.
biological model	Model of explaining behavior as caused by biological changes in the chemical, structural, or genetic systems of the body.
psychoanalytical model	Model based on the work of Freud and his followers. Typically explains disorder behavior as the result of repressing thoughts and memories in the unconscious mind.
behaviorist model	Explanation of disorder behavior as being learned just like normal behavior.
cognitive model	Model that explains abnormal behavior as resulting from illogical thinking patterns.
DSM-IV-TR	Diagnostic and statistical manual of mental Disorders, Version Four, Text Revision. Manual written and used primarily by psychologists and psychiatrists as a guide in diagnosing and assessing psychological disorders.
anxiety disorders	Disorders in which the main symptom is excessive or unrealistic anxiety and fearfulness.

phobias	An irrational, persistent fear of an object, situation, or social activity.
social phobias	Fear of interacting with others or being in social situations that might lead to a negative evaluation.
specific phobias	Fear of objects or specific situations or events.
agoraphobia	Fear of being in a place or situation from which escape is difficult or impossible.
obsessive compulsive disorder	Disorder in which intruding, recurring thoughts or obsessions create anxiety that is relieved by performing a repetitive, ritualistic behavior (compulsion).
panic disorder	Disorder in which panic attacks occur frequently enough to cause the person difficulty in adjusting to daily life.
generalized anxiety disorder	Disorder in which a person has feelings of dread and impending doom along with physical symptoms of stress, and lasts six months or more.
magnification	The tendency to interpret situations as far more dangerous, harmful, or important than they actually are.
all-or-nothing thinking	The tendency to believe that one's performance must be perfect or the result will be a total failure.
overgeneralization	The tendency to interpret a single negative event as a never-ending pattern of defeat and failure.
minimization	The tendency to give little or no importance to one's successes or positive events and traits.
somatoform disorders	Disorders that take the form of bodily illnesses and symptoms, but for which there are no real physical disorders.
hypochondrias	Somatoform disorder in which the person is terrified of being sick and worries constantly, going to doctors repeatedly, and becomes preoccupied with every sensation of the body.
somatization disorder	Somatoform disorder in which the person dramatically complains of a specific symptom, such as nausea, difficulty swallowing, or pain for which there is no real physical cause.
conversion disorder	Somatoform disorder in which the person experiences a specific symptom in the somatic nervous system's functioning, such as paralysis, numbness, or blindness, for which there is no physical cause.
dissociative disorders	Disorders in which there is a break in conscious awareness,

memory, the sense of identity, or some combination.

dissociative amnesia	Loss of memory for personal information, either partial or complete.
dissociative fugue	Traveling away from familiar surroundings with amnesia for the trip and possible amnesia for personal information.
dissociative identity disorder	Disorder occurring when a person seems to have two or more distinct personalities within one body.
mood disorders	Disorders in which mood is severely disturbed.
dysthymia	A moderate depression that lasts for two years or more and is typically a reaction to some external stressor.
cyclothymia	Disorder that consists of mood swings from moderate depression to hypomania and lasts two years or more.
major depression	Severe depression that comes on suddenly and seems to have no external cause.
bipolar disorder	Severe mood swings between major depressive episodes and manic episodes.
schizophrenia	Severe disorder in which the person suffers from disordered thinking, bizarre behavior, hallucinations, and is unable to distinguish between fantasy and reality.
delusions	False beliefs held by a person who refuses to accept evidence of their falseness.
hallucinations	False sensory perceptions, such as hearing voices that do not really exist.
flat affect	A lack of emotional responsiveness.
disorganized	Type of schizophrenia in which behavior is bizarre and childish, and thinking, speech, and motor actions are very disordered.
catatonic	Type of schizophrenia in which the person experiences periods of statue-like immobility mixed with occasional bursts of energetic, frantic movement and talking.
paranoid	Type of schizophrenia in which the person suffers from delusions of persecution, grandeur, and jealousy, together with hallucinations.
undifferentiated	Type of schizophrenia in which the person shows no particular pattern, shift from one pattern to another, and cannot be neatly classified as disorganized, paranoid, or catatonic.

residual	Type of schizophrenia in which there are no delusions and hallucinations, but the person still experiences negative thoughts, poor language skills, and odd behavior.
positive symptoms	Symptoms of schizophrenia that are excesses of behavior or occur in addition to normal behavior; hallucinations, delusions, and distorted thinking.
negative symptoms	Symptoms of schizophrenia that are less than normal behavior or an absence of normal behavior; poor attention, flat affect, and poor speech production.
personality disorders	Disorders in which a person adopts a persistent, rigid, and maladaptive pattern of behavior that interferes with normal social interactions.
antisocial personality disorder	Disorder in which a person has no morals or conscience and often behaves in an impulsive manner without regard for the consequences of that behavior.
borderline personality disorder	Maladaptive personality pattern in which the person is moody, unstable, lacks a clear sense of identity, and often clings to others.
seasonal affective disorder (SAD)	A mood disorder caused by the body's reaction to low levels of sunlight in the winter months.

HINTS

1. Assume that you have been given the task of conducting a diagnostic interview based on the guidelines laid out in the DSM-IV-TR. You need to be sure to ask the individual you are interviewing questions that address each of the five axes. Come up with at least one question for each axis and write it below.

Axis 1: _____

_____

Axis 2: _____

_____

Axis 3: _____

_____

Axis 4: _____

_____

Axis 5: _____

_____

2. Six different categories of psychological disorders are presented in this chapter. In order to help yourself organize the new terms, try creating a table of the different disorders, including a general description of each category and the specific disorders within the category. The first category has been completed for you as an example.

Disorder Type	General Description	Specific Examples
Anxiety disorders	*A psychological disorder in which the main symptom is an intense fear or anxiety.*	*social phobias, specific phobias, agoraphobia, obsessive-compulsive disorder, generalized anxiety disorder, panic disorder*
Somatoform disorders		
Dissociative disorders		
Mood disorders		
Schizophrenia		
Personality disorders		

3. In addition to understanding the disorders themselves, it is important to understand the different theories as to the causes of each disorder. Your textbook discusses four models of explanation for each disorder. They are biological, psychoanalytical, behavioral and cognitive. In order to enhance your understanding of these models, briefly describe how each of them would explain the disorders listed below.

Model	Depression	Schizophrenia	Dissociative Identity Disorder
Psychoanalytic			
Behavioral			
Cognitive			
Biological			

Suggested answers for Question 3

Model	Depression	Schizophrenia	Dissociative Identity Disorder
Psychoanalytic	*anger turned inwards and then repressed*	*severe breakdown of the ego and regression back to child-like state*	*motivated forgetting*
Behavioral	*learned helplessness*	*bizarre behavior that has been shaped through reinforcement*	*behavior shaped through positive reinforcement such as attention from others*
Cognitive	*negative and self-defeating thoughts*	*severe form of illogical thinking*	*thought avoidance*
Biological	*brain chemical imbalance (in neurotransmitters such as serotonin and dopamine)*	*chemical imbalance and brain structure abnormalities*	*variation in brain activity between different "personalities"*

SAMPLE EXAM

For the following multiple choice questions, select the answer you feel best answers the question and explain the rationale or reason for your selection in the space provided.

Objective 14.1

1. It is probably accurate to assume that in ancient times signs of mental illness were believed to be caused by_____.
    a) imbalance of body fluids
    b) demons
    c) improper diet
    d) social forces

    Rationale:
    B is the correct choice because people in ancient times perceived signs of mental illness as caused by demons. Hippocrates, a Greek physician, viewed the imbalance of body fluids as the cause of mental illness, but Hippocrates, time period is not considered "ancient times."

Objective 14.2

2. What is the primary difficulty with applying the criterion of "social norm deviance" to define abnormal behavior?
    a) Norms are difficult to enumerate.
    b) Cultures accept and view all behaviors as normal.
    c) Behavior that is considered disordered in one culture may be acceptable in another.
    d) Norms do not guide behavior except in rare instances.

    Rationale:
    B is the correct answer. Behavior that is considered disordered in one culture may be acceptable in another. D is incorrect because most people do allow social norms to guide much of their behavior.

3. Which of the following is NOT a criterion used to decide if a pattern of behavior should be considered to be a psychological disorder?
    a) The behavior is physically exhausting.
    b) The behavior causes subjective distress.
    c) The behavior goes against the norms of the society.
    d) The behavior is maladaptive.

    Rationale:

    _____

    _____

Objective 14.3

4.   The biological model views psychological disorders as resulting from_____.
        a) distorted thought patterns
        b) repressed memories
        c) underlying behavioral issues
        d) physiological causes

    Rationale:

    _____

    _____

Objective 14.4

5.   The psychoanalytic model holds that abnormal behavior is the result of _____.
        a) learning
        b) repressed thoughts
        c) biology
        d) biochemical imbalances

    Rationale:

    _____

    _____

6.   Alan went to see a psychologist to get some help overcoming his anxiety in public. The
    psychologist spent a lot of time discussing the specific thoughts Alan has when he is in public and
    trying to help him change those thought patterns. The psychologist could be best described as
    adhering to the _____.
        a) cognitive perspective
        b) behaviorist model
        c) psychoanalytical perspective
        d) biological model

    Rationale:

    _____

    _____

7. Disorders such as koro, susto, and amok are considered _____.
    a) restricted syndromes.
    b) naturalistic syndromes
    c) sociocultural disorders
    d) culture-bound syndromes

    Rationale:

    _____

    _____

Objective 14.6

8. _____is used to help psychological professionals diagnose psychological disorders.
    a) The Diagnostic and Statistical Manual of Mental Disorders
    b) The Physician's Desk Reference
    c) The Textbook of Psychological Disorders
    d) The Textbook of Physiological Disorders

    Rationale:

    _____

    _____

Objective 14.7

9. When a psychologist or psychiatrist is using the DSM-IV-TR as a guide to evaluating a client, he or she would assess the client on each of five _____.
    a) axes
    b) stages
    c) phases
    d) steps

    Rationale:

    _____

    _____

10. In any given year in the United States, approximately how many adults over age 18 experience a mental disorder?
    a) 5%
    b) 22%
    c) 52%
    d) 76%

    Rationale:

    _____

    _____

11. Which of the following statements is true about anxiety?
    a) It is never considered realistic or normal.
    b) Some anxiety is realistic when its source is obvious and understandable.
    c) It always manifests itself as a disorder.
    d) It is unusual for a mentally healthy person to experience anxiety.

    Rationale:

    _____

    _____

12. Over the past few years, Sam has become extremely fearful of going to any public place such as a restaurant, concert, or even the grocery store. There are many days when Sam does not even leave his house for fear that he might be caught somewhere that would not be easy to escape from. Which anxiety disorder would Sam most likely be diagnosed with?
    a) a specific phobia
    b) obsessive-compulsive disorder
    c) generalized anxiety disorder
    d) agoraphobia

    Rationale:

    _____

    _____

13. Liza has an anxiety disorder. She is currently seeing a therapist who believes that anxiety disorders are a result of illogical, irrational thought processes. Liza is probably seeking treatment from a_____.
    a) behaviorial psychologist
    b) cognitive psychologist
    c) psychoanalyst
    d) psychologist with a biological perspective

    Rationale:

    _____

    _____

14.   The cognitive process of magnification could be most accurately described as
  a)   interpreting a single negative event as a never-ending pattern of defeat
  b)   making mountains out of molehills
  c)   giving little or no emphasis to one's successes or positive events
  d)   throwing the baby out with the bath water

Rationale:

_____

_____

Objective 14.10

15.   A person who is preoccupied with every sensation of her body, worries excessively about getting ill, and continuously goes to doctors who never find anything physically wrong with her is likely to be diagnosed with _____.
  a)   hypochondriasis
  b)   conversion disorder
  c)   somatization disorder
  d)   psychophysiological disorder

Rationale:

_____

_____

16.   Disorders that take the form of a physical illness that has no real physical cause are referred to as
  a)   dissociate disorders
  b)   schizophrenia
  c)   somatoform disorders
  d)   mood disorders

Rationale:

_____

_____

Objective 14.11

17.   What did Freud believe about somatoform disorders?
  a)   They are caused by the repression of disturbing thoughts, conflicts, or memories.
  b)   They result from magnifying symptoms and allowing false beliefs to dominate one's thinking.
  c)   They are the result of positive and negative reinforcement.
  d)   They are due to an imbalance of the neurotransmitters GABA and serotonin.

Rationale:

_____

_____

18. Disorders in which there is a break in conscious awareness, memory, the sense of identity, or some combination are called _____.
    a) paraphilias
    b) anxiety disorders
    c) somatoform disorders
    d) dissociative disorders

Rationale:

_____

_____

19. Dissociative identity disorder is a psychological disorder more commonly known as
    a) amnesia
    b) fugue or flight disorder
    c) schizophrenia
    d) multiple personality disorder

Rationale:

_____

_____

Objective 14.13

20. Which of the following perspectives claims that shaping may play a big role in the development of some cases of dissociative identity disorder?
    a) behavioral
    b) humanistic
    c) biological
    d) psychoanalytic

Rationale:

_____

_____

Objective 14.14

21.   Spanos conducted studies to determine the validity of dissociative identity disorder. He found that ordinary college students, under hypnosis, showed signs of a second personality. Based on his studies, what did he conclude about the disorder?
    a)   Many of the diagnoses were incorrect, as professionals had been fooled by the clients' tendency to play the role of a multiple personality.
    b)   Many cases had clearly been caused by childhood trauma.
    c)   Many cases were a misdiagnosis of other psychological disorders.
    d)   Very few cases had been misdiagnosed.

Rationale:

_____

_____

Objective 14.15

22.   Disorders characterized by disturbances in emotion are known as _____ disorders.
    a)   conversion
    b)   somatoform
    c)   mood
    d)   dissociative

Rationale:

_____

_____

23.   An individual diagnosed with dysthymia would most likely exhibit which of the following symptoms?
    a)   cycles of being sad, then happy, then sad.
    b)   mild depression over a period of several years
    c)   severe depression that appears very rapidly without any apparent reason
    d)   periods of excessive excitement followed by days or weeks of severe depression

Rationale:

_____

_____

24.   Which of the following is the biological explanation for mood disorders?
      a)   They are a result of learned helplessness.
      b)   They are a result of anger turned inward on oneself.
      c)   They are a result of distortions in thinking.
      d)   They are a result of an imbalance of brain chemicals.

Rationale:

_____

_____

Objective 14.17

25.   A person suffering from disordered thinking, bizarre behavior, and hallucinations, who is unable to distinguish between fantasy and reality, is likely suffering from_____.
      a)   schizophrenia
      b)   bipolar disorder
      c)   a dissociative disorder
      d)   passive-aggressive personality

Rationale:

_____

_____

26.   The condition in which a person shows little or no emotion is referred to as _____.
      a)   flat affect
      b)   hallucinations
      c)   delusions
      d)   disorganization

Rationale:

_____

_____

Objective 14.18

27.   The primary feature of _____ schizophrenia is severe disturbance of motor behavior.
      a)   disorganized
      b)   catatonic
      c)   residual
      d)   paranoid

Rationale:

_____

_____

28.   Which of the following symptoms would NOT be considered a negative symptom of schizophrenia?
         a)   lack of affect
         b)   poor attention
         c)   social withdrawal
         d)   hallucinations

Rationale:

_____

_____

Objective 14.19

29.   Sal has decreased levels of the neurotransmitter dopamine in his prefrontal cortex. Which disorder might he be at risk of experiencing?
         a)   antisocial personality disorder
         b)   agoraphobia
         c)   schizophrenia
         d)   dissociative fugue

Rationale:

_____

_____

Objective 14.20

30.   Disorders that affect the entire life adjustment of a person are referred to as
         a)   somatoform disorders
         b)   dissociative disorders
         c)   mood disorders
         d)   personality disorders

Rationale:

_____

_____

31.   A person with antisocial personality disorder would be likely to engage in which of the following behaviors?
         a)   lying to other people without worrying about the consequences
         b)   display excessive and inappropriate emotions
         c)   report hallucinations
         d)   completely withdraw from society

Rationale:

_____

_____

32.   Which of the following statements represents the biological view of personality disorders?
        a)   They are due to an inadequate resolution of the Oedipus complex.
        b)   They are a type of learned behavior.
        c)   They have physiological causes.
        d)   They are due to disturbances in family relationships.

Rationale:

_____

_____

Objective 14.22

33.   _____ is a mood disorder that is caused by the body's reaction to low levels of light present in the winter months.
        a)   panic disorder
        b)   bipolar disorder
        c)   dysthymic disorder
        d)   seasonal affective disorder

Rationale:

_____

_____

SAMPLE EXAM ANSWERS & RATIONALES

1.   b   B is the correct choice because people of ancient times perceived signs of mental illness as caused by demons. Hippocrates, a Greek physician, viewed the imbalance of body fluids as the cause of mental illness, but Hippocrates' time period is not considered "ancient times."

2.   b   B is the correct answer; behavior that is considered disordered in one culture may be acceptable in another. D is incorrect because most people do allow social norms to guide much of their behavior.

3.   a   The three main criteria for a behavior to be considered a psychological disorder are that it deviates from social norms, is maladaptive, and causes the individual personal distress or discomfort.

4.   d   The biological model emphasizes physiological or physical causes for psychological disorders. The other three choices represent the cognitive, psychoanalytical and behavioral models for a, b, and c, respectively.

5.   b   Originating with the theories of Freud, psychoanalysts view disorder behavior as resulting from thoughts that are below the level of conscious awareness.

6.   a   Cognitive psychologists tend to treat disorders by attempting to change the person's thought patterns.

7.   d   Koro, susto, and amok are considered culture-bound disorders because they occur only in particular cultures.

8.   a   The DSM helps psychological professionals diagnose psychological disorders, while the Physician's Desk Reference is used by medical professionals to diagnose physiological problems.

9.   a   The DSM-IV-TR uses a system of five different axes for evaluations.

10.   b   According to recent studies, approximately 22% of the U.S. adult population experiences a mental disorder in a given year.

11.   b   This statement is true because some types of anxiety are normal.

12.   d   Agoraphobia is an anxiety disorder characterized by an extreme fear of going in public places that would be difficult to escape from if necessary.

13.   b   Cognitive psychologists view anxiety disorders as a result of distorted thought processes, while behaviorists view anxiety disorders as a result of learning.

14.   b   Magnification is the tendency to interpret a situation as being far more harmful, dangerous, or embarrassing than it actually is, or in other words, making a big deal out of something that is actually very small.

15.   a   Someone with hypochondriasis is excessively worried about getting ill and frequently goes to see doctors. People with somatization disorder do not worry so much about every aspect of their health; they complain in dramatic terms about one particular symptom.

16.   c   The term "somatic" literally means bodily.

17.   a   Freud viewed somatoform disorders as the physical symptoms of repressed thoughts, conflicts, or memories. Cognitive psychologists believe somatoform disorders result from faulty thought processes, such as magnifying symptoms and allowing false beliefs to dominate thinking.

18.   d   Dissociative disorders are characterized by a break in conscious awareness, memory, the sense of identity, or some combination.

19.   d   Multiple personality disorder is no longer used by psychologists but is still very common in the general public.

20.   a   Behavioral psychologists emphasize shaping through positive and negative reinforcement as a factor in the development of some cases of dissociate identity disorder.

21.   a   Spanos found that many supposed cases of dissociative identity disorder had been misdiagnosed.

22.   c   Mood disorders are characterized by disturbances in emotion, while somatoform disorders take the form of bodily ailments that have no physical cause.

23.   b   Dysthymia can be thought of as a mild version of depression, while cyclothymia more closely resembles a mild version of bipolar disorder.

24.   a   The biological explanation emphasizes an imbalance of brain chemicals.

25.   a   Disordered thinking, bizarre behavior, hallucinations, and inability to distinguish between fantasy and reality are all symptoms of schizophrenia. Bipolar disorder is characterized by mood swings between depression and mania and does not involve hallucinations or inability to distinguish between fantasy and reality.

26.   a   The word "affect" is used to mean emotion or mood.

27.   b   Severe motor disturbance is a feature of catatonic schizophrenia. Symptoms of residual schizophrenia include negative beliefs, poor language skills, and unusual ideas and perceptions.

28.   d   Negative symptoms of schizophrenia reflect a decrease in normal function (such as lack of social interactions or displays of emotions). Hallucinations represent an excess or addition in normal function and would be classified as a positive symptom of schizophrenia.

29.   c   Schizophrenia is associated with an imbalance of dopamine.

30.   d   Personality disorders do not just affect a single aspect of a person's life, but rather affect the person's entire life adjustment.

31.   a   Antisocial personality disorder is characterized by an individual who acts "against society." For example, an individual might commit a crime without feeling any remorse.

32.   c   The biological perspective focuses on physiological causes for psychological disorders, while cognitive-learning theorists do believe that the behavior displayed by people with personality disorders is learned through reinforcement, shaping and modeling.

33.   d   Seasonal affective disorder occurs primarily during the winter months. Dysthymic disorder consists of similar symptoms but is not seasonal in nature.

APPLY IT

This section will help you use the concepts you are learning in this class to improve your study skills.

As you near the end of the semester, you may be preparing for finals or other exams. For this application, spend some time thinking about the test-taking techniques that you use and exploring some tips that you may not have tried. You have most likely developed some strategies for test-taking whether you realize it or not. Think about how you take a test and list a few of the strategies that you use here.

- _____

- _____

- _____

Now read through the following suggestions and select one or two to try for your next exam.

Tip	Rationale
Arrive to the test on time	Arriving late or at the last minute can add additional stress that could interfere with your recall of the information.
Before answering any questions, unload the information	If there were specific lists or a large amount of information you learned for the exam, find a place on the paper and write it all down before you begin answering questions. This way you won't have to worry about trying to keep them all "in your head" while you are answering other questions.
Read the directions carefully	There may be important information included in the directions as to exactly what the examiner is looking for. Also pay attention to the point value for each question so you can spend more time on the high point questions.
Budget your time wisely	Before you start answering the first question, quickly scan through the entire test to get an idea of how many questions there are and where most of the high-point questions are located. This can help you use your time most effectively.
Look for clues	Often multiple choice questions can be quickly narrowed down. Eliminate obviously wrong selections first. Most multiple questions are written to contain the correct selection along with the main distracter. Also, look for grammatical correctness as well as clues from other questions.
Answer all the questions	Sometimes partial credit is given for answers that are close – especially on short-answer and essay questions.
Use all of the class time	If you finish early, go back over the exam to make sure you answered all the questions and didn't make a simple mistake that could take points away.

15.1   What are the two ways in which
       psychological disorders can be treated?

15.2   How were psychological disorders treated
       in the past?

15.3   What were the basic elements of Freud's
       psychoanalysis?

15.4   How is psychoanalysis conducted and
       viewed today?

15.5   What are the basic elements of Roger's
       person-centered therapy?

15.6   What is Gestalt therapy?

15.7   How are humanistic therapies viewed
       today?

15.8   How do behavior therapists use classical
       conditioning to treat disordered behavior?

15.9   How do behavior therapists use operant
       conditioning to treat disordered behavior?

15.10 How successful are behavior therapies?

15.11 What is cognitive therapy?

15.12 What are the goals of cognitive-behavioral
       therapies?

15.13 What is rational-emotive behavior therapy?

15.14 How successful are cognitive and cognitive-
       behavior therapies?

15.15 What are the advantages and disadvantages
       of group therapy?

15.16 What are the different types of group
       therapy?

15.17 For whom is group therapy most likely to be
       a useful form of treatment?

15.18 Does eye-movement desensitization
       reprocessing really work?

15.19 How effective is psychotherapy?

15.20 Is psychotherapy's effectiveness affected by
       cultural, ethnic, or gender differences?

15.21 What are the various types of drugs used to
       treat psychological disorders?

15.22 How is electroconvulsive therapy used to
       treat severe psychological disorders?

15.23 What is the history of psychosurgery, and
       how is it used today?

15.24 What are the dangers of treating children
       and adolescents with antidepressant drugs?

SUMMARY

Therapy for psychological disorders consists of treatment methods aimed at making people feel better and function more effectively. The two main types of therapy are **psychotherapy,** which consists of talking things out with a professional, and **biomedical therapy** which consists of using biological methods such as medication to treat a psychological disorder. Psychotherapy techniques can be roughly divided into **insight therapies,** which have the goal of self-understanding, and **action therapies,** which focus on changing an individual's behaviors. Biomedical therapies consist mainly of the use of drugs, surgical techniques, or electroconvulsive therapy. Early treatment of the mentally ill often consisted of fatal attempts to "rid" the individual of the physical impurities causing the abnormal behavior. It was not until 1793 that Philippe Pinel began the movement of humane treatment of the mentally ill.

Psychoanalysis is an insight therapy developed by **Sigmund Freud** with the goal of revealing the unconscious conflicts, urges and desires that Freud assumed were the cause of the psychological disorder. Freud utilized a number of techniques in his attempt to reveal the unconscious. **Dream interpretation** involved an analysis of the actual or **manifest content** of a dream as well as the hidden or **latent content**. Freud felt the latent content of dreams could reveal unconscious conflict. In addition, Freud used **free association**, or allowing the patients to freely say whatever came to their minds, to uncover the repressed material; **resistance**, in which patients became unwilling to discuss a topic any further; and **transference**, in which the therapist became a symbol of a parental authority figure. Today, psychoanalytic therapy is often referred to as **psychodynamic therapy** and is more direct, places more emphasis on transference, and is usually much shorter than traditional psychoanalysis. Individuals with anxiety, somatoform or dissociative disorders are more likely to benefit from psychodynamic therapy than individuals with other types of disorders.

Humanistic therapy is also an insight therapy, but unlike psychoanalysis, humanistic therapy focuses on conscious experiences of emotion and an individual's sense of self. The two most common humanistic therapies are person-centered therapy and Gestalt therapy. **Carl Rogers** developed **person-centered therapy,** which has the goal of helping an individual get their real and ideal selves to more closely match up. According to Rogers, the role of the therapist is to provide the unconditional positive regard which was missing in the individual's life. He felt the therapy should be **nondirective,** with the individual doing most of the work and believed the four key elements of **reflection, unconditional positive regard, empathy** and **authenticity** were crucial for a successful person-therapist relationship. **Fritz Perls** believed that people's problems arose from hiding important parts of their feelings from themselves and developed another humanistic therapy called **Gestalt therapy**, a directive form of insight therapy. Gestalt therapy focuses on the client's feelings and subjective experiences and uses leading questions and planned experiences such as role-playing to help the person reveal the feelings they may be hiding from themselves. Humanistic therapies have been found to be more successful with individuals who are able to express their thoughts and feelings in a logical manner and are not necessarily the best choice for individuals with more severe psychological disorders.

  Behavior therapies use action-based therapy to change behavior based on basic principles of classical and operant conditioning. The abnormal behavior is not seen as a symptom, but rather seen as the problem itself. **Behavior modification or applied behavior analysis** refers to the use of conditioning techniques to modify behavior. Behavior therapies that rely on classical conditioning include systematic desensitization, aversion therapy, and flooding. **Systematic desensitization** consists of a three-step process that utilizes **counter-conditioning** in order to reduce fear and anxiety. First, the client learns deep muscle relaxation technique, then creates a list of anxiety producing events called a hierarchy of fear, and finally confronts the anxiety producing event while remaining in a relaxed state. **Aversion therapy** uses classical conditioning to decrease a behavior by pairing an aversive (unpleasant) stimulus with the stimulus that normally produces the unwanted behavior. For example, the drug Antabuse produces severe nausea when paired with alcohol so that the individual learns to associate drinking alcohol with getting sick; the CS (alcohol) is now paired with an undesirable UCS (nausea) instead of the desirable UCS (drunkenness). **Flooding** involves rapid and intense exposure to an anxiety producing object in order to produce extinction of the conditioned fear response. Behavior therapies that utilize operant conditioning include participant modeling, token economies, contingency contracts and extinction techniques such as the use of a time-out. **Participant modeling** has been used to successfully treat phobias and obsessive-compulsive disorders by having the client watch and mimic a model demonstrating the desired behaviors. In a **token economy**, clients are reinforced with tokens for behaving correctly and can later exchange the tokens for things they want, such as food, candy, or special privileges. A **contingency contract** is a written statement of specific required behaviors, contingent penalties, and subsequent rewards. **Extinction techniques** such as time-outs work by removing the reinforcement for a behavior. In adults, simply refusing to acknowledge a person's behavior is often successful in reducing the frequency of that behavior. Behavior therapies have been effective in the treatment of disorders including overeating, drug addictions and phobias.

  Cognitive therapy is an action therapy that focuses on helping people change the distorted thinking and unrealistic beliefs that lead to maladaptive behaviors. Common distortions in thought include **arbitrary inference** (or "jumping to conclusions"), **selective thinking, overgeneralization, magnification and minimization,** and **personalization. Cognitive behavioral therapy (CBT)** is a type of cognitive therapy in which the goal is to help clients overcome problems by learning to think more rationally and logically. Albert Ellis developed a version of CBT called **rational-emotive behavioral therapy** in which clients are taught to replace their own irrational beliefs with more rational, helpful statements. Cognitive therapies have considerable success in treating disorders such as depression, stress disorders, anxiety disorders and some types of schizophrenia.

  An alternative to individual therapy is **group therapy**, in which a group of clients with similar problems gather together and discuss their problems under the guidance of a single therapist. Types of group therapies include **family counseling** and **self-help (or support) groups**. The advantages of group therapy are lower cost, exposure to the ways other people handle the same kinds of problems, the opportunity for the therapist to see how that person interacts with others, and the social and emotional support from the people in the group. The disadvantages are a person may not feel as free to reveal embarrassing or personal information, the therapist's time must be shared during the session, a shy person may have difficulty speaking up in the group setting, and people with severe disorders such as schizophrenia may not tolerate a group setting. Group therapy seems to be most successful as a long-term treatment intended to promote the development of skilled social interactions.

Francine Shapiro developed a therapy technique called **eye-movement desensitization reprocessing (EMDR)** in which clients attempt to decrease their fears, anxieties, and disturbing thoughts by moving their eyes rapidly back and forth. Although EMDR has been a popular treatment for post-traumatic stress disorder, the effectiveness of the treatment has yet to be firmly established and has not been found to be any more effective than other more traditional techniques such as simple muscle relaxation or exposure therapy.

The effectiveness of the various psychotherapy techniques is difficult to determine due to various time frames required for the different therapies, alternate explanations of "effectiveness," the lack of adequate control groups, experimenter bias, and the inaccuracies of self-report information. Most psychological professionals today take an eclectic approach to psychotherapy, which involves using a combination of methods to fit the particular client's needs. The most important aspect of successful psychotherapy appears to be the relationship between the client and the therapist, also referred to as the **therapeutic alliance**. Differences in culture between the therapist and the client can make it difficult for the therapist to understand the exact nature of the client's problems. Several studies have found that members of minority racial or ethnic groups drop out of therapy at significantly higher rates than the majority group clients. Barriers to effective psychotherapy include differences in language, cultural values, social class and nonverbal communication. A new form of therapy that is delivered via the Internet, call **cybertherapy**, is now available.

Biomedical therapies directly affect the biological function of the body and include the three categories of drug therapy, shock therapy, and surgical treatments. **Psychopharmacology** refers to the use of drugs to control or relieve the symptoms of a psychological disorder and is often combined with psychotherapy for a more effective outcome. Psychopharmacological drugs can be divided according to the disorders they treat, including drugs for psychotic disorders, anxiety disorders, manic symptoms of mood disorders, and depression. Drugs used to treat psychotic symptoms such as hallucinations, delusions and bizarre behaviors are called **antipsychotic drugs** and include typical neuroleptics, atypical neuroleptics and partial dopamine agonists. In general, these drugs work to decrease dopamine levels in the brain. The newer drugs tend to have fewer negative side effects than the older typical neuroleptics. The two kinds of drugs currently used to treat anxiety disorders include the traditional **antianxiety drugs** such as the minor tranquilizers, or benzodiazepines, including Xanax, Ativan, and Valium, and **antidepressant drugs** to be discussed in more detail shortly. The most common treatment for the manic symptoms of bipolar disorder is the antimanic drug lithium. The exact mechanism of lithium is still not clearly understood. Antidepressant drugs can be divided into three separate categories; the monamine oxidase inhibitors (MAOIs) such as Marplan and Nardil, tricyclic antidepressants such as Tofranil and Elavil, and the selective serotonin reuptake inhibitors (SSRIs), such as Prozac and Zoloft. **Electroconvulsive therapy** (or ECT), also known as shock therapy, is still in use today to treat severe cases of depression, schizophrenia, and mania. The treatment involves delivery of an electric shock to one or both sides of a person's head, causing a release of neurotransmitters and almost immediate improvement in the individual's mood. One of the main side effects of ECT is at least a short-term loss of memory. **Psychosurgery** involves operating on an individual's brain to remove or destroy brain tissue for the purpose of relieving symptoms of psychological disorders. One of the earliest psychosurgery techniques is the prefrontal lobotomy, which is no longer performed today. The main psychosurgery technique in use today is the bilateral cingulotomy, which destroys the cingulated gyrus and has been shown to be effective in about one-third of cases of depression, bipolar disorder, and obsessive-compulsive disorder. This procedure is only performed with the patient's full and informed consent after all other treatment options have been exhausted.

A recent controversy involves the use of antidepressant drugs for the treatment of depression and anxiety in adolescents. It is not clear whether or not these drugs may lead to an increased risk of suicide in the adolescent patient. Currently the Food and Drug Administration requires a "black box" warning on these drugs urging close monitoring of a child or adolescent taking the medication.

KEY POINTS

- Define two main types of theory and briefly discuss the history of treatment of the mentally ill.
- Introduce the major types of psychotherapy, including psychoanalysis, humanistic, behavior, cognitive, and group therapy.
- Discuss the assessment of the effectiveness of the psychotherapy treatments.
- Describe the biomedical approaches of treating psychological disorders including the use of drugs, electroconvulsive therapy and psychosurgery.

KEY CONCEPTS

therapy	Treatment methods aimed at making people feel better and function more effectively.
psychotherapy	Therapy for mental disorders in which a person with a problem talks with a psychological professional.
biomedical therapy	Therapy for mental disorders in which a person with a problem is treated with biological or medical methods to relieve symptoms.
insight therapies	Therapies in which the main goal is helping people to gain insight with respect to their behavior, thoughts, and feelings.
action therapies	Therapies in which the main goal is to change disordered or inappropriate behavior directly.
psychoanalysis	An insight therapy based on the theory of Freud, emphasizing the revealing of unconscious conflicts.
Sigmund Freud	1856-1939. Founder of the psychoanalytic school of thought, which focuses on the role of the unconscious on behavior.
dream interpretation	The analysis of the elements within a patient's reported dream as a means of revealing unconscious conflicts and desires.
manifest content	The actual content of one's dream.
latent content	The symbolic or hidden meaning of dreams.
free association	Freudian technique in which a patient was encouraged to talk about anything that came to mind without fear of negative evaluations.
resistance	Occurs when a patient becomes reluctant to talk about a certain topic, either changing the subject or becoming silent.

transference	In psychoanalysis, the tendency for a patient or client to project positive or negative feelings for important people from the past onto the therapist.
psychodynamic therapy	A newer and more general term for therapies based on psychoanalysis, with an emphasis on transference, shorter treatment times and a more direct therapeutic approach.
humanistic therapy	Psychotherapy focused on conscious, subjective experiences of emotion and people's sense of self.
Carl Rogers	1902-1987. Humanist psychologist who focused on the role of the self-concept and positive regard on personality development.
person-centered therapy	A non-directive insight therapy based on the work of Carl Rogers in which the client does all the talking and the therapist listens.
nondirective	Therapy in which the therapist remains relatively neutral and does not interpret or take direct actions with regard to the client, instead remaining a calm, non-judging listener while the client talks.
reflection	Therapy technique in which the therapist restates what the client says rather than interpreting those statements.
unconditional positive regard	Refers to the warmth, respect, and accepting atmosphere created by the therapist for the client in client-centered therapy.
empathy	The ability of the therapist to understand the feelings of the client.
authenticity	The genuine, open, and honest response of the therapist to the client.
Fritz Perls	1893-1970. Developed and popularized Gestalt therapy.
Gestalt therapy	Form of directive insight therapy in which the therapist helps the client to accept all parts of their feelings and subjective experiences, using leading questions and planned experiences such as role-playing.
behavior therapies	Action therapies based on the principles of classical and operant conditioning and aimed at changing disordered behavior without concern for the original causes of such behavior.
behavior modification or applied behavior analysis	The use of learning techniques to modify or change undesirable behavior and increase desirable behavior.
systematic desensitization	Behavior technique used to treat phobias, in which a client is asked to make a list of ordered fears and taught to relax while concentrating on those fears.
counter-conditioning	Replacing an old conditioned response with a new one by

changing the unconditioned stimulus.

aversion therapy	Form of behavioral therapy in which an undesirable behavior is paired with an aversive stimulus to reduce the frequency of the behavior.
flooding	Technique for treating phobias and other stress disorders in which the person is rapidly and intensely exposed to the fear-provoking situation or object and prevented from making the usual avoidance or escape response.
participant modeling	Technique in which a model demonstrates the desired behavior in a step-by-step, gradual process while the client is encouraged to imitate the model.
token economy	The use of objects called tokens to reinforce behavior in which the tokens can be accumulated and exchanged for desired items or privileges.
contingency contract	A formal, written agreement between the therapist and client (or teacher and student or parent and child) in which goals for behavioral change, reinforcements and penalties are clearly stated.
extinction techniques	The removal of a reinforcer to reduce the frequency of a behavior.
cognitive therapy	Therapy in which the focus is on helping clients recognize distortions in their thinking and replace distorted, unrealistic beliefs with more realistic, helpful thoughts.
arbitrary inference	Distortion of thinking in which a person draws a conclusion that is not based on any evidence.
selective thinking	Distortion of thinking in which a person focuses on only one aspect of a situation while ignoring all other relevant aspects.
overgeneralization	Distortion of thinking in which a person draws sweeping conclusions based on only one incident or event and applies those conclusions to events that are unrelated to the original.
magnification and minimization	Distortions of thinking in which a person blows a negative event out of proportion to its importance (magnification) while ignoring relevant positive events (minimization).
personalization	Distortion of thinking in which a person takes responsibility or blame for events that are unconnected to the person.
cognitive behavioral therapy (CBT)	Action therapy in which the goal is to help clients overcome problems by learning to think more rationally and logically.
rational-emotive behavioral therapy (REBT)	Cognitive-behavioral therapy in which clients are directly challenged in their irrational beliefs and helped to restructure their

thinking into more rational belief statements.

group therapy	Type of therapy in which a group of clients meet together with a therapist.
family counseling	A form of group therapy in which family members meet together with a counselor or therapist to resolve problems that affect the entire family.
self-help groups (support groups)	A group composed of people who have similar problems and who meet together without a therapist or counselor for the purpose of discussion, problem-solving, and social and emotional support.
eye-movement desensitization reprocessing (EMDR)	Controversial form of therapy for post-traumatic stress disorder and similar anxiety problems in which the client is directed to move the eyes rapidly back and forth while thinking of a disturbing memory.
therapeutic alliance	The relationship between therapist and client that develops as a warm, caring, accepting relationship characterized by empathy, mutual respect, and understanding.
cybertherapy	Psychotherapy that is offered on the Internet. Also called online, Internet, or Web therapy or counseling.
psychopharmacology	The use of drugs to control or relieve the symptoms of psychological disorders.
antipsychotic drugs	Drugs used to treat psychotic symptoms such as delusions, hallucinations, and other bizarre behavior.
antianxiety drugs	Drugs used to treat and calm anxiety reactions, typically minor tranquilizers.
antidepressant drugs	Drugs used to treat depression and anxiety.
electroconvulsive therapy (ECT)	Form of biomedical therapy to treat severe depression in which electrodes are placed on either one or both sides of a person's head and an electric current that is strong enough to cause a seizure or convulsion is run through the electrodes.
psychosurgery	Surgery performed on brain tissue to relieve or control severe psychological disorders.

1. An important task in this chapter is to understand the differences between the multiple types of therapy. Listed below are several of the psychotherapies discussed in the chapter. For each therapy, indicate the type of therapy (insight or action), the role of the therapist (directive or nondirective), the school of thought most likely to use this technique, and the overall goal of the therapy. The first psychotherapy has been filled in as an example.

Therapy	Type of therapy	Role of therapist	School of thought	Goal of therapy
Traditional Psychoanalysis	*Insight*	*Nondirective*	*Psychoanalysis*	*Uncover unconscious conflicts*
Person-centered therapy				
Gestalt therapy				
Rational-emotive behavioral therapy (REBT)				
Systematic Desensitization				

Which of the therapies listed above would you find most helpful? _____

Why? _____

_____

2. At least six specific behavior therapies are discussed in this chapter. The therapies can be divided into those that rely on classical conditioning and those that utilize the principles of operant conditioning. Recall that classical conditioning involves the learning of an association between two events or stimuli, while operant conditioning uses reinforcement to change the frequency of a behavior. For each of the situations listed below, explain how the conditioning procedure is used to modify the individual's behavior.

Classical Conditioning Therapies

	CS	UCS
SITUATION #1 Systematic desensitization for a woman who is extremely fearful of birds	*originally the CS is the bird*	*originally the UCS is some event that was traumatic, such as seeing someone attacked by a bird*
	Once treatment begins, the CS may begin as simply as a picture of a bird in a magazine and then slowly step up to eventually having a bird in the same room as the woman.	*The new UCS is the deep relaxation techniques that the patient learned prior to being exposed to the CS.*
SITUATION #2 Aversion therapy for a man who is trying to stop smoking.		
SITUATION #3 Systematic desensitization for a student who has extreme test anxiety, which often triggers panic attacks in the student.		

	Desired Behavior	Reinforcement
SITUATION #1 Token economy in a group home for individuals with schizophrenia	*Self care behaviors such as showering, brushing teeth, combing hair, or positive social interactions.*	*Token for each desired behavior. Tokens can be "cashed in" for reinforcers such as extra TV time or other privileges.*
SITUATION #2 Contingency contract between a woman with depression and her therapist.		
SITUATION #3 Token economy for an teenage boy living at home with his parents		

3. Rational-emotive behavior therapy is commonly used for individuals with depression and anxiety. The therapy is based on the idea that an individual has adopted irrational beliefs that have in turn led to their condition of anxiety and depression. The goal of the therapy is to identify the irrational beliefs and teach the individual how to respond with more rational thought processes. In order to better understand the process, assume you are a therapist using the REBT technique and your client makes the following irrational statements. List a suggestion for a rational belief the client could adopt instead. The first one has already been completed.

Irrational Belief	**Rational Belief**
1. I must be loved, or at least liked, and approved by every significant person I meet.	*I want to be loved or liked by some of the people in my life, and I know I may feel disappointed or lonely when that doesn't happen, but I can cope with those feelings.*
2. I must be completely competent, make no mistakes, and achieve in every possible way, if I am to be worthwhile.	
3. It is dreadful, nearly the end of the world, when things aren't how I would like them to be.	
4. Human unhappiness, including mine, is caused by factors outside of my control, so little can be done about it.	
5. If something might be dangerous, unpleasant, or frightening, I should worry about it a great deal.	
6. My problem(s) were caused by event(s) in my past, and that's why I have my problem(s) now.	
7. I should be very upset by other people's problems and difficulties.	

SAMPLE EXAM

For the following multiple choice questions, select the answer you feel best answers the question and explain the rationale or reason for your selection in the space provided.

Objective 15.1

1.   Therapies directed at changing the disordered behavior are referred to as _____.
        a)   action therapies
        b)   insight therapies
        c)   biomedical therapies
        d)   relationship therapies

Rationale:
A is the correct choice; action therapy emphasizes changing behavior, whereas insight therapy emphasizes understanding one's motives and actions.

2.   Which of the following is the best example of biomedical therapy?
        a)   use of antidepressants to treat depression
        b)   use of insight therapy for social phobia
        c)   psychoanalysis to help treat an anxiety disorder
        d)   flooding treatment for an individual with obsessive compulsive disorder

Rationale:
A is the correct choice; any medical treatment that is directed at changing the physiological functioning of an individual is classified as a biomedical therapy. All of the remaining choices are examples of types of psychotherapy treatments.

Objective 15.2

3.   Approximately how long ago were the first efforts made to treat the mentally ill with kindness, rather than subjecting them to harsh physical treatment?
        a)   20 years ago
        b)   100 years ago
        c)   200 years ago
        d)   500 years ago

Rationale:

_____

_____

4. Psychoanalysis was a therapy technique designed by _____.
    a) Alfred Adler
    b) Carl Rogers
    c) Fritz Perls
    d) Sigmund Freud

    Rationale:

    _____

    _____

5. Freud believed one of the indications he was close to discovering an unconscious conflict was when a patient became unwilling to talk about a topic. He referred to this response in the patient as
    a) transference
    b) latent content
    c) dream analysis
    d) resistance

    Rationale:

    _____

    _____

6. Which of the following individuals would be <u>least</u> likely to benefit from psychoanalysis?
    a) Mary, who has a somatoform disorder
    b) Kaleem, who suffers from a severe psychotic disorder
    c) Pasha, who has panic attacks
    d) Lou, who suffers from anxiety

    Rationale:

    _____

    _____

7. The modern psychoanalyst provides more guidance to the patient, asks questions, suggests helpful behaviors, and gives opinions and interpretations. This type of role for the therapist is described as a _____ approach.
    a) free association
    b) directive
    c) biomedical
    d) nondirective

    Rationale:

    _____

    _____

Objective 15.5

8.   What did Carl Rogers view as a cause of most personal problems and unhappiness?
     a)   Reinforcement of maladaptive behavior patterns..
     b)   Unrealistic modes of thought employed by many people.
     c)   Mismatch between an individual's ideal self and real self.
     d)   Unresolved unconscious conflicts occuring between the id and superego.

     Rationale:

     _____

     _____

9.   Which of the following was NOT one of the four key elements Rogers viewed as necessary for a successful person-therapist relationship?
     a)   reflection
     b)   unconditional positive regard
     c)   authenticity
     d)   resistance

     Rationale:

     _____

     _____

Objective 15.6

10. What is a major goal of the Gestalt therapist?
     a)   to facilitate transference
     b)   to eliminate the client's undesirable behaviors
     c)   to provide unconditional positive regard
     d)   to help clients become more aware of their own feelings

     Rationale:

     _____

     _____

Objective 15.7

11. Which of the following is a limitation of humanistic therapy?
     a)   Clients do not need to be verbal.
     b)   There is not enough empirical research to support its basic ideas.
     c)   It cannot be used in a variety of contexts.
     d)   The therapist runs the risk of having his or her words misinterpreted by the client.

     Rationale:

     _____

     _____

12. In the aversion therapy technique known as rapid smoking, the client takes a puff on a cigarette every five or six seconds so that the nicotine now produces unpleasant responses such as nausea and dizziness, and eventually the cigarette itself produces a sensation of nausea in the client. In the terms of classical conditioning, the cigarette functions as the _____ and the nicotine is the _____.

    a) UCS, CS
    b) CS, UCS
    c) CR, UCS
    d) CS, UCR

    Rationale:

    _____

    _____

13. Which method of treating phobias involves progressive relaxation and exposure to the feared object?

    a) extinction
    b) punishment
    c) token economy
    d) systematic desensitization

    Rationale:

    _____

    _____

14. In a token economy, what role does the token play in shaping behavior?

    a) the tokens are used as punishment to decrease the maladaptive behavior
    b) the tokens are used to reinforce the desired behavior
    c) the token is the actual behavior itself
    d) the token represents the written contract between the client and therapist

    Rationale:

    _____

    _____

15. What is an advantage of using operant conditioning in treating undesirable behaviors?
      a) The results are usually quickly obtained.
      b) Clients can get an understanding of the underlying cause of the problem.
      c) Unconscious urges are revealed.
      d) Clients can change distorted thought patterns that affect behavior.

   Rationale:

   _____

   _____

Objective 15.10

16. Which of the following is one of the criticisms of behavior therapy?
      a) It focuses on the underlying cause of behavior and not the symptoms.
      b) Therapy typically lasts for several years and is very expensive.
      c) It focuses too much on the past.
      d) It only relieves some symptoms of schizophrenia but does not treat the overall disorder.

   Rationale:

   _____

   _____

Objective 15.11

17. What is the goal of cognitive therapy?
      a) To help clients gain insight into their unconscious.
      b) To help people change their ways of thinking.
      c) To change a person's behavior through shaping and reinforcement.
      d) To provide unconditional positive regard for the client.

   Rationale:

   _____

   _____

18. Which of these clients is the most likely candidate for Aaron Beck's form of cognitive therapy?

      a) Albert, who suffers from mania.
      b) Barbara, who suffers from depression.
      c) Robert, who suffers from schizophrenia.
      d) Virginia, who has been diagnosed with dissociative identity disorder.

   Rationale:

   _____

   _____

Objective 15.12

19.   Which approach assumes that disorders come from illogical, irrational cognitions and that
       changing the thinking patterns to more rational, logical ones will relieve the symptoms of the
       disorder?
        a)   cognitive-behavioral
        b)   person-centered
        c)   psychoanalytic
        d)   Gestalt

Rationale:

_____

_____

Objective 15.13

20.   According to Albert Ellis, we become unhappy and depressed about events because of _____.
        a)   our behaviors
        b)   our irrational beliefs
        c)   the events that happen to us
        d)   other people's irrational beliefs

Rationale:

_____

_____

21.   Which of the following is the best example of an irrational belief that a therapist using rational-
       emotive behavioral therapy would challenge you to change?
        a)   It is disappointing when things don't go my way.
        b)   If I fail this test, it will hurt my grade in this class but I will try to make it up on the
            next exam.
        c)   There must be something wrong with Bob since he turned down my invitation for a
            date.
        d)   Everyone should love and approve of me and if they don't, there must be something
            wrong with me.

Rationale:

_____

_____

Objective 15.14

22.   Which of the following is an advantage of cognitive and cognitive-behavioral therapies?
       a)   Clients do not need to be verbal.
       b)   They treat the underlying cause of the problem.
       c)   They are less expensive and short-term than typical insight therapies.
       d)   The therapist decides which of the client's beliefs are rational and which are irrational.

       Rationale:

       _____

       _____

Objective 15.15

23.   An advantage to group therapy is that groups _____.
       a)   are a source of social support
       b)   allow countertransference to occur
       c)   provide unconditional approval to the group members
       d)   allow an extremely shy person to feel more comfortable speaking up

       Rationale:

       _____

       _____

Objective 15.16

24.   In family therapy, the therapist would most likely _____.
       a)   focus on one individual who has been identified as the source of the problem
       b)   have each family member come in for therapy individually
       c)   provide unconditional approval to all the family members
       d)   focus on the entire family system to understand the problem

       Rationale:

       _____

       _____

25.   Which of the following is NOT true about self-help support groups?
       a)   Self-help groups do not have leaders.
       b)   Currently there are only a limited number of self-help groups operating in the United States.
       c)   Self-help groups are typically not directed by a licensed therapist.
       d)   Self-help groups are usually free to attend.

       Rationale:

       _____

       _____

26.   An advantage of group therapy is that it _____.
        a) can provide help to individuals who may be unable to afford individual psychotherapy
        b) can be helpful to individuals who are uncomfortable in social situations
        c) can only be used alone and not in combination with any other form of therapy
        d) can be helpful to those who have difficulty speaking in public

Rationale:

_____

_____

Objective 15.18

27.   _____ is a controversial form of therapy in which the client is directed to move the eyes
rapidly back and forth while thinking of a disturbing memory.
        a) Eye-movement desensitization reprocessing
        b) Systematic desensitization
        c) Eye-memory therapy
        d) Eye therapy

Rationale:

_____

_____

Objective 15.19

28.   Most psychological professionals today take a(n) _____ view of psychotherapy.
        a) group treatment
        b) humanistic
        c) eclectic
        d) behavioral

Rationale:

_____

_____

29.   The most important aspect of a successful psychotherapy treatment is
        a) the length of the session
        b) the specific approach of the therapist
        c) the relationship between the client and the therapist
        d) the severity of the disorder

Rationale:

_____

_____

30. Studies that have examined cultural and ethnic factors in the therapeutic relationship have found that
     a) members of minority racial or ethnic groups are more likely to continue treatment until the problem has been resolved.
     b) members of the majority racial or ethnic group usually have lower prevalence rates of disorders.
     c) members of minority racial or ethnic groups drop out of therapy at a higher rate than members of the majority group.
     d) members of minority racial or ethnic groups rarely or never seek therapy.

Rationale:

_____

_____

31. Which of the following has NOT been found to be a barrier to effective psychotherapy when the cultural background of client and therapist is different?
     a) language differences
     b) differing cultural values
     c) nonverbal communication
     d) severity of the disorder

Rationale:

_____

_____

Objective 15.21

32. Antipsychotic drugs treat symptoms such as _____.
     a) hopelessness, sadness, and suicide ideations
     b) excessive worry, repetitive thoughts, and compulsive behavior
     c) hallucinations, delusions, and bizarre behavior
     d) manipulation, lying, and cheating

Rationale:

_____

_____

33. In what way is the new class of antidepressants known as the SSRIs an improvement over the older types of antidepressants?
     a) they work faster
     b) they are more effective
     c) they target a larger number of different neurotransmitters
     d) they have fewer side effects

Rationale:

_____

_____

34.   For which disorder was electroconvulsive therapy originally developed as a treatment?
         a)   panic
         b)   schizophrenia
         c)   bipolar disorder
         d)   cyclothymia

       Rationale:

       _____

       _____

35.   Which of the following is the appropriate definition of psychosurgery?
         a)   information given to a patient about a surgical procedure before the surgery in order to
              prevent anxiety
         b)   surgery that is performed on brain tissue to relieve or control severe psychological
              disorders
         c)   surgery that severs the spinal cord of the patient
         d)   a procedure in which a brief current of electricity is used to trigger a seizure that
              typically lasts one minute, causing the body to convulse

       Rationale:

       _____

       _____

36.   Psychosurgery is no longer performed in the United States.

         a)   True; long-term studies highlighting the serious negative side effects of lobotomies led
              to the discontinuation of all psychosurgery techniques in the United States.
         b)   False; although frontal lobotomies are no longer performed, bilateral cingulotomies
              are still carried out on patients that have not been helped by any other treatment.
         c)   False; frontal lobotomies are still performed on a small number of patients in the
              United States today.
         d)   True; all forms of psychosurgery have been banned in the United States.

       Rationale:

       _____

       _____

37.   Which of the following statements about antidepressants taken by children and adolescents is true?

        a)   They are known to be very effective.
        b)   They are not very effective.
        c)   Their effects are clearly understood.
        d)   Their effects are not clearly understood.

Rationale:

_____

_____

SAMPLE EXAM ANSWERS & RATIONALES

1. a Action therapy emphasizes changing behavior, whereas insight therapy emphasizes understanding one's motives and actions.

2. a Any medical treatment that is directed at changing the physiological functioning of an individual is classified as a biomedical therapy. All of the remaining choices are examples of types of psychotherapy treatments.

3. c In 1793 Philippe Pinel unchained the mentally ill inmates at an asylum in Paris, France and began the movement of humane treatment for the mentally ill.

4. d Freud was the founder of psychoanalysis, while Rogers developed person-centered therapy.

5. d Resistance occurred when a patient became unwilling to discuss a concept. In transference, the patient would transfer positive and negative feelings for an authority figure in their past onto the therapist.

6. b People with severe psychotic disorders are less likely to benefit from psychoanalysis than are people who suffer from somatoform or anxiety disorders.

7. b A directive approach involves asking questions and suggesting behaviors. The more traditional psychoanalyst typically takes a more nondirective approach in which the therapist remains neutral and does not interpret or take direct actions with regard to the client.

8. c Rogers believed the closer the match between a person's ideal and real selves, the happier the person. It was Freud, not Rogers, who viewed unresolved unconscious conflicts between the id and superego as the cause of personal problems.

9. d Rogers felt a therapist must provide the four elements of reflection, unconditional positive regard, empathy, and authenticity for successful treatment.

10. d The major goal of Gestalt therapists is to help clients become more aware of their feelings. Providing unconditional positive regard is the primary goal of person-centered therapy, not Gestalt.

11. b The humanistic therapist does not run the risk of having his or her words misinterpreted by the client because the therapist uses reflection as the main means of communication. Unfortunately, at this point, there is not enough empirical evidence to support or refute the basic ideas of humanistic therapy.

12. b Both the cigarette and nicotine are stimuli, so choices "c" and "d" can be immediately eliminated. In rapid smoking, the cigarette serves as the conditioned stimulus and the nicotine serves as the unconditioned stimulus.

13. d Systematic desensitization involves progressive relaxation and exposure to the feared object, while extinction involves the removal of a reinforcer to reduce the frequency of a particular response.

14. b In a token economy, the tokens are the reinforcers used to shape and strengthen the desired behaviors.

15. a Operant conditioning is not concerned with the cause of the problems; rather it is concerned with changing behavior. However, operant conditioning does provide rapid change in behavior in comparison to other therapies.

16. d Behavior therapy may help relieve some symptoms but does not treat the overall disorder of schizophrenia.

17. b Cognitive therapy focuses on changing an individual's <u>cognitions</u> or thought processes.

18. b Beck's cognitive therapy is especially effective in treating distortions related to depression.

19. a Cognitive behavioral therapists are concerned with helping clients change their irrational thoughts to more rational and positive thoughts. A person-centered

therapist believes disorders come from a mismatch between the ideal self and the real self and a lack of unconditional positive regard.

20.   b   Ellis believes irrational beliefs cause dissatisfaction and depression.

21.   d   Irrational beliefs typically have one thing in common; they are all-or-none types of statements.

22.   c   Cognitive and cognitive-behavioral therapies are relatively inexpensive and are short-term.

23.   a   Group therapy provides social support for people who have similar problems. However, an extremely shy person is not likely to do as well in group therapy.

24.   d   Family therapy focuses on the entire family as a part of the problem.

25.   b   Currently, there are an extremely large number of self-help groups in the United States.

26.   a   Group therapy can provide help to those who may be unable to afford individual psychotherapy.

27.   a   EMDR is a form of therapy in which the client is directed to move the eyes rapidly back and forth while thinking of a disturbing memory. Systematic desensitization gradually exposes the client to the feared object while using relaxation techniques to reduce anxiety.

28.   c   An eclectic view is one that combines a number of different approaches to best fit the needs of the client.

29.   c   A number of studies have found that the client-therapist relationship (also called the therapeutic alliance) is the best predictor of successful treatment.

30.   c   Members of minority groups are much more likely to drop out of therapy when compared to members of majority racial and ethnic groups.

31.   d   The severity of the disorder has not been found to be a cultural barrier for treatment.

32.   c   Hallucinations, delusions and bizarre behaviors are defined as psychotic behaviors and are treated with antipsychotic drugs. Antidepressant drugs, not antipsychotic drugs, treat feelings of hopelessness, sadness, and suicide ideations.

33.   d   The speed of action and effectiveness is similar between the three classes of antidepressants, but the main difference is the number of negative side effects. The SSRIs actually target only one neurotransmitter: serotonin.

34.   b   ECT was originally designed to induce seizures in schizophrenics.

35.   b   Severing the spinal cord would lead to the very negative side effect of paralysis of the body. Psychosurgery is performed on brain tissue.

36.   b   Frontal lobotomies are no longer performed; however, bilateral cingulotomies are still performed on severe cases in which no other treatments have been found to be effective.

37.   d   Currently, the effects of antidepressants in children are not clearly understood.

APPLY IT

This section will help you use the concepts you are learning in this class to improve your study skills.

Many of the therapies presented in this chapter focus on the power our thoughts have on influencing how we feel and behave. In this application, you will utilize the concepts of rational emotive behavioral therapy to try to reduce any anxieties you might have regarding exams and grades. Rational emotive behavioral therapy is a type of cognitive behavior therapy in which individuals are taught to identify their own irrational beliefs and replace them with more rational and helpful statements.

Step 1. Identify some of your current irrational beliefs. Many irrational beliefs include all-or-nothing type of statements (e.g. All of my classes should be exciting and engaging) and often assign devastating results to normal occurrences (e.g. Getting a C on this test proves I am a horrible student and shouldn't even be in school).

List some irrational beliefs that you engage in with regard to school here:

1. _____

2. _____

3. _____

4. _____

Step 2. Now try to convert your irrational beliefs to a more realistic and rational belief. For example, I don't expect all of my classes to be "my favorites," but I can still try to get something out of them. Or, I got a C on this test, which is disappointing, but maybe I'll make an appointment with the professor to talk about the test and see what I did wrong.

Convert the irrational beliefs above into more rational beliefs.

1. _____

2. _____

3. _____

4. _____

Step 3. Try to pay attention to your thoughts throughout the day and catch yourself when you slip into an irrational belief; try replacing it with a more rational belief and see how that affects your anxiety levels.

A.1	Why do psychologists use statistics?	A.5	How can statistics be used to determine if
A.2	What types of tables and graphs represent patterns of data?		differences in sets of data are large enough to be due to something other than chance variation?
A.3	What types of statistics examine central tendencies in data?	A.6	How are statistics used to predict one score from another?
A.4	What types of statistics examine variations in data?	A.7	Why are skills in statistics important to psychology majors?

SUMMARY

Statistics provide the tools for describing and analyzing the data psychologists collect through systematic observation and experimentation. The tools are divided into two categories; descriptive statistics summarize the data, while inferential statistics use a small sample to make a guess (or "inference") about a larger group.

Descriptive statistics are used to describe the frequency, central tendency and variability for sets of data. Data can be organized in a table or graph using a **frequency distribution**. Two common frequency distribution graphs are the **histogram** and the **polygon**. The shape of the frequency distribution graph can be used to describe the data. A symmetrical, bell shaped curve is referred to as a **normal curve**. A graph with most of the data points at the lower end is described as **positively skewed,** and a graph with most scores at the high end and just a few at the lower end is called **negatively skewed**. A **measure of central tendency** is one number that most accurately represents a "typical" score. The three measures of central tendency of the **mean**, **median** and **mode**. The mean is the arithmetic average and is found by adding up all the scores and dividing by the total number of scores. The median is the score that is in the exact middle of a distribution with half the score above the median and half the scores below. The median is more appropriate than the mean when there are extreme scores in the distribution. The mode is simply the most frequently occurring score. **Measures of variability** indicate how "spread out" the scores are from each other. The **range** is calculated by finding the difference between the highest and lowest scores in a data set. The **standard deviation** indicates how far, on average, each score is from the mean. The higher the standard deviation, the further spread out the scores are. A **z-score** indicates how many standard deviation an individual score is away from the mean. The z-score is calculated by subtracting the mean from the score and dividing by the standard deviation.

Inferential statistics use data from a small sample to make guesses about a larger population. Statistical tests indicate the probability that a specific result is due to random variability or if the result indicates a real difference. When the result is found to be due to real differences between the groups, it is said to be **statistically significant**. Some of the statistical tests include the t-test, analysis of variance, and chi-square. A correlation is a measure of the relationship between two or more variables, and a **correlation coefficient** is a number that indicates the strength and direction of the relationship.

KEY POINTS

- Explain the difference between descriptive and inferential statistics.
- Introduce descriptive statistics for frequencies, central tendency and variation.
- Describe the concept of statistical significance.
- Discuss the inferential statistic for correlation data.

KEY CONCEPTS

statistics   A set of procedures for collecting, describing and analyzing data.

descriptive statistics	A way of organizing and summarizing numbers so that patterns can be determined.
frequency distribution	A table or graph that shows how often different numbers of scores appear in a particular set of scores.
histogram	A bar graph showing a frequency distribution.
polygon	A line graph showing a frequency distribution.
normal curve	A special frequency polygon in which the scores are symmetrically distributed around the mean. The mean, median and mode are all located on the same point. Also referred to as a bell curve.
positively skewed	A distribution of scores in which the scores are concentrated in the low end of the distribution.
negatively skewed	A distribution of scores in which the scores are concentrated in the high end of the distribution.
measure of central tendency	Numbers that best represent the most typical score of a frequency distribution.
mean	The arithmetic average of a distribution of numbers.
median	The middle score in an ordered distribution of scores.
mode	The most frequently occurring score in a distribution.
measures of variability	Measurements indicating the degree of difference within a distribution, or, in other words, how spread out the distribution is.
range	The difference between the highest and lowest score in a distribution.
standard deviation	The square root of the average squared deviations from the mean of scores in a distribution.
z-score	A number indicating how far an individual score is from the mean in terms of standard deviations.
inferential statistics	Statistical analyses of two or more sets of data to reduce the possibility of error in measurements and to determine if the differences between the data sets are greater than chance variation would predict.
statistically significant	Indicating a difference between groups that is due to more than just chance.

correlation coefficient   A number that represents the strength and direction of a relationship between two variables.

APPENDIX B LEARNING OBJECTIVES

SUMMARY

There are several types of professionals in the field of psychology. A **psychiatrist** has a medical doctorate (M.D.) degree, specializes in the diagnosis and treatment of individuals with psychological disorders, and has the ability to write prescriptions and perform medical procedures. A **psychoanalyst** is a psychiatrist or psychologist with additional training in the theories of Freud. **Psychiatric social workers** usually have a master of social work (M.S.W.) degree or a licensed clinical social work (L.C.S.W.) degree and often work in clinical settings. A **psychologist** has either a doctor of philosophy (Ph.D.) or a doctor of psychology (Psy.D.) degree.

Some psychologists do research that is directed at discovering basic principles of human behavior. This is referred to as basic research, and the following description provides an overview of some of the major areas of specialization within the field of psychology that focus on basic research. **Clinical psychology** is the area of psychology in which a psychologist would diagnose and treat individuals with mild to severe psychological disorders. The treatment in clinical psychology consists of listening and talking to the patient. **Counseling psychology** is similar to clinical psychology in the treatment; however, counseling psychologists usually work with people with less severe problems. **Developmental psychology** focuses on the study of change, and psychologists in this area work in academic settings conducting research and teaching. **Experimental psychology** deals with learning, memory, thinking and perception, and also consists of conducting research and teaching in an academic setting. **Social psychology** focuses on how human behavior is affected by the presence of others. Psychologists in this field may work in an academic setting or for federal agencies and businesses. **Personality psychology** studies the differences in personality among individuals; psychologists in this area work in an academic setting. **Physiological psychology** is also referred to as neuroscience or biopsychology and focuses on the study of the biological bases of behavior. Most psychologists in this field work in academic settings. **Comparative psychology** focuses exclusively on animals and animal behavior.

Other psychologists spend more time engaged in research designed to find solutions to practical problems in the here and now. This type of research is referred to as applied research. **Applied psychology** refers to using findings from psychological research to solve real-world problems and is applicable to a large number of areas in the field of psychology. The following areas of specialization are particularly focused on applied psychology: **Health psychology** focuses on the relationship of human activities to physical health and tries to come up with programs to improve physical health. A health psychologist may work in a hospital, clinic, medical school, academic setting or private practice. **Educational psychology** is concerned with the study and enhancement of human learning. Educational psychologists would most likely do research and develop new learning techniques. **School psychology**, on the other hand, is focused on using the results of the research and applying them in an actual school system. A school psychologist works directly with children in a school setting. **Sports psychology** focuses on helping athletes prepare mentally for participation in sports. A sports psychologist may have their own private practice or work within an athletic organization. **Forensic psychology** is the practice of

346

psychology related to the legal system. Forensic psychologists may aid either the prosecution or the defense and may do consulting work in addition to a regular private practice. **Environmental psychology** focuses on the relationship between human behavior and the environment in which the behavior takes place. Environmental psychologists may work with other professionals, such as urban or city planners or economists, for example. **Industrial/organizational (I/O) psychology** is concerned with the relationships between people and their work environments. I/O psychologists are often hired by businesses to deal with hiring and assessment of employees. **Human factors psychology** is a specific area within I/O psychology that focuses on designing machines, furniture, and other devices to be the most effective for human use. Management theories have been developed to understand and motivate workers. Older theories assumed the only motivating force for workers was money, whereas newer theories view work as something that can be meaningful to employees.

Many techniques have been developed in the field of sports psychology to help athletes obtain their peak performance.

KEY POINTS

- Define the concept of applied psychology.
- Describe the types of careers that are available in the area of psychology.
- Discuss specific areas of specialization within the field of psychology.

KEY CONCEPTS

psychiatrist	A medical doctor who specializes in the diagnosis and treatment of psychological disorders.
psychoanalyst	Either a psychiatrist or a psychologist who has special training in the theories of Sigmund Freud and his method of psychoanalysis.
psychiatric social workers	A social worker with some training in therapy methods who focuses on the environmental conditions that can have an impact on mental disorders, such as poverty, overcrowding, stress, and drug abuse.
psychologist	A professional with an academic degree and specialized training in one or more areas of psychology.
clinical psychology	The diagnosis and treatment of people with psychological disorders that may range from mild to severe.
counseling psychology	Area of psychology in which the psychologists help people with problems of adjustment.
developmental psychology	Study of the changes in the way people think, relate to others, and feel as they age.
experimental psychology	Research and experiments in the areas of learning, memory, thinking, perception, motivation, and language.
social psychology	Psychology that focuses on how human behavior is affected by the

presence of other people.

personality psychology	The study of the differences in personality among people.
physiological psychology	Area of psychology in which the psychologists study the biological bases of behavior.
comparative psychology	The study of animals and their behavior for the purpose of comparing and contrasting it to human behavior.
applied psychology	The use of psychological concepts in solving real world problems.
health psychology	Psychology that focuses on the relationship of human behavior patterns and stress reaction to physical health.
educational psychology	The study of human learning and development of new learning techniques.
school psychology	Psychological work done directly in the schools, including doing assessments, educational placement, and diagnosing educational problems.
sports psychology	Psychology that aims to help athletes and others to prepare themselves mentally for participation in sports activities.
forensic psychology	Area of psychology concerned with people in the legal system, including profiling of criminals, jury selection, and expert witnessing.
environmental psychology	Psychology that focuses on how people interact with and are affected by their physical environments.
industrial/organizational (I/O) psychology	Area of psychology concerned with the relationships between people and their work environment.
human factors psychology	Area of industrial/organizational psychology concerned with the study of the way humans and machines interact with each other.